For Francie and Max

Preface and Acknowledgments

This book aims to offer both an empirically-anchored theory of news and democracy and a normative exploration of the desirable and possible. This approach reflects my orientation as a political scientist trained in the field of public policy analysis. The central purpose of this new discipline is to understand and make recommendations on how to improve government. The book thus blends empirical with normative analysis, in the conviction that explicitly weaving the "is" and "ought" offers the best way to illuminate the actual and potential impacts of journalism on American democracy. In my view, normative concerns should direct the gaze of empirical analysis, and an empirical theory of the press must undergird normative critiques.

The combined approach clarifies a central conundrum: traditional free press ideals and most critiques of the media assume that journalists control the creation of the news. But, in empirical fact, journalists do not enjoy the independent command over the news process that they would need to fulfill the normative ideals. As the book explains, however much they try, journalists do not have the power to improve journalism in the ways critics demand—and they themselves would like.

This diagnosis illustrates the policy-analytical orientation at work, employing social scientific research and insight not just to build theory but to enhance our understanding of the paths and obstacles to improving the governmental process. I can understand why some people prefer a strict separation, with quantitative empirical research unadulterated by value judgments or recommendations for improvement. Yet a division of labor seems reasonable. Especially in studying the media, scholars ought to have the leeway to use varied techniques. It would be ironic indeed if students of a "free press" all had to conform to one scholarly method, one research paradigm.

In fact, the dominant role expectations for journalists and social scientists present similar dilemmas. On the one hand, journalists and social scientists are supposed to follow objectivity rules and mirror reality without judging or affecting it. Yet on the other, they are supposed to explore reality dauntlessly and independently so as to illuminate the truth in all its complexity. For scholars, at least, the tension between these two demands can be resolved by making the values and goals supporting the analyses explicit and clear, and that is what I do here.

A further consequence of my analytical strategy is a commitment to going beyond quantitative data where necessary. I believe that the influence of the media is so complicated and subtle that quantitative data cannot reveal all its facets. If limited solely to quantifiable information, I believe, social science can miss some of the reality of American journalism. In studying the news media, genuine empirical accuracy demands going beyond the numbers to qualitative data and informed speculation.

Thus I write in the spirit of Donald McCloskey's advice to social scientists. McCloskey, himself a distinguished economist, argues (in *The Rhetoric of Economics*) that social scientists should not be bound by an inaccurate ideal of "hard" science to exploring an artificially limited range of phenomena using a narrow range of quantitative techniques. Rather, quoting Wayne Booth, he says they should perform a " 'careful weighing of more-or-less good reasons to arrive at more-or-less probable or plausible conclusions—none too secure but better than what would be arrived at by chance or unthinking impulse.' " The task, he says (again from Booth) is to practice " 'the art of discovering good reasons, finding what really warrants assent, because any reasonable person ought to be persuaded.' "

I have attempted to make this book accessible to journalists, politicians, and others who might be in a position to apply its insights in making practical decisions. The book is therefore designed to help build social science theory while remaining approachable by those outside the scholarly community. The major adjustment for the non-specialist is the presentation of statistical analyses in appendices. Scholars should read these segments, which help to support the arguments in social scientific terms. While each appendix explains the meaning of the statistics in ways that should be comprehensible to the layperson, those uncomfortable with regression coefficients and t-tests can skip the appendices without losing the major points. To avoid cluttering the text, I also placed many of the scholarly qualifications and amplifications in discursive endnotes. Again those with scholarly interests should attend carefully, but the general reader can consult the endnotes only when he or she desires elaboration of a particular point.

Following custom and necessity, I relied heavily on family, friends, and colleagues in writing this book. Above all, my wife Francie and son Max made this book possible. As I wrote, every so often I would glance away from the computer screen, gaze at my pictures of these two, and gain the strength to write on. I finished the first outline of the book just before Max was born and sent off the manuscript right around his second birthday. He filled the time between with the most profound pleasure and pride. And in ways we can only partially comprehend, he has deepened the love of his parents for each other.

Among my colleagues and friends I cite first, for invaluable support far exceeding the call of collegial duty, those who served as my departmental chairmen: Joel Fleishman, Bob Behn, and Phil Cook. Each provided encouragement at crucial junctures. For reading the prospectus of the book and making helpful suggestions, I thank David Barber, Jay Blumler, Ben Compaine, Max McCombs, and Russ Neuman. I also appreciate the willingness of several colleagues to read and converse about selections from early versions of the manuscript: Phil Cook, Rod Hart, John McConahay, Michael Rice, Sudhir Shetty, and Leon Sigal. Seminar audiences at the universities of Iowa, Southern California, and Texas, and at Columbia University's Gannett Center, offered stimulating responses to my ideas. Five people read and commented carefully on the whole manuscript, significantly improved the book, and earned my gratitude: Clay Steinman and John Nelson, professors respectively at Florida Atlantic University and the University of Iowa; Sheri Gravett, Ph.D. candidate at Duke University; and Rachel Toor and Stephanie Sakson-Ford, editors at Oxford University Press.

The research reported here enjoyed funding from three sources whose support I gratefully acknowledge. Most important was the John and Mary R. Markle Foundation, which bestowed two separate grants. I especially thank the foundation's president, Lloyd Morrisett, who showed faith in me when it mattered most. Also helpful were grants from the University of Wisconsin Institute for Research on Poverty and the Duke University Research Council.

I received research assistance from a talented succession of students at Duke, especially: Kelly Barfield, Kate Berry, Jeri Cabot, Will Davis, Gerri Fried, Sheri Gravett, Julie Rosenberg, and Carrie Teegardin.

Although I could not have written the book without this support and assistance, I must accept full responsibility for the analysis and conclusions that appear here.

Durham, N.C.   R.M.E.
October 1988

Contents

DEMOCRACY
WITHOUT
CITIZENS

Introduction

In theory, democracy in the United States benefits from a vigorous marketplace of ideas created by an energetic "free press." The press is supposed to enhance democracy both by stimulating the citizenry's political interest and by providing the specific information they need to hold government accountable. But America's "free press" cannot be free. Restricted by the limited tastes of the audience and reliant upon political elites for most information, journalists participate in an interdependent news system, not a free market of ideas. In practice, then, the news media fall far short of the ideal vision of a free press as civic educator and guardian of democracy.

Despite their institutional shortcomings, the news media do influence politics significantly. This book weaves an explanation of the media's simultaneous dependence and strength into a theory of news, public opinion, and democracy in the United States. The theory explains how the media can wield the power to alter public policy and cripple presidencies—yet cannot harness that power to serve democratic citizenship and promote government accountability as free press ideals demand.

Four paradoxes in the press's performance challenge any faith that competition in a free market of ideas nourishes democracy. The first emerges from the burgeoning, over the past twenty years or so, of a large variety of new video and print media outlets.[1] The media—both the print and electronic press[2]—are as free as ever; more competitors jam the "idea marketplace" than ever.

Moreover, computer and communication technology have enhanced the ability of journalists to obtain and transmit information rapidly and accurately. If free press ideals were valid, logic would lead us to expect the public to be participating in politics more intelligently than ever.

Yet scholarly research clearly establishes that, despite any improvement in access to news, Americans do not know more about politics now than they did twenty years ago. They vote less. According to some observers, the public's knowledge of facts or reality has actually deteriorated, so that more people are prone to political fantasy and myth transmitted by the very same news media.[3] Of course the press by itself is not responsible for the way people think and act in politics. Still, the state of citizenship in the United States raises serious questions about free press ideals.

The second paradox concerns the puzzling inability of a powerful press to hold government to account. Consider the record. Every president of the United States since 1964 has ended his term seriously weakened, drained of authority, or defeated.[4] If the flourishing and aggressive free press had been doing the job the ideals demand, if the media had highlighted the right information from the start, the foreign entanglements and scandals that crippled each administration might have ended before they escalated. I do not mean to suggest that these were the only causes of presidential failure. For Lyndon Johnson, Richard Nixon, and Ronald Reagan, I believe they were the most important single forces behind the loss of leadership. For Jimmy Carter and Gerald Ford, economic problems were probably more important; but their scandals and crises surely made Americans less patient with economic travail than they might have been.

The press did report energetically and often critically about many of these presidents' actions. Yet, paradoxically, despite their frequently bellicose and suspicious stance toward authority figures, the media failed to make the government's decisions visible and leaders accountable at the very times spirited inquiry was most desperately needed.[5] News coverage challenging these presidents' most disastrous decisions was too little, too obscure, too late.

Conventional wisdom holds the reverse. From Johnson's Vietnam through Nixon (and Ford's) Watergate,[6] Carter's Iran hostage tragedy, and Reagan's Iran-contra affair, the common view is that each of the debacles showed the media at their indomitable best, their most assertive and independent. But the point of a free press is to prevent rulers from damaging the nation and destroying themselves, not to let them plunge the country into disaster now and make them pay with their political fortunes later. The press certainly provided restrospective accountability in each of these cases, which was far better than nothing, but far inferior to what free press ideals presume.

In each case, most of the media failed to investigate nascent signs that something was rotten in Washington. Each time, journalists depended far too much on the president's line, whether it be framing Vietnam as a limited war, Watergate a third-rate burglary, the Iran hostage-taking a world-historical crisis, or Oliver North a minor functionary.

While this portrait of the impact of journalism defies orthodoxy, it is the one academic research best supports. Myths about the "living-room war" notwithstanding, the press did not emphasize the critical perspective on the Vietnam War. Daniel Hallin's definitive probe reveals that, especially before the Tet offensive of 1968, the media failed even to give equal weight to those who challenged the president's factual claims and policy agenda.[7] Around the Tet period itself, the negative and even despairing[8] media coverage helped topple Lyndon Johnson, the creator of the policy.[9] But American involvement continued for several more years, in some respects at an intensified level (e.g., the bombing), while, as Hallin shows, the bulk of the press failed to offer repeated, detailed, critical assessments of Richard Nixon's policies.

Watergate would become an enormous story after Nixon's re-election, but during 1972, when the crimes were actually committed and when understanding them could have altered election-year politics, most media presented only sporadic reports. Although media treatment was not the only reason, Watergate never became a major issue in the election and only a very small minority of the public—in one survey during late August 1972 a mere 1 percent—apparently thought Nixon himself involved in the scandal.[10] Kurt and Gladys Lang conclude that, during

1972, "With a few notable exceptions, the rest of the [print] press did not join the [*Washington*] *Post* in its dogged pursuit of the Watergate story."[11] The same was true of television. Detailed content analyses for 1972 are not available, but existing data show, for example, that for the seven-week period preceding the election, the three evening news shows devoted a total of about 155 minutes to Watergate-related stories. The average newscast offered only about ninety seconds on the issue.[12] By comparison, the networks spent 394 minutes on the much narrower scandal surrounding President Carter's brother Billy over a seven-week period in 1980.[13]

Turning to the Iran hostage episode, Carter apparently pumped the incident up to stimulate public support. If the media had not cooperated in elevating the situation, the hostages might have become old news. Jimmy Carter might not have lived to regret his promotion of this incident to the center of American politics for a year,[14] where it finally became a symbol of his weakness. The media treatment was not inevitable, was not compelled by the "reality." After all, when North Korea kept 82 American hostages from the Navy ship Pueblo for most of 1968, the story generated only one-fifth as much network coverage as the Iran hostages obtained.[15] Unlike the Vietnam, Watergate and Iran-contra cases, here the media's problem was less omission and neglect than over-attention; but in all cases, journalists found themselves surrendering to the president's manipulation of the news agenda. Had the press made more independent news judgments, the nation's attention in the critical election year of 1980 might have been focused on less emotional issues of more lasting significance.

Finally, until the Iran-contra scandal broke open in November 1986, the Reagan administration simply denied all allegations about Oliver North's activities in support of the Nicaraguan contra rebels during the congressional ban on such aid, as it did reports of U.S. dealings with Iran. Members of Congress accepted the denials, and so did the media.[16] Thus even though a handful of enterprising reporters occasionally wrote about these matters before late 1986, the press in general did not pick up the leads and as a practical matter the scandal did not exist until then. Arguably, had the media turned their spotlight on North and the

National Security Council earlier, the nation might have been spared the fall from grace of yet another president.

If the primary objective of news organizations were fulfilling free press ideals, they would have pounced in unison, much sooner, and much more vigorously, on the provocative evidence a few journalists had managed to unearth in the cases of Vietnam, Watergate, and Iran-contra. And they would not have converged as they did to blow up the Iran hostage incident. Yet I believe that the media could not have done anything much different; they do not have the ability to make fulfillment of free press ideals their overriding goal. A central task of this book is to explain why.

Different coverage might have stimulated popular pressure, emboldened members of Congress and other Washington elites to challenge the administration, and ultimately pushed the presidents to change course earlier. Certainly free press ideals envision just such a scenario. While individual journalists made an admirable attempt to counter the tide in each of the cases beginning with Vietnam, their lonely reports were not enough; sporadic individual stories or editorials rarely are. The high-volume, high-visibility coverage that is usually needed for media reports to move the political process might not have prevented these disasters. But the passivity of the press as a whole, the omissions as much as the misleading denials and propaganda, in many senses helped to lull the public—and the president—into acceptance until it was too late.

Although the experience beginning with Vietnam should have sent journalists clear signals, the media repeatedly fell into the same trap, and that highlights the third paradox. Journalists' failure at their central mission of holding government to timely account has persisted despite critics' continual indictments of the media for falling short of free press ideals. The criticisms have cited not only the media's openness to manipulation by presidents but a host of other derelictions: providing horse-race coverage rather than news that educates the public during election campaigns; personalizing and sensationalizing the news; practicing me-too, pack journalism in which every reporter says basically the same thing; and neglecting trends to focus on daily events.[17] These practices continue despite the clear vulnerability of the media to the pressures of officials, interest groups, and audiences, all of whom frequently express anger at media failings. And the recapitulation recurs in the face of journalists' own frustrations and sincere desires to improve.[18] It is paradoxical that a "free" press, especially one as committed to its ideals and unfettered by government regulation as the American press, cannot seem to profit from its mistakes and reform the way it gathers and reports the news.

The final paradox concerns the media's power in politics. The media's contributions to electing and undoing presidents suggest that their clout has grown.[19] Politicians and others on the receiving end of news coverage often claim the media exercise their sway by deliberately slanting coverage to promote one view or another—by injecting bias into the news. Yet journalists themselves insist they only hold up a mirror to reality. They say they hew strictly to objectivity, reporting only what their sources say and do. In this they acknowledge what the other paradoxes suggest: the autonomy of the press is limited. The paradox is that critics and journalists are both right. The national press corps is biased and objective, a passive, dependent reflector and an active force.

The media's influence arises from the effect of their messages upon the political thinking of the public and the elite. But, as we shall see, neither individual journalists nor news organizations truly control the versions of reality that their messages construct. The news product is powerful, but the power of its producers is fragmented and problematic.

The book seeks to explain these four paradoxes:

- *Abundance without growth:* The failure of citizenship to grow along with the increase in the number of media outlets and improvement in the nation's information infrastructure;
- *Aggressiveness without accountability:* The faltering of accountability journalism, the seeming inability of the vigorous Washington press corps to provide news that holds government to timely and consistent account, despite the trend toward increasingly skeptical if not cynical reporting;
- *Pressure without reform:* The seeming inability of the media at the national level[20] to overhaul their practices in the face

of continual and often self-voiced criticism for failing to enhance citizenship and make government more accountable, despite the clear vulnerability of news organizations to pressures
from audiences and from elites; and

- *Power without control:* The paradoxical coexistence of journalistic vulnerability, dependence, and devout adherence to
objectivity norms on the one hand with the growing power of
the press to influence the fate of politicians and policy proposals on the other.

Given the way politics is practiced in the late twentieth-century
United States, the media become crucial to any theory that government can be made responsive to genuine, independently considered (rather than manipulated) public preferences.[21] America
lacks effective political parties or other mechanisms to mobilize
the participation of the average person in politics. The only real
avenue of participation available and acceptable to most people
is voting regularly and knowledgeably. For most, the information
necessary for intelligent voting can come only from the mass
media, or from friends who themselves scan the news. There are
few alternative sources of information about candidates, policy
issues, or government actions. Even where the public experiences
a problem directly, as in the cases of inflation or crime, participating intelligently demands that they understand government policy
toward the dilemma. It is not enough that they know inflation
and crime are high; rational citizens must know who and what
is responsible, and what can be done.[22]

Unfortunately, this burden is too great; the media cannot live
up to the demands that modern American democracy imposes
on them. That point is the source of this book's title and a major
theme of the chapters to follow.

In describing and explaining the inability of journalism to fill
the institutional vacuum in American democracy, I am not attacking news organizations or individual journalists. On the contrary, I argue that many critics and scholars of journalism, and
even journalists themselves, have unfairly blamed the press for
sins that are beyond its power to redeem. Yet however unrealistic,
the critics' standards are desirable goals, ideals worth striving
toward in the interest of a healthier democracy.[23] Understanding

more precisely why the press cannot fulfill the ideals is a prerequisite to making progress. Thus while this book offers rather few accolades to the press as an institution, it attempts precisely to convey a sympathetic grasp of the journalistic predicaments I identified in my discussion of the four paradoxes.

By way of a critique of the notion of a "marketplace of ideas," Chapter One illuminates the central dilemma that spawns the paradoxes, although a full portrait requires the entire book. In essence, the dilemma is this: to become sophisticated citizens, Americans would need high-quality, independent journalism; but news organizations, to stay in business while producing such journalism, would need an audience of sophisticated citizens. Understanding this vicious circle of interdependence reveals that the inadequacies of journalism and democracy are the "fault" neither of the media nor of the public. Rather, they are the product of a process, of a close and indissoluble interrelationship among the media, their messages, their elite news sources, and the mass audience.

In support of this argument, Chapter One first probes the nature of market demand that news organizations face and must satisfy; it reveals that few Americans spend much time shopping in any "marketplace of ideas" for political information. More important, using data on knowledge, voting, and public opinion, the chapter discloses the grave implications of journalism's dilemma for representative democracy. The data suggest that journalism's inability to fulfill free press ideals does indeed impair the health of American democracy.

The next three chapters explain how the media can seem at the same time passive and aggressive, impotent and powerful, objective and biased, civic-minded and utterly unhelpful to informed citizenship. They illuminate the reasons for journalism's continuing inability to use its considerable influence more effectively in promoting citizenship and accountability.

To take a familiar example of media power that does little to advance citizenship or democracy, consider the overwhelming publicity boost usually received by the media-certified winners of the Iowa presidential caucuses and New Hampshire primaries.[24] The kind of influence journalists wield is exemplified by the media's ability and inclination to shower the "winners" of Iowa and New Hampshire with attention even while hewing to objectivity guidelines. The coverage arises neither from a malignant media conspiracy to promote specific candidates nor from a philosophical meditation on how the press can best advance democracy. It continues despite years of criticism of the unhealthy effect that the Iowa-New Hampshire show has on presidential politics.

The irrational concentration on Iowa and New Hampshire is an unfortunate but inescapable result of competition. Thus, though all journalists might like to de-emphasize the two events, none can.[25] The coverage represents power exerted by the media that the media themselves cannot control, in the absence of an agreement among politicians and news moguls to change the rules and suspend the incentives that competition creates. In other words, only if all the major national media could agree on minimizing attention to Iowa and New Hampshire would any of them feel free to downplay the first two tests of strength in the presidential campaign. Any individual outlet that did so unilaterally would risk confusing or losing its audience, and antagonizing the winners of the two contests.

Chapters Two and Three develop the argument that the power of the press is often in nobody's hands, that the national media do not fully govern the political influence of their own stories. The chapters criticize the standard notion of media bias and present a model that explains the origins and nature of news slant; they show how images conveyed by the media—but only partially under their control—help to determine the fates of presidents, policies, and parties. The model is illustrated by comparative analyses that explain how and why Ronald Reagan seemed consistently to receive more positive press than Jimmy Carter.

Using a national survey and newspaper content study, Chapter Four employs theories of cognitive psychology to dissect the nature of media influence over public opinion. The chapter explains how news slant and editorials shape both the public's actual opinions and the widely shared perceptions of the "public mood" that may influence the political process even more than public opinion itself.

The first four chapters, Part I of the book, show that news organizations operate in a system of interdependence, yet exercise considerable power in politics. Overcoming the media's dilemma and making journalism better thus becomes crucial to enhancing American democracy. That is the subject of Part II. Historically, the two main mechanisms for improving journalism have been reliance upon healthy, competitive economic markets, and use of government regulation to nourish or simulate such competition. Most policy discussions start with a belief that economic competition protects the marketplace of ideas, thereby enhancing the press's contributions to democracy. If anything, this faith has grown more ardent in recent years. Part II shows that, rather than improving journalism, economic competition can reinforce interdependence and dampen movement toward free press ideals.

Chapter Five explores the common, pessimistic reaction to rising newspaper monopoly—and the overly optimistic faith that newspaper competition yields something like a marketplace of ideas. According to data on ninety-one papers across the nation, economic competition makes little systematic difference to newspaper quality. Analysis reveals little reason to expect otherwise.

Chapter Six examines the conventional perception that rising competition in the television industry unequivocally benefits democracy. The most important policy decision to emerge from this notion is the Federal Communications Commission's abolition of the broadcast Fairness Doctrine. The doctrine was the government policy that intervened most directly to enhance news programming. The commission argued that the recent increase in electronic media outlets has created a genuine competitive market that will guarantee diversity and autonomy in political information much more effectively than government regulation ever could. The chapter reveals that well-intentioned criticism and policy analysis of the news media which ignores the dilemma of interdependence can undermine democracy.

There may be ways to disrupt the circle of interdependence, enhance the press's autonomy, and strengthen the accountability of government to a more informed citizenry. Some sort of external shock might upset the gridlocked relationships of media, elites, and audiences, strengthen the public's desire for accountability journalism, and enhance the media's ability to provide it. Chapter Seven suggests means of delivering the shock. The probability of success may be low; the proposals will provoke political antagonism, and implementation would be fraught with pitfalls. But Americans must address the real source of the shortcomings of the news. Otherwise, the apparently compulsive repetition of news practices that clash with the ideals that every journalist holds dear will persist, along with the dearth of democratic citizenship.

I

UNDERSTANDING MEDIA INFLUENCE

1

The Dilemma of Journalism: Democracy Without Citizens

Beyond the metaphorical marketplace of ideas lie two markets that are quite real: the economic and the political. In ideal visions of the marketplace of ideas, competition in these two markets drives journalism to excel. In practice, the competition prevents journalists from supplying the kind of news that would allow the average American to practice sophisticated citizenship. Because most members of the public know and care relatively little about government, they neither seek nor understand high-quality political reporting and analysis. With limited demand for first-rate journalism, most news organizations cannot afford to supply it, and because they do not supply it, most Americans have no practical source of the information necessary to become politically sophisticated. Yet it would take an informed and interested citizenry to create enough demand to support top-flight journalism. This vicious circle of interdependence makes the metaphor of an idea marketplace a poor reflection of the reality, and the dilemma, of American journalism. The dilemma in turn has baleful implications for democratic representation.

The problem begins in the economic market, where news organizations compete for the audiences and advertising revenues necessary to maintain profitability and stay in business. The nature of both demand and supply cements interdependence and diminishes the press's autonomy. On the demand side, news organizations have to respond to public tastes. They cannot stay in business if they produce a diverse assortment of richly textured ideas and information that nobody sees. To become informed and hold government accountable, the general public needs to obtain news that is comprehensive yet interesting and understandable, that conveys facts and outcomes, not cosmetic images and airy promises.[1] But that is not what the public demands.

Because of my focus on democracy and citizenship, "news" for the purpose of this book is political coverage provided by the media aimed at mass audiences.[2] While some prestige newspapers approach the ideal on occasion, coverage of politics in most newspapers, in the news magazines, and on television—most news intended for mass consumption—falls short of this standard. In the main these outlets offer the relatively superficial, diverting, or entertaining news the public seems to want—or at least has tolerated all these years. This is the demand facet of the vicious circle: the unsophisticated mass audience demands or accepts current news formats, or in many cases wants no news at all; the dearth of informative "accountability news" perpetuates an unsophisticated audience.

On the supply side, economic competition encourages news organizations to minimize costs and generate growing profits. The least expensive way to satisfy mass audiences is to rely upon legitimate political elites for most information. Besides profit maximization and cost minimization, other reasons for dependence upon elite sources include the cultural legitimacy of elites and the "facts" they supply; the shared social class positions and outlooks of many media owners and political elites; the definition of news as yesterday's or tomorrow's government actions, and the control elites exert over those activities; and the frequent dearth of non-elites with newsworthy information. Profit seems to me to be the primary concern, however; if using other news sources were significantly more profitable, it is doubtful the media would be nearly as dependent on elites as they are.[3]

Even without economic incentives, the media would have reasons to please audiences and use elites. Making audiences happy, for example, yields prestige, influence, and a sense of serving the public's interests. The point is not that economics alone causes the dilemma of interdependence, but that economic pressures strengthen it and weaken journalism's ability to achieve free press ideals.

The deep impact of economic requirements on news practices is not always recognized. Some scholars deny that profit goals have much of a direct effect on journalists. But economic pressures do shape the values that guide the creation of news—brevity, simplicity, predictability, timeliness. As one example, timeliness is so important to the news because it keeps the audience coming back. If the news is not timely, it is less important to watch or read on any given day. To attract the consumer every day, a daily news outlet has to imply that missing it will hurt. The focus on what just happened, the emphasis on getting scoops and beating the opposition to a story that everyone would have reported anyway in a day, says that knowing what just happened is the crucial thing. The requirement of timeliness also deepens the dependence of reporters on easily accessible, familiar elites; with more time, reporters could cover a wider range of sources.

The elites who make most of the national news are the ones who control policy outcomes in Washington: top officials in the White House and executive branch agencies, members of Congress and powerful congressional staffers, representatives of important interest groups, and some party spokespersons, think-tank experts, former government officials, and elder statesmen still involved in politics. The supply side of the journalist's dilemma is that most of these convenient and logical sources have a stake in what is reported. News reports can advance or undermine the policy proposals they want enacted or privileges they want maintained. The information they provide is tainted. The news largely consists of information supplied by sources who may sincerely support democracy in the abstract, but who must in each specific encounter with the press subordinate that ideal to the protection of their own political interests.

The continuing dependence of reporters on self-interested elites helps perpetuate the journalistic status quo, and this is where the political market comes in. In this market, elites and journalists vie with each other for control of the news. Each side peddles something the other needs. The elites have newsworthy political information, the indispensable raw material needed to construct the news. Journalists can provide publicity that can be slanted favorably or unfavorably. Elites seek to exchange a minimal amount of potentially damaging information for as much positively slanted coverage as they can obtain. Journalists seek to extract information for stories that generate acclaim or acceptance from editors and colleagues.[4] Government sources and journalists join in an intimacy that renders any notion of a genuinely "free" press inaccurate.

Because of the competitive nature of the political market and the inattentive, perplexed nature of the public, elites have little choice but to manipulate journalists. Elites who want to succeed politically cannot afford to debate complicated truths in a marketplace of ideas. Nor can officials volunteer information for the public to use in holding them to account, in the naïve faith that ordinary people will understand the complexities. If politicians do make that mistake, their competitors in the political market will almost certainly pounce and seize the advantage. So news organizations wind up depending upon elites whose primary goal when talking with reporters is to manage publicity rather than illuminate the truth.

To escape this dependence, a news organization would almost have to reinvent the news. It would have to develop a new definition of news, uncover novel sources of information, legitimize the definition and sources for mass audiences, and invest heavily in new techniques of news gathering and reporting—with little guarantee of enhanced profit and considerable danger of economic loss.[5]

Hence pressures from the two markets bolster each other and sustain the dilemma of journalism. Competition in the political market enforces the requirement that elites manage news; competition in the economic market enforces cost minimization and profit maximization, which means news organizations must depend upon elites and make news attractive to the largest number of consumers.

These relationships curtail elites' own political independence as they dampen the media's and the public's. Of course democracy is all about curbing elites' independence and requiring them to respond to the public's desires. But the media may not advance true responsiveness. The media system encourages elites to fashion rhetoric and take actions that accord with journalistic values and limitations rather than with responsive public policy.[6] For example, clever politicians shun complex proposals or ideas that opponents in the political market can easily turn into negative media symbols,[7] however much sense they make. Recall Walter Mondale's politically disastrous proposal in 1984 to raise taxes.[8] A frustrated and tense governing elite arises, a leadership class unable to break through the media wall without resorting to simplification and news management. The "marketplace of ideas" shrinks, and the public fails to understand what government is doing and what the stakes are. That returns us again to the origin of the vicious circle in the unsophisticated mass audience.

Genuine accountability news requires proper historical context, diverse perspectives, and explicit linkages to the officials responsible for policy outcomes. Such reporting allows ordinary Americans to understand how the actions or plans of government affect their vital interests and concerns. The typical newspaper or news broadcast fails to do much of this, and therefore flunks the test of the marketplace of ideas. For example, scholars find that coverage of presidential campaigns generally emphasizes the horse race (who's gaining, who's fading, and why) much more than the policy issues or records of the candidates. With occasional exceptions, most other elective offices garner little news of any sort either during or between elections.[9] Except for emergencies and scandals, decisions by regulatory agencies and other bureaucracies (e.g., the Federal Reserve or Department of Housing and Urban Development) receive even less news coverage.[10] Despite their asserted devotion to facts, news reports often fail even to reflect reality very well.[11] For example, reporting on Vietnam waned well before the intensity of the war itself,[12] "crime waves" often hit page one without any corresponding surge in actual crime rates;[13] and the press often characterizes "moods" in public opinion that contradict scientific surveys.[14]

I am not saying that the media can ever reach an ideal, that the average American will ever become a sophisticated political analyst, or that elites will ever completely refrain from managing the news. I am merely saying journalism's dilemma has stymied movement along the endless path toward the ideal.[15]

A major reason for the gap between the ideal and the actuality of journalism is that the metaphor of an "idea marketplace" is loaded with unsupported and insupportable assumptions and expectations.[16] The metaphor assumes enough ideas circulate to allow the public to choose those that truthfully depict reality or advance the social good. The model does not explain why the media would necessarily highlight the good ideas and downplay the bad. Nor does it say how or why the public would seek more of the good and discard the bad. There is no evidence that the truth or quality of any idea is the primary value guiding the manufacture or consumption of news.[17] Media organizations have scant incentive or ability to elevate truth over other news values. Their elite sources and their audiences often disagree about truth anyway. Elites, audiences, and advertisers might find unpalatable truths offensive. The safest bet is to stand by the practices that go under the label "objectivity." Despite the connotation of the word, these practices sharply limit the ability of journalists to offer audiences explicit assessments of truth, distortion, and falsehood.[18]

As most observers acknowledge, the primary product of journalism in any case is not ideas. The product is news. In practice, news slights ideas in favor of recent acts, events, decisions, and results in the competitive horse race of politics.

Even if journalism did feature analyses of ideas from many perspectives, or of historical context and trends rather than yesterday's ephemera,[19] a proper "marketplace of ideas" could not be a market at all. In a real market, producers supply what consumers like, and stop supplying what they do not like. If news producers followed this practice, the media would supply only the popular ideas, an obvious insult to the free press ideal. Suppliers in the marketplace of ideas are emphatically not supposed to behave the way producers in real markets do. If they did, novel notions would not circulate widely; only low-profit (or non-profit) media could afford to tell unpopular truths in an unpopular style, since for mass-targeted media, unpopular is, by definition, unprofitable. Mass-circulation media would say largely the same fashionable and expected things. It is unfortunate that journalism in the real competitive economy resembles this portrait more than it does the chimerical ideal.

This discussion should clarify the impossible double bind that popular and critical expectations of the press create for journalists. The media are expected both to be market-driven, profit-oriented organizations, which ensures they will please audiences (and therefore advertisers), and to be autonomous, free of fear or favor, which ensures they can provide truth. Similarly, critics usually want the media to be passive purveyors of "accurate" facts; when they disagree with the facts reported, they also demand that the media become active seekers and explainers of information. These contradictions are rarely noted explicitly, but they tend to be present in most critical discussions of the press. For reasons that will become increasingly clear, not only are these expectations logically impossible to fulfill; it is practically impossible for the media to fulfill any single one of them, at least consistently, except for making a profit.

Citizenship and Free Press Ideals

Even the sincere, intelligent, energetic professionals who staff most of our better news outlets seem incapable of providing enough high-quality accountability news to enable citizenship to thrive. To be sure, a citizen can usually put together the key facts by reading and carefully analyzing the best newspapers and magazines. But few people take the time. Short of the ideal, an effective citizen must at least possess basic information on political leaders and vote consistently, using that information. Even on this score the public falls short. The result of deficient citizenship is not only that major improvements in journalism are stymied, but that politics is rendered less representative, less democratic than it might be if knowledge and participation were higher.

The marketplace of ideas appears to call for citizens to obtain their news from more than one source, for example, to read more than one newspaper, and to look at each of four news categories: state/local, national, and international news, as well as editorial comments. The most detailed data on the public's use of the news media come from the 1974 national survey by the University of Michigan Center for Political Studies (CPS), which portrays a public that fails to meet these expectations.

Respondents who said they read two or three newspapers and all four types of news coverage "frequently" represent only 5.6 percent of the sample. Those who read the four catetgories frequently but only in one paper represent 6.5 percent of the sample, for a total of no more than 12 percent who are frequent readers.[20] To take another angle, slightly under one in seven Americans (13.7 percent) report reading two or more papers and watching the national evening news frequently. All of these data are based on self-reports and imprecise categories like "frequently"; they almost certainly overestimate media use. Most people believe it desirable to show interest, and many inflate their claims of good citizenship.[21] The number who attend carefully and habitually to a variety of media is probably lower than the data suggest.

Similar results emerge from less detailed questions on the 1984 Michigan CPS survey. For example, those who report watching the national news on TV five, six, or seven days during the previous week and regularly reading two or three newspapers total 15.5 percent of the sample, close to the 1974 result.[22] In the past decade, newspaper circulation per household and the ratings of national news shows have both decreased markedly. These data suggest that no more than 15 percent of the public fulfills the standard of extensive and intensive use of a variety of media to monitor news of public affairs.[23] The American public simply does not partake of a marketplace of ideas as free press ideals would have them do.[24]

More important than how people describe their use of the media is the result: their level of civic information and participation in politics. The evidence generally contradicts ideal visions of citizenship. Most of the population finds politics a remote and unengaging concern.[25] The low level of American voting participation is well known.[26] The CPS study of 1974 included verified data on voting,[27] although voting alone cannot measure citizenship.[28] The most realistic measure combines participation and knowledge: voting knowledgeably. To gauge this *sine qua non* of effective citizenship, I developed a leadership knowledge index. If unaware of which leaders prefer what, people cannot reliably represent themselves in democracy.[29] Knowing the stands of the major candidates is the only way consistently to match one's votes to one's priority concerns. Otherwise, any connection between vote and policy preferences is likely to be loose and unreliable.

I constructed a leadership knowledge index from the respondents' identification of the political stands in 1974 of three well-known leaders: Richard Nixon, Gerald Ford, and George Wallace.[30] Scores ran from 0 to 14 correct responses. I coded generously. For example, respondents received credit when they said Nixon was a moderate or slightly to the right on handling urban unrest; it could be argued he was a firm conservative.[31]

Those voting in 1974 and giving correct answers on at least 7 of the 14 candidate placements ("high knowledge") amounted to just 13.4 percent of the sample. At the other extreme, 42.7 percent of the sample both failed to vote in 1974 and managed no more than zero to six correct answers ("low knowledge"). Ignorant nonvoting is the most frequent response.[32] The portion of the sample in each category is:

	Vote	No Vote
High knowledge	13.4%	16.5%
Low knowledge	27.4%	42.7%

More recent surveys provide parallels.[33] In the 1980 Michigan survey, on perhaps the most important issue of the campaign, 52 percent of the respondents could not place Ronald Reagan's position on the inflation-unemployment tradeoff and 14 percent placed him on the wrong side (unemployment priority). Similarly, 42 percent could not place Reagan on the general liberal-conservative scale and 8 percent said he was a liberal; the same percentages could not place Carter or said he was a conservative.[34] After four years of the Reagan presidency, in 1984, 43.5 percent still either failed to identify Reagan as a conservative or could not place him at all.[35]

The 1984 survey also asked respondents which party had majorities in the House and Senate before and after the 1984 election. The election did not alter party dominance; the Democrats had controlled the House for thirty years, the Republicans had run the Senate for four. With four chances to give a correct answer (House and Senate pre-election, House and Senate post-election), only 19.7 percent got four correct and 6.0 percent got three. About half the sample knew one or two answers, and a quarter, none.[36] Or consider this: the percentage of the public unable to name any congressional candidate in their district was 45 percent in 1956.[37] In 1984, 68 percent failed.[38] If there are any trends in the data, they are not toward more knowledge or voting, despite rising education and the growing number of media outlets.[39]

Does Citizenship Matter to Democracy?

It has become commonplace for scholars to assert that the public's deficiencies in knowledge and participation do not prevent Americans from receiving adequate democratic representation. In order to reach this conclusion, scholars lower the standards of citizenship to match existing, depressed levels of political knowledge and turnout. The reasoning and data behind this judgment are in my view incomplete.

Much of the optimism about representation comes from comparing policy preferences of voters and nonvoters. Some scholars have found similar opinions among both groups. Even with 100 percent participation, they claim, elections would probably give us the same officials and presumably the same public policies. Unless one believes participation is an end in itself, by this account, the inability of most Americans to reach ideal citizenship becomes relatively insignificant.[40]

The analysis of Wolfinger and Rosenstone is probably the best known.[41] Comparing seven stands of self-reported voters and nonvoters in 1972, they find no significant differences and conclude that voters accurately represent nonvoters. For the next national election year, 1974, validated voting reports and more extensive measures of belief are available. These include a series of indexes of respondents' sentiments about a variety of political groups, and an index of liberal-conservative stance on policy issues.

The data indicate that the current electorate does not represent the entire public, and that knowledge (or its absence) may influence political attitudes. (Appendix A offers statistical tests and details.) Again, the analysis considers four groups: knowledgeable voters, "ignorant" voters, knowledgeable nonvoters, and "ignorant" nonvoters. The *knowledgeable nonvoters* are significantly more liberal than *knowledgeable voters* (on five of six political belief indexes) and *ignorant voters* (on all six indexes). Contrary to the popular conclusion in political science, then, voters probably do not fully represent those who stay home. Nor do election outcomes accurately reflect what would happen if everyone voted. If the knowledgeable nonvoters were to start voting, the distribution of opinions in the electorate would change and elections might turn out differently. Or if the groups were to switch roles, with, for example, those who now vote in ignorance staying home while knowledgeable nonvoters cast ballots, majorities might back different candidates.

The data also suggest the possibility that the preferences of nonvoters with little knowledge might change if they came to know more. *Knowledgeable* nonvoters are significantly more liberal than *ignorant* nonvoters. If ignorant nonvoters became knowledgeable, all else being equal, they might develop new opinions. If they then participated, the beliefs represented at the ballot box might change still more.[42]

The data are far from definitive. The difference between the knowledgeable and the ignorant could be traceable to forces not measured here. The data certainly do not prove that the public would select more liberal candidates if knowledgeable participation increased. For one thing, the data come from a single, off-year election. Given the complexities of voting, an expanded electorate might even choose more conservatives. Only a more complicated statistical analysis of data from several elections could establish definitively how increases in knowledge and participation would affect the electorate. Developing such a model would take this book far beyond its central focus on the media.

But Wolfinger and Rosenstone and others rely upon simplified models to conclude that voters do represent nonvoters.[43] My major point is to warn against drawing such conclusions from static analyses of current nonvoters and voters. If people now lacking political knowledge developed more insight, their preferences might change, and so might the political complexion of the electorate.[44] It seems fair to conclude that the outcome of elections held under current conditions of political ignorance and withdrawal may not represent the desires a larger and more informed electorate would register at the polls.

These findings are equally relevant to scholars who look only at voters and emphasize that even ignorant participants can represent themselves adequately by employing shortcuts that require little information.[45] For example, Brady and Sniderman say voters can develop clear feelings of liking and disliking candidates even on the basis of sketchy knowledge.[46] Using these likes and dislikes they can evaluate different candidates and reliably choose those who best suit their feelings. But concluding that voters now represent themselves sufficiently assumes that current levels of knowledge yield the proper shortcuts, that they like and dislike the "right" politicians given their general political goals and interests.[47] It is difficult to take at face value political ratings by people whose awareness of the players and policies is so limited that they cannot name a congressional candidate or identify the majority parties in Congress. The optimistic assumption also omits those—in many elections the majority—who do not vote and thus do not represent themselves at all.

The importance of more sophisticated levels of knowledge becomes clear when one looks at the larger picture of voting and representation. Consider this hypothetical scenario. The minority party in Congress is large and skilled enough to veto initiatives of a disunified majority party that also controls the presidency. As a result, the legislature kills or waters down policies which the president and congressional leadership want. Serious economic problems result that might have been avoided if the president's bills had passed. The economic difficulties are the minority party's fault. But the natural response of people with low information would be to blame the majority party (the one "in power") for the country's economic problems, vote them out, and reward the minority party—those truly blameworthy—with more seats in Congress. In such circumstances, citizens would have to possess sophisticated political understanding to avoid voting against their own interests.[48]

If not "without" citizens, the United States is demonstrably a democracy where people who participate regularly and knowledgeably form a distinct minority. As a result, it may be a democracy that represents the general public less well than Americans deserve.[49]

Even if most Americans will never reach the ideal, I believe that more knowledgeable participation is possible and desirable.

The media currently help to thwart any significant movement in that direction. Their baleful contribution is not the media's fault; nor is it the public's, nor even the elites'. If they attempted to produce more independent accountability news, media organizations would confront paltry demand, high costs, and sizable risks.

The marketplace of ideas may inspire the journalist's spirit; the grubby daily grind in the political and economic markets dominates the journalist's product. Despite the lessons of the recent past, the pressures from news critics, and their own best instincts and efforts, they continue to purvey easily digestible, elite-dominated news. Based on unrealistic assumptions of autonomous media serving an independent, active, and knowledgeable citizenry, the concept of a marketplace of ideas does more to mystify than to clarify journalism's influence in politics and contributions to democracy. Mutual dependency diminishes the ability of journalists, the public, and even elites to reach their democratic potential. Journalism falls far short of the free press ideal; too much of the public remains ignorant and disconnected from politics; and elites compulsively and often successfully manage the news to foil accountability.

2

Objectivity, Bias, and Slant
in the News

One of the major consequences of the failure to recognize the interdependence of the media, elites, and audiences is that discussions of the press's political influence tend to become mired in heated disputes about "bias." On one side are politicians and the public, who tend to trace episodes of unfavorable coverage to bias; on the other are scholars and journalists themselves, who insist that newsworkers do follow the objectivity guidelines designed to minimize bias.[1] There the argument usually rests, unresolved. Neither claiming that objectivity rules are violated nor certifying that they are obeyed reveals much about how the media's messages influence politics.

Objectivity rules contain two primary requirements. *Depersonalization* demands that reporters refrain from inserting into the news their own ideological or substantive evaluations of officials, ideas, or groups. *Balance* aims for neutrality. It requires that reporters present the views of legitimate spokespersons of the conflicting sides in any significant dispute, and provide both sides with roughly equivalent attention.[2] Exceptions aside,[3] journalists for the national press try to follow these rules of objectivity; audiences expect as much.[4] In theory, objectivity limits the role of the journalist to depicting reality for people to judge themselves, and prevents the newsperson from influencing people's political thoughts and behavior. According to professional lore, the impact of any news report must therefore come from the facts it describes, not from the journalistic choices (of sources, quotes, emphases) it embodies.

The problem is that facts do not speak for themselves. Choosing how to put facts together and which to emphasize inevitably affects what audiences perceive as reality. As many philosophers and scholars have shown, cultural concepts, literary conventions, psychological drives, economic interests, and linguistic codes work together to form people's perceptions of reality.[5] Journalists follow the work rules[6] that objectivity lays down, but they cannot realize the aims of objectivity. The objectivity creed contains yet simultaneously camouflages codes and conventions that journalists use in making their news choices. These selections do impart a slant to the news and influence politics—but not in the manner usually alleged by critics.

On Liberal Bias in the News

Despite the conventional academic wisdom that genuine objectivity is impossible in any discourse, participants in the political market continue to score points by claiming that journalists violate objectivity. Critics on the right are far more visible and vigorous than those on the left. They assert that national journalists insert their personal views and fashion their reporting to damage the right. A few academics, notably Robert Lichter and Stanley Rothman, have developed some evidence which they believe supports the existence of liberal bias.[7] Conservative politicians, from Vice President Spiro Agnew in 1969 through Reagan advisor Patrick Buchanan and Senator Jesse Helms (R.-N.C.) during the 1980s, made a crusade of the charge that liberals consciously dominate the news.

Perhaps the most influential manifestation of the conservative campaign against liberal bias in the 1980s was the effort led by Senator Helms against CBS television. Representatives of CBS, ABC, and NBC denied they were intimidated or even influenced. Yet in the wake of Helms's campaign, all three found partners to form much larger corporations with deeper pockets. (Other forces also played a major role in these combinations, especially federal deregulation.)

The profitable survival of the networks and their lucrative government-licensed stations depends in significant measure on general public trust or quiescence. The ideology of objectivity secures trust by reassuring audiences that the networks' political clout is limited and justified. So, even as they denied Helms's allegations, network executives confronted clear incentives to deflect charges of liberal bias. Although it would be difficult to prove, the pressure might have promoted news more favorable to conservatives.[8]

Dissecting the conservatives' campaign, consider first the charge of personalization, the assertion that the leftist personal beliefs of journalists lead them to advance liberal causes by intentionally slanting the news. In making this claim, the critics assume journalists enjoy much more autonomy than they do.

The studies cited most frequently are those of Rothman, Lichter, and Lichter.[9] Polling a non-random sample that vastly overrepresented perhaps the most liberal segment of journalism (Public Broadcasting station personnel in Boston, New York, and Washington), the authors discovered opinions significantly to the left of the general public on several issues. Of the 234 journalists surveyed, 41 worked for PBS, as compared, for example, with 23 who worked at the *New York Times* and 29 at CBS.[10] There is no consensus formula for obtaining a sample that properly represents the national media, but this one is clearly skewed. For example, if ratings were the criterion, the "CBS Evening News" garners at least ten times more viewers than PBS's "MacNeil/Lehrer NewsHour," so if 41 journalists from PBS were surveyed, the study should have sampled 410 CBS personnel instead of 29.

Other studies do suggest that journalists of the national media are more liberal on average than the general public on some issues, but reporters also reject radicalism, and they come much closer to public sentiment than do Jesse Helms and his followers.[11] In any case, most scholars have failed to find any liberal personalization in national news coverage. The routine processes of news selection and editing normally combine with career pressures and professional rules to purge personal ideological sentiments from the national news. On the local level, newspapers and broadcast stations may violate objectivity codes more often. But these deviations are controlled by the local owners,

publishers, or editors, not the journalists in the field.[12] Editors
enforce the owner's biases largely through the editing and play
(or censorship) of the stories that reporters turn in. Where local
newspapers do exhibit a consistent tilt, most often they seem to
favor conservatives or Republicans, not liberals.[13]

The other charge leveled by conservatives is that the news is
out of balance. The question of imbalance is more complicated
than that of personalization—and much more complex than either
the news critics or the defenders have acknowledged. Even if journalists' personal beliefs do not enter their stories, other forces
could in theory produce liberal imbalance in the news. An example of solid research that might support the claim of liberal imbalance is Clancey and Robinson's study of 1984 presidential
campaign coverage. A detailed consideration of their work reveals
the extraordinary difficulty of measuring stories against any meaningful standard of balance. Enforcing strict balance along all dimensions is usually impossible, without violating the original purpose of objectivity—without deliberately skewing the facts.

When critics claim that news is biased because it lacks balance,
they imply that giving equal time to another side would accurately reflect reality. They ignore the serious ambiguity that journalists face in applying objectivity rules to the practical choices
they confront. Objectivity rules cannot guarantee "correct" depictions of a reality that is the focus of continuous controversy.[14]

Clancey and Robinson found that, on matters relating to "candidate quality," from September 1984 through Election Day,
ABC, CBS, and NBC gave President Reagan 7,230 seconds of
"bad press." Mondale received only 1,050 negative seconds. The
figures indicate reporting that is highly skewed against Reagan.
But that inference would be problematic. The authors of the
study, respected academics, interpret their data cautiously and
deny that their findings reveal deliberate liberal bias. Their data
suggest more intriguing conclusions.

Mondale supporters might say that Mondale's superior coverage accurately reflected the developments of the latter part of the
campaign. They might point to Reagan's poor debate perfor-
mances, to his knowledge gaps on major policy issues, and to in-
dications of widespread corruption in his administration culmi-
nating in the October indictment of Labor Secretary Raymond

Donovan. They could argue that truthful coverage of reality as it developed during the autumn campaign produced any negative balance on Reagan's "candidate quality" ledger.

Reaganites might counter that Mondale's subservience to special interests, the financial mess of vice presidential candidate Geraldine Ferraro, and Jimmy Carter's unhappy legacy were far more damning, especially in comparison with Reagan's record of relative peace and prosperity. The Clancey-Robinson study would provide them with evidence of enormous bias in campaign news.

Even disinterested observers might see the 7 to 1 ratio in negative reporting as prejudicial. They might call for more balance. But the proper standard is unclear. If networks aimed for mathematical equality, providing the same number of seconds of "bad news" about each candidate's quality, they would have had to ignore some of Reagan's public statements and actions while playing up trivial Mondale blunders. Few would endorse such a practice; most would condemn it as deliberate distortion. The problem illustrates the media's difficulty in attaining the balance mandated by objectivity rules. Thus, ironically, strict balance violates its own purpose: to ensure that the news offers a neutral, factual mirror of reality.

The Clancey-Robinson study looked at another aspect of coverage: "horse race" stories assessing the candidates' chances to win. Mondale received 5,880 seconds of unfavorable coverage, Reagan, 1,200. The polls showed that Mondale's chances for victory were slim. Reality might have justified this ratio. But to remain consistent, critics who demanded equal treatment on candidate quality regardless of campaign reality would have to call this 5 to 1 ratio in horse-race news anti-*Mondale* bias.

To take yet another angle on the data, toting up "good press" in both candidate quality and hore-race stories, Reagan's positive press amounted to 6,270 seconds, Mondale's to 3,780 seconds. By this accounting, Reagan obtained considerably more favorable coverage than Mondale. On the other hand, adding together bad and good press for the entire ticket on both dimensions yields a Reagan-Bush net of 3,470 seconds of negative press. Mondale-Ferraro's press was also negative on balance, at 4,160 seconds. By this measure, both tickets looked just about equally bad; the news seems balanced.

Critics could use these data selectively to support any of three conclusions. Data that first seemed to reveal a strong anti-Reagan imbalance turn upon closer examination into an index of either an anti-Mondale tilt or a balanced portrait. Yet none of the interpretations seems acceptable, given the limitations of the data.

These considerations bring up the central problem in using conventional content analysis to study news bias: the lack of detailed knowledge about the influence of news on public opinion. When content analysts place a story in the "good press" or "bad press" category, they must make assumptions about the impact of that story on public attitudes. When they say a particular report or series of reports constitutes "bad press," presumably they mean the coverage caused a greater number of people to feel more unfavorable than more positive toward a candidate. But social scientists are just beginning to understand how news stories and editorials affect citizens' thinking and voting. Until understanding improves, nobody will be able to draw definitive conclusions about good and bad press.

Consider again the Clancey-Robinson data. Judging from the election, the 7,230 seconds of "bad press" on Reagan's quality as a candidate had little negative impact. In retrospect, the "bad press" seems not so bad at all. Even if the coverage looks as though it should have hurt Reagan, it did not. The venom in Mondale's lesser volume of "bad press" may have poisoned attitudes more effectively. Then Mondale would be the one who received the bulk of effectively "bad press," even though there were fewer seconds of it. Conclusions about bias become even murkier.[15]

Reagan's overwhelming win suggests that content analysis sometimes looks at the wrong aspect of the message when it simply counts seconds. Message dimensions vary in their impact on public evaluations of presidential candidates. The amount of time devoted to a message is not the only measure of its potential influence. A network might air ten ninety-second stories that contain strong attacks on a president for inaccessibility to the press; it might also show ten twenty-second stories that each feature the president as a strong leader. Most content analyses would weigh all coverage equally. Analysts would consider the 900 critical seconds to outweigh by far the 200 favorable. They would categorize the coverage as negative. Yet few but the journalists may care about press access, and most Americans may care greatly about strong leadership, in which case the net impact of the twenty stories might be favorable—just the opposite of what the raw data suggest.

Without a model of media effects, analysts may be mistakenly evaluating media messages. Content analysis requires some theory to explain which messages are potent, which less significant to public opinion. Absent such a theory, there is no acceptable intellectual basis for concluding that the national media consistently promote the left or indeed any view.

Objectivity, News Slant, and the Political Market

Despite the flaws in the argument that a consistent liberal bias pervades the press, the critics' distemper has roots in a valid point: journalism does exercise selectivity and influence. Even though, contrary to critics' claims, journalists do cling to the rules of objectivity and avoid deliberate bias, they often find themselves making choices that slant the news. By this I mean that their reports, while not ideologically biased, typically provide partial accounts that assist some causes while damaging others.

Slant emerges from choices that journalists must make in constructing their narratives. There is no easy way for journalists to reach some sort of ultimate balance or absolute depersonalization in all aspects of their message. As an example, one story must open the network news every evening. The lead story appears to have a greater influence on audiences than other news.[16] If that story happens to report a positive development for a president, for example, the decision to make it the lead imports a more favorable slant to the coverage than placing it at the end of the broadcast. Similarly, positioning a newspaper story on the right-hand side of page one, above the fold, gives it greater impact.[17]

An example of slant is the national media's coverage of the Iowa caucus and New Hampshire primary. Allocation of space and time usually tilts heavily in favor of perceived winners, at least in the immediate aftermath of the events. In 1984, for example, the *Washington Post* and *New York Times* each mentioned

Gary Hart 13 times in headlines after the Iowa caucus and before the New Hampshire primary. The *Post* mentioned Walter Mondale 13 times, the *Times*, 11.[18] After highlighting the perceived winners, the papers diverged more, but they all demoted those candidates who seemed to be falling behind. John Glenn received only seven headlines from the *Times*, three from the *Post*. Acting in accord with standard news values, which usually emphasize a two-person contest, the editors who selected and decided how to play stories helped to slant the news against Glenn and for Hart. Iowa and New Hampshire had too few delegates for Glenn's poor showing to damage his mathematical chances significantly, but the media emphasis mattered, not the mathematics. A different slant on the Iowa and New Hampshire results, say one that reflected the actual number of delegates selected, might have kept Glenn's candidacy afloat, and he might have triumphed in states with later primaries and more congenial electorates; we will never know.

As the examples suggest, however strictly they uphold objectivity standards, reporters and editors often participate willy-nilly in slanting the news to favor one side or another. Most individual journalists do not enjoy enough independence to make such choices as deciding which story should be the lead on the basis of what selection advances their pet candidates or causes. Rather, it is the professional norms of journalism and the economic interests of their news organizations that govern the slant of the news by guiding the decisions on lead stories, space or time allocation, and the rest.[19]

An unacknowledged and perhaps even unrecognized function of objectivity is to make it easier to influence these decisions—to make journalism safe for the elite news managers who populate the political market. Even if elites do not consciously realize it, the rules of objectivity offer would-be news managers two key advantages: predictability, since virtually all national media play by the same rules, and access, since in practice objectivity means journalists have to interview legitimate elites on all major sides of a dispute. Objectivity thus facilitates the manipulation of news slant. With knowledge of objectivity rules and other news norms (such as the one focusing disproportionate attention on Iowa and New Hampshire during presidential campaigns), elites can concentrate their resources where it will most benefit their press coverage, devise interview responses in advance, package pronouncements for maximum impact, and in general develop more effective strategies for obtaining favorable slant.[20]

The influence of objectivity rules means that truth often has less impact on the slant of a news report than skill at managing news. Even when one side offers a feeble argument and flimsy facts, as long as its spokespersons are considered important and respectable, and as long as they know how to play the political market skillfully, journalists will give them a say. Depending on the circumstances, this can either help or harm news managers. When they have only weak or even absurd points to make, they may be grateful that objectivity rules allow them to obtain coverage that treats their claims with surprising deference. When those same people have truth and logic on their side, however, they may be frustrated to find that reporters accord their opponents' ludicrous propositions serious attention.

Employing their knowledge of news rules and practices, manipulating information and events insofar as possible, competitors in the political market attempt to induce reporters to make news choices that help their cause and hurt their opponents. Those selections, normally decided on the basis of professional norms and practices, not personal preferences, determine news slant. The choices tend to yield slanted news despite reporters' close adherence to objectivity rules, and it is the slant that influences politics.

Journalists cannot do much about either their vulnerability to the political market or their inadvertent exercise of political power through choices that slant the news. This situation frustrates political leaders. It convinces many that the news is deliberately biased against them. It heightens their tendency to manage news, to take a cautious and calculating approach to journalists, a pose that limits journalistic independence even more. But limited as journalists' control over news may be, the next two chapters reveal that the slant of their coverage is politically potent.

3

Straight Talk on Slanted News: "Bias" and Accountability in Reporting Carter and Reagan

In 1980, the nation learned that President Carter's brother had been representing the Libyan government without registering as a foreign agent. The "Billygate" scandal dominated the network news for weeks. In 1984, Secretary of Labor Raymond Donovan became the first sitting cabinet member ever indicted, for allegedly participating in a fraud conspiracy involving at least one reputed member of organized crime. The story vanished after only a few days. Consider another contrast. When nine servicemen died in 1980 trying to rescue the American hostages in Iran, President Carter received a negative drumbeat of personal criticism in the press. When 241 U.S. Marines died in 1983 from a suicide bomb attack in Beirut, President Reagan largely escaped such condemnation.

Why did the two scandals and two deadly foreign crises receive such disparate treatment? The answer is not simply "reality." News decisions are not linked in any simple fashion to reality, nor could they be. Defining reality is problematic and journalists' depictions of it are heavily contested. Journalists have to decide which scandals should lead the evening news and justify repeated follow-ups and which should receive perfunctory play, when coverage of foreign policy mistakes should revolve around the president and when it should focus mostly on his subordinates. It is precisely through choices such as these that the media exert their influence.

Scholars need to take the observation that media "construct reality" beyond the generalization to ask: What are the rules and procedures used in the construction process, and how specifically do the media come to transmit or omit politically crucial information? This chapter develops a tentative, exploratory model designed to explain how the media convert the raw and malleable ingredients of reality into politically influential news.

Journalism's decisions arise in part from the doomed effort to produce news that serves two conflicting ideals: mirroring reality and holding government accountable. According to the mirror standard, journalism should be objective; that is, it should passively reflect and exert no political influence apart from reality. But following the accountability or watchdog standard requires that the media actively select the information they transmit; that the news reflect not just any reality, but the specific data needed to hold the government accountable. If people do use news reports in evaluating government, the media inevitably become influential. Journalists attempt to resolve the contradiction between being a passive mirror and an influential watchdog through the rules and procedures they use to select and evaluate political information. The result is what I call slanted news.

As the examples suggest, news slant becomes visible when we compare news stories to each other—not to reality. Typically, observers wishing to illustrate media impact use content analysis to show how the news deviates from some sense or index of reality. Comparing stories to each other, assessing the political information in each, minimizes fruitless debates over accuracy and fairness; these are usually conflicts over values which cannot be resolved.

The cases explored in this chapter involve two presidents, Carter and Reagan, in situations of scandal and crisis. Comparing stories does not demand that the events be identical "in reality." Rather, the assessment assumes that the stories have *comparable journalistic potential*. There are two requirements for such a comparative focus. The developments reported in the stories must have similar projected impacts on public opinion; both events must have either predictably positive impacts on a president's standing or predictably negative effects. And, journalists must be able to portray both occurrences similarly without violating their mirror or watchdog duties.

In terms of the first criterion for comparable potential, scholars have found that the public tends to evaluate chief executives by common standards such as competence, integrity, and personality.[1] Americans apply these precepts in judging several conditions: economic "misery" (inflation plus unemployment); battle deaths of U.S. servicemen; scandals; success in obtaining congressional passage of legislation; and actions in foreign crises.[2] A president's popularity is determined by a combination of real events and conditions and how the media cover them.[3] Press reports can enhance or stifle a boon, reduce or deepen a disaster.[4]

This body of research seems to predict that scandals, and crises that lead to seemingly futile U.S. battle deaths, are likely to lower a president's approval ratings.[5] News of these developments seems to have the potential to diminish public support of chief executives. The actual effects, however, will depend in significant measure on the tenor of the coverage.

The underlying reality of any two events inevitably differs, but much of the variation in news treatment can be linked to the journalistic process. When scholars claim the media construct reality, they suggest that were two events somehow to be identical, they could still generate different portrayals in the press. The premise here is that these differences in media response are consistent and predictable.

This brings up the second part of the definition of comparable journalistic potential. Any event offers an assortment of data which journalists have to shape into a narrative. Seeking always to balance the watchdog and mirror roles, journalists must decide how to tell the story, and their choices ultimately convey politically influential information. News slant, then, is defined as the contrast in treatment of events with comparable journalistic potential, on dimensions likely to affect public opinion.

Slant can be positive or negative, but it is always a relative concept. The news is negatively slanted if, based on an underlying theory of public opinion, coverage of one event will have a more negative impact on the audience's sentiments than that of the other. For example, when the media give repeated and prominent treatment to one scandal and not another, coverage of the first is negatively slanted: it is more likely to diminish public approval of the president. News can, of course, be slanted positively as well.

Why then did Billygate but not Donovan become an important focus of network attention and an instance of negative slant for Carter? The answer to the question illuminates the way that journalists manage to influence politics despite their dependence on elites, susceptibility to manipulation, and obedience to norms of objectivity. In other words, the answer helps resolve the paradox of a news industry that cannot control the considerable power its products exert.

The exploration begins with scandal news. President Carter's scandal is the failure of his brother Billy to register as an agent of the Libyan government.[6] President Reagan's scandals involve charges against Labor Secretary Donovan. In 1982, congressional committees and a special counsel investigated and cleared Donovan. Then, in 1984, a grand jury indicted him for grand larceny and fraud. Donovan and his codefendants won acquittal on May 25, 1987, but of course journalists covering the story in 1982 and 1984 did not know what the jury would find. I also present but discuss more briefly a second contrast, between coverage of the alleged turpitudes involving White House counselor (later Attorney General) Edwin Meese and those involving Carter's budget director, Bert Lance. Both allegedly engaged in irregular and possibly illegal financial transactions; both were powerful advisors and intimate friends of the president. In the later section on foreign crisis reporting, I compare coverage of the failed rescue mission in Iran (April 1980) with the U.S. Marine barracks bombing in Beirut (October 1983).

The study works with four dimensions of news slant. The list is not exhaustive, but includes some of the more important ways news coverage conveys information that influences public opinion. This chapter illustrates the first three dimensions.

Importance describes the prominence, repetition, length, and duplication of news stories across different media. This is the pre-eminent dimension of slant. Stories that do not receive important treatment rarely have much impact on public opinion, no matter what their traits on the other dimensions.

Criticism measures the amount and types of negative evaluation a story subject receives. The watchdog role demands that journalists convey such critiques where appropriate. The standards of assessment are embedded within journalism's expectations of how a proper leader or interest group should act.

Linkage describes the connections that a story makes between the subject of the report and aspects not strictly part of the news event. For example, whether a story about an administration decision links it explicitly to the president can affect his political standing.

Perspective is determined by the reporter's use of sources.[7] When a president's perspective suffuses a story, he or his allies are sources for the bulk of the information and thereby guide many of the reporter's ostensible news decisions. Perhaps the most important aspect of perspective is diversity of sources. Stories with many conflicting sources convey a variety of views; stories with one source tend to convey one interpretation.[8]

The Importance of Being Billy

The most significant dimension of news slant is importance. Importance judgments reflect the amount and prominence of treatment a news event receives. In this section I explore importance in coverage of the scandals on the three major networks, ABC, CBS, and NBC.[9]

Research on the special impact of lead stories[10] suggests that important treatment amplifies a story's effect on public opinion. Even if the words and pictures are precisely the same, the 90 seconds that open a TV news show usually have more influence on politics than do the 90 seconds that close it. Elites may also assume lead stories affect public opinion and act accordingly. Conversely, news near the end of a show may not create a stir commensurate with the information it conveys; many in the audience may assume it is less important for them to think about those stories than the lead. Sensing this, elites may pay less heed to later stories too.

In my calculations, *placement* of the story in the broadcast is measured by the number and percentage of times the story enjoys lead status. *Length* is the average time devoted to each story in seconds, and the total amount of time the coverage takes up; *repetition,* the number of stories on the scandal within a single program (omitting anchor introductions); and *duplication,* the total number of days the story runs on all three networks. The more time taken to present information on an event, the more repetition and duplication, the more likely it will catch the public's attention and affect its beliefs.

President Carter's scandals received more important treatment on most dimensions. Billygate was the subject of 118 stories in the concentrated period of seven weeks (May–June 1980); Bert Lance, 91 stories over seven weeks (August–September 1977); Donovan, 40 stories over three different phases (two in 1982, one in 1984); and Meese, 49 stories in five weeks (March–April 1984).

As summarized in Table 1, Billygate attracted 394 total minutes of reporting, Lance 318 minutes, Donovan 102 minutes, and

Table 1. Importance of Billygate, Lance, Donovan, and Meese

| | Length | | | | Placement | |
	Total Coverage (min.)	Average Story (sec.)	Duplication[a]	Repetition[b]	Lead[c]	Lead ratio[d]
Billy Carter	394	200	41	53	38	26.4%
Bert Lance	318	210	19	52	31	22.5%
Donovan	102	153	18	6	8	6.6%
Meese	84	102	24	3	8	7.6%

Note: All figures refer to combined totals for ABC, CBS, and NBC evening news. Figures come from Vanderbilt Television News Archives network news indexes.

[a] Number of days the story received coverage on all three networks.

[b] Number of times a network covered different aspects of the story in separate reports by different correspondents (excluding anchor).

[c] Number of times story served as lead on one of the networks.

[d] Number of times story served as lead divided by number of times it could have served as lead. That is, the number of days the story endured times three networks. Billygate, for example, endured for 48 days; on each day it could have served as lead on any of three networks, so it had 48×3 or 144 opportunities to be the lead story. The figures are 38/144, 31/138, 8/120, and 8/105 for Billygate, Lance, Donovan, and Meese respectively.

Meese 84 minutes. The average length of Billy stories was 200 seconds, compared with 210 for Lance, 153 for Donovan, and 102 for Meese.

Switching from one to another correspondent and repeating variations on the theme several times within one broadcast conveys greater importance to the story than the normal one correspondent per news event. The number of times Billy was the subject of multiple correspondent stories within a single show was 53, and for Lance, 52. For Donovan, multiple reporting occurred only five times, for Meese, three. On 41 days out of the 48 during which Billygate was big news, all three networks ran stories on the scandal. This was true for Lance 19 times in 46 days. Donovan received triple-network treatment 18 out of 40 days, and Meese, 24 out of 35 days. The Billy Carter issue led the evening news 38 times, Lance 31 times, Donovan 8 times, and Meese 8 times. Thus Billy was the subject of lead stories 26 percent of the time, a percentage nearly four times greater than either Donovan or Meese.

A slightly different definition of the Donovan "story" makes for an even more striking contrast. The biggest scandal was the indictment, because it demonstrated that a grand jury and the district attorney believed Donovan might have committed a crime. The other stories had occurred two years earlier and had little bearing on the indictment. There were only 16 stories on the indictment itself, lasting a total of 41 minutes. The average story was 154 seconds long. On only two days was the Donovan indictment mentioned by all three networks; and it served as a lead story only five times. The networks offered no independent investigation of the charges. Compared with the firestorm over Billygate, the first-ever indictment of a sitting cabinet member did not become a major scandal. Nor did the 1982 special prosecutor's investigation, during which a witness died mysteriously and congressional staffers received death threats, unusual happenings that could have made the Donovan scandal more newsworthy than Billy Carter.[11]

Television caused Billygate to appear much more important than Donovan, making it in actuality more significant to politics. The treatment converted an unfortunate reality into worse news for President Carter. In the wake of this scandal, his approval rating dropped to 21 percent—an all-time low for any president since surveying began.[12] If television had accorded Billygate and Lance the relatively low importance granted Donovan and Meese, Carter might have suffered less political injury. If journalists had magnified Donovan and Meese, President Reagan, who appointed and refused to fire both men, might have experienced political damage. Instead, he won landslide reelection a month after Donovan's indictment.[13]

Explaining Slant in Scandal News

Importance judgments are explained by four forces. The first two are the evaluation and the production biases. These biases embody journalistic norms that guide the gathering and assessment of newsworthy information. I will discuss the other two forces, event context and media-management skill, shortly. I consider the biases "institutional" because individual journalists might not approve or even consciously apply them. Yet the national journalistic community responds predictably and consistently to news events in ways that suggest the biases are real. Because of the unstated nature of the biases, I infer their existence from the content of the news itself.[14]

Although it describes a myth, the marketplace of ideas has a real world function: providing the crucible for the professional creed of journalism. Embedded in the doctrine is a primary duty to make government actions visible and comprehensible and thereby help the public evaluate political leaders. The creed also encourages journalists to approach this task with profound skepticism about the motives of politicians.[15] This watchdog mandate produces the two tendencies that I combine under the rubric of evaluation biases: favoring popularity and favoring power.

According to the popularity bias, presidents should enjoy public esteem. When journalists believe a president is unpopular, relatively negative news slant tends to arise. Journalism's watchdog commitment appears to encourage reporters both to highlight evidence of public coolness toward a president and to convey criticisms of unpopular leaders. On the other hand, when they perceive a president as popular, journalists become more hesitant to convey damaging information.[16]

According to the power bias, a president should know how to get things done in Washington. If he does not know how to work the levers of power, he cheats the majority who elected him of the policies he promised to enact. When journalists think a president is incompetent at using power, they pass on this judgment through news slant.

I call these the evaluation biases because they both attempt to give the public the most pertinent information needed to assess how well the president is performing. The unstated theory seems to go as follows: if a president does not enjoy public approval, he must by definition be doing something the public dislikes; he must be failing to represent the public correctly, and the public should know that in evaluating him. If he does not have a solid "professional reputation"[17] for using power to get things done in Washington, he is failing to move government to represent the desires of the public that elected him, and they should know this when judging his performance.

Applying these institutional biases allows reporters and editors to conform to objectivity rules while appearing to hold presidents accountable, thus smoothing over the conflict between the mirror and the watchdog roles. Journalists cannot offer explicit judgments about the wrongheadedness of a president's policies and actions without breaching objectivity. But they can evaluate popularity and power, and provide their appraisals for audiences to use in evaluating presidents.

However, journalists normally do not either make or report assessments of popularity and power independently. Their sense of a president's professional power and public approval tends to come from their interactions in the political market. Elite sources—interest group leaders, members of Congress, experts, agency officials—determine their press strategies in substantial measure by gauging presidential power and popularity. To protect their own interests, when elites think the president is popular and wields power skillfully, they tend to withhold or moderate criticism in talking with journalists. If elites think he is slipping, or if an untoward event provides an opening, elite opponents provide reporters with critical assertions. Hence the evaluation biases of national journalism are a joint product of internalized, professional values and of newsgathering routines. When elites are openly critical of a president, it signals to journalists that his effectiveness or popularity must be threatened. Equally important, as a practical matter, elite criticism provides reporters with sources who are willing to say negative things.

The most important single indicator of presidential popularity and power for journalists appears to be support by members of the president's party. It may also be the most significant single force behind news slant. Almost by definition, to be powerful in Washington and popular in the country, a president must have his own team consistently on his side. When Republicans coat their president in Teflon and Democrats do not leave a scratch, journalists' reasoning points to a popular and powerful leader. When the president's ostensible allies volunteer hostile observations on their leader, the opposite occurs.

Here is how this model applies to Billygate and to the Donovan scandal. I focus on these two because they offer the most revealing contrasts. As Billygate began, I believe journalists regarded Carter as neither effective in Washington nor popular in the nation. He was fighting for renomination amid serious Democratic unrest. Billygate appeared further to threaten Carter's standing. Apparently sharing this assessment, unhappy Democrats and ambitious Republicans eagerly peddled Billygate information and comments to reporters. That ensured novel news developments almost daily, keeping the story hot. An incumbent with more public popularity and a better reputation for wielding power effectively might have been able to dismiss the charges as irrelevant to the presidency. Instead, the active opposition from both parties fed journalists' own negative evaluations and supplied their stories with legitimate, newsworthy quotes and data.

Conversely, when the Donovan allegations surfaced, Washington elites seemed to believe Reagan to be both popular with the public and powerful in Washington. Even Democrats held off, perhaps because they assumed attacking Reagan would not help them. Journalists' judgments built on those of their sources: Reagan was doing well in the political game. With all indicators in 1984 predicting landslide re-election, he had virtually no opposition among Republican elites. This served as an index of his high professional standing in Washington and his public approval, drying up potential sources of critical data or comment that might have made Donovan more newsworthy. Republicans hoping to board the Reagan juggernaut had no incentive to feed the Donovan story—unlike many Democrats who hoped to prevent Carter's renomination in 1980 by playing up Billygate. Also, Democrats may have become reluctant to press the corruption issue against Reagan in 1984 after the financial difficulties of their vice presidential nominee made headlines, some of them alluding to ties with organized crime.[18]

The evaluation biases comprise only part of the explanation for the divergent coverage. Also important are the three tendencies I call the production biases. If the ideals of the marketplace of ideas create evaluation biases, production biases spring from the economic market. The primary business purpose of news organizations is to package audiences' attention for sale to the advertisers, who foot most of the bill (they provide about 75 percent of the revenue for daily newspapers and nearly 100 percent for television).[19] The production biases grow out of the need to manufacture news that attracts and retains mass audiences. This is no easy task. The news media compete for the audience's attention with entertainment media and many other activities. Apart from a few distinguished exceptions, in order to produce news that appeals broadly enough to succeed in this competition, the media enforce three production biases: simplification, personalization, and symbolization.

The simplification bias leads the media to generate more copy on stories that are simple to report—convenient, inexpensive, and safe, rather than inconvenient, costly, and risky. The media also prefer stories that are simple to understand. Journalism conveys a simple message more readily and accurately than a complicated one, because institutionally it finds the information easier to process, and it deems simple messages more accessible and attractive to audiences. Because of the simplification bias, news stories often tend to strip the context from ideas or actions.[20] There is no necessary ideological bias to the removal of context; the specific situation determines who benefits and who loses.[21]

The second of the production biases is personalization. In order to encourage audience interest and identification, journalists tend to explain events by reference to the actions of individuals rather than to institutional, historical, or other abstract forces. To lend drama and provide a concrete narrative framework, journalists favor news that clearly involves well-known individuals in conflict. If the story takes an archetypal form (David vs. Goliath, Good vs. Evil), so much the better.

Symbolization is the third production bias. Journalism welcomes symbols that condense widely shared, familiar meanings and carry broad political connotations. A dramatic action, intriguing personality, or stirring slogan can supply a symbol. Underlying the symbolization bias appears to be the assumption that audiences easily grasp such symbols and enjoy the pleasure of recognition they afford.[22] A symbol can stand for a familiar stereotype or shared public understanding of the subject covered in the story. As we will see, the news often stereotypes presidents and summarizes them using symbols. A symbol can also connote a wider cultural value or archetype, such as patriotism or individualism.

Sadly for President Carter, the bad news involving his brother fit the production biases well. Billygate was a simple story to report, a simple story to understand. Making reporters' jobs easier, sources seeking to undermine the president continued to serve up new Billygate tidbits for their own self-interested reasons. The accusation against Billy was uncomplicated: failure to register as a lobbyist for an unpopular foreign country. As a well-known character in the news, the irrepressible presidential sibling who flouted and embarrassed his brother supplied a perfect symbol of presidential weakness. Too, Billygate offered a story of familiar personalities in conflict. Beyond this, it enacted an archetypal saga of tension between brothers with roots as old as the biblical tale of Cain and Abel; Billygate was a soap opera set in the White House. Billy personalized and symbolized the stereotype common in Washington and around the country of President Carter as ineffectual.

The Donovan story clashed with the production biases. It required much more difficult, costly, and risky journalism. Unlike Billygate, no legitimate elite sources were peddling "Donovangate" revelations. The chief potential news sources were district attorneys and grand jury participants sworn to secrecy (and alleged conspirators). Unlike the politicians milking Billygate, the Donovan sources had every incentive to avoid reporters. The alleged scam was Byzantine: a complex shell game difficult to convey in 150 seconds of television. In contrast to the colorful Billy Carter, Donovan was a drab, shadowy personality unknown to most Americans. The purpose of symbolism in journalism is to summarize vividly a widely held impression. Donovan and his purported dark associations did not fit the established image of the sunny, "morning again in America" Reagan presidency the way Billy seemed to summarize the stereotype of the Carter reign.

The production biases seem conducive to reinforcing stereotypes. Simplification, personalization, and symbolization are all strategies people use in selecting and making sense of the infinite amount of data with which the world confronts them. These cognitive techniques help to blend new developments with existing knowledge and beliefs, to make novel information comprehensible in terms of stored experience. Journalists themselves have these needs to assimilate the new in terms of the familiar, and they know audience members are even more in need of such assistance. Hence journalism seems often to search for and emphasize information that confirms stereotypes, such as those of Carter as weak and Reagan as popular, and to neglect or downplay information that contradicts conventional wisdom.

Sometimes bad news is congruent with the production biases, sometimes good. Under the right circumstances, production biases can outweigh evaluation biases and cause negative stories to appear about a president the press generally treats gently. Coverage of the Reagan administration's quandary over tax exemptions for racially prejudiced schools illustrates the production biases at work against the president. Applying moderately complicated legal reasoning, administration officials instructed the Internal Revenue Service to reverse previous policy and grant Bob Jones University and similar discriminatory schools tax exemptions. The IRS, they reasoned, did not have clear statutory authority to withhold exemptions on civil rights grounds. These officials felt the IRS could begin abusing its power, withdrawing exemptions from women's colleges and other institutions. They favored legislation explicitly authorizing the IRS action. However, the press simplified the issue, treating it almost exclusively as the Reagan administration supporting taxpayer "subsidies" (in the form of exemptions) for racist schools. Without the complicated context, and building upon the potent, familiar symbolism and stereotype of old-South racism, news slant was quite negative.[23] Media pressure, fed by public criticism from Republicans, grew, and the administration reversed its decision.

Beyond the evaluation and production biases are the two other forces that contribute to slant. One is the event context. Some events become lead stories largely because they happen on a slow news day. A story may also obtain repeated play because it occurs over a time when no other events compel attention. Or a story may generate attention because related events have occurred recently, suggesting a possible pattern. Other stories are buried by an avalanche of bigger news. Whether the event context helps or hurts a president depends on whether the story in question reveals something he would like emphasized or slighted.

For politicians, a cyclical event sets a context of particular import: elections. A development that emerges during a campaign may receive more attention than one that happens earlier or later. For example, Billygate came at a bad time in the electoral cycle for President Carter. The Billygate scandal's potential to damage his shaky standing in the campaign made it more newsworthy. The Democratic convention was nearly at hand, the election itself less than four months off. A year or two earlier, Billygate might have received less attention.

For Reagan, the initial Donovan investigations (1982) arose well before the re-election campaign. But the context of the October 1984 indictment was potentially quite damaging. Had Reagan's reputation for effectiveness been weak and his popularity low in 1984, as Carter's was in 1980, the timing could have devastated his re-election chances. To reverse the point, given how the press treated Billygate, if one of Carter's sitting cabinet members had become the first in history to be indicted, a month before election day, reporting might well have tilted strongly against Carter compared with the coverage Reagan actually received.[24]

The final explanation of slant is skill in news management. Controlling the way facts and events influence the slant of the news is a major preoccupation of the White House. Unflattering reality may insert itself at inopportune times with inexorable force, and opponents in the political market actively contest the president's efforts. But presidential press staffs slave away to pump up journalists' perceptions of their man's popularity and effectiveness; to fashion simple, symbolic good news; and to time their actions and words for the right context.

Ronald Reagan's press staff exhibited unusual mastery at these tasks. Reagan's personal amiability and the absence of a unified Democratic message and strategy made the job easier. At the opposite extreme, Jimmy Carter's press officers made many mistakes. Carter's chilly relationship with the Washington press corps made his administration more vulnerable to attacks by the savvy, united Republican opposition.

The contrast between the coverage of the scandals surrounding Bert Lance and Edwin Meese could also illustrate the four forces behind news slant. As Table 1 shows, the Lance affair was accorded nearly as much importance as Billygate, and considerably more than Meese (or Donovan). Lance, a close personal friend and advisor of Carter, was director of the Office of Management and Budget. Between July and September 1977, the Senate held a series of hearings featuring allegations that Lance acted improperly when a bank president. Meese, perhaps the president's closest friend and advisor in the first term White House, faced allegations in March and April 1984, during confirmation hearings on his nomination for Attorney General, that he had received unsecured personal loans from persons who later obtained jobs and other favors from the federal government and failed to disclose income on disclosure statements and tax returns.

When the Lance scandal exploded, Carter was still quite popular (around 66 percent approval rating),[25] but his professional reputation had already deteriorated, and, perhaps most important, elites of his own party deserted him. He had offended fellow Democrats from his first day in office; his proposals floundered in Congress. The willingness of a Senate controlled by Democrats to hold public hearings excoriating one of the president's closest associates probably signaled to journalists the weakness of Carter's support even among Democratic elites. The hearings also offered a source of revelations which satisfied journalists' needs for new data to keep the daily scandal narrative flowing. Whereas the Democratic Senate leadership under Carter established a high-profile committee probe that kept the presses humming, the Republicans who controlled the Senate confirmation process during the 1984 Meese scandal called off the hearings as soon as a special prosecutor was named, arresting the news flow.

Beyond the weakness of support from Washington Democrats, which put the evaluation biases to work against Carter, the production biases also hurt him. Lance appeared to symbolize old-style cronyism of the sort Carter had campaigned against. Feeding an impression of hypocrisy, Carter appointed and then stuck by a man whose business dealings seemed shady if not criminal. Also, Lance's banking practices were complicated, not simple enough to unravel in the normal TV report or even newspaper analysis. Finally, the president's dogged public loyalty to Lance provides another example of the Carter administration's mismanagement of the press. Carter might well have diffused the scandal early and preserved his distance if he had fired Lance immediately rather than repeatedly proclaiming his support of the budget director.

It might be argued that the difference in slant is traceable to Lance's alleged misdeeds being more serious than Meese's. The sums of money at issue were considerably greater for Lance; if money is the measure, the alleged ethical breaches of Meese were less serious. But by another standard, that of range of power in government, any character and behavior flaws in Edwin Meese were more serious since his purview had encompassed all of domestic and foreign policy, not just the budget—and he was under consideration to be the nation's chief law enforcer. Even if the accusations against Lance were the more serious, there is no standard of reality by which one could conclude Lance's trespasses were three or four times more serious than the charges against Meese. And if gravity of offense were the primary explanation of slant in scandal news, Billygate should have generated the least attention of any of these four scandals. As someone who did not even hold public office, Billy and his deficiencies had the least serious implications for the well-being of the public. As did Billygate and Donovan, the Lance and Meese affairs offered journalists an assortment of facts, on the basis of which they could have covered both stories as highly important, treated either one as considerably more important than the other, or portrayed both as relatively minor.

Foreign Crisis and News Slant

A comparison of the foreign crisis coverage received by Carter and Reagan in *Time* and *Newsweek* illustrates two other aspects of news slant: linkage and criticism. Linkage is the connection of presidents to events that reflect positively or negatively upon their leadership. Criticism consists of information on policies or actions that suggest a president's failure to perform according to public expectations.

In both the Iran rescue and the Beirut bombing, Americans died from sudden, hostile action. Different presidential decisions might have averted the deaths. Both crises raised grave questions about the wisdom of U.S. policy and the competence of the U.S. military—and thus about the president.

The differences between the crises are also important. Carter's Iran rescue attempt occurred in a brief period as a result of a specific presidential act. It was an invasion of a foreign country with a clear mission; its failure was simple to see. Reagan's stationing of U.S. Marines in Lebanon came at the request of that country's government. Since the policy lacked a clearly defined purpose, the press had no simple measure of its success or failure. The president had chosen the original policy of troop deployment months before the barracks attack. He had not issued a separate and distinct command setting up the possibility of the barracks bombing.

But these contrasts convey only a partial appreciation of the reality of the two crises. I shall amplify that point after discussing the findings.

Fundamental to journalism's watchdog role is critical evaluation of political officials' behavior. Conveying just the right amount of criticism is tricky. If they criticize too much or too harshly, journalists may face attacks for violating objectivity. On the other hand, if they criticize too little they fail at the watchdog function, risk derision from professional colleagues, and remain vulnerable to charges of bias from the president's opponents.

When he must defend himself against recurring criticism, a president may appear weak or guilty, even if he is not. Audiences may discount his responses as self-serving. A president under repeated, high-importance critical siege almost never looks good. One measure of criticism is a simple count of assertions that criticize administration policy. Another is a count of criticisms that mention the president by name rather than attack only the policy or event.

In explaining events, reporters omit a great many qualifications, nuances, and complexities. They employ several devices intended to convey the relevance or meaning of the news simply. These cues assert connections between the news and an element that may not be strictly part of the newsworthy development. One device is linkage.

The most important linkage element for a president is probably personal connection: drawing explicit or implicit connections between events or actions and the president. Merely naming the president links him to a story. Just by mentioning the president's name, stories about unfortunate policy developments suggest presidential responsibility. Stories that do not contain the name discourage the audience from associating the president with the event. Thus counting the number of times a president's name appears in the coverage measures linkage.

Institutional biases and media skill both directly affect linkage. When a president appears popular with the public, opponents fear that slamming him personally may backfire. Stories critical of administration policies are therefore less likely to mention the president, more likely to blame subordinates. One mark of media skill is the president's ability to manage journalists' perceptions of his personal involvement. Linkage to the president almost automatically elevates importance judgments. Lack of a presidential news peg can relegate news to a single appearance in the back pages. Carter and his staff often seemed to claim credit as energetically for bad events as for good, giving journalists a reason to elevate the importance of negative news and link it to the president. In the Billygate case, for example, Carter made the mistake of actively intervening, and his role became part of the scandal. Reagan remained aloof from the Meese and Donovan affairs.[26]

To measure crisis linkage, I analyzed the two issues of *Time* and *Newsweek* that immediately followed the rescue attempt and barracks bombing. I counted the number of times the name Carter or Reagan, or "the President," appeared in the coverage. I assumed that the more the stories mention a president's name, the more likely audiences would use the event in judging him. For criticism I counted explicit or implicit negative evaluations of the president's policies, decisions, or ideas. While the sheer number of criticisms is important, I also noted specifically the ones appearing in juxtaposition with the president's name.

As Table 2 shows, Carter fared two and one-half times worse in linkage than Reagan. His name (or "the president") appears 242 times in coverage of Iran: Reagan's appears only 91 times in Lebanon reporting.

The magazines painted the rescue mission as a marked personal failure for Carter. Coverage of the Lebanon bombing invoked and rebuked Reagan much less. *Time* and *Newsweek* focused on Carter as the cause of the disaster. Much of the analysis concerned

Table 2. Linkage and Criticism in Crisis

Subject	Linkages[a]	Criticism[b]	Personal Criticism in Paragraphs[c]
Carter and Iran rescue	242	84	62
Reagan and Beirut bombing	91	45	16

[a] Number of mentions of the president by name or title.

[b] Includes explicit or implicit criticisms of the president's actions, policies, or ideas, which mention him by name (or call him "the president") or which do not mention a president by name but in context clearly refer to his activities or goals. The criticism must be of the president's own decisions, strategies, or goals. Criticism of the specific acts of subordinates (e.g., tactics on the battlefield) does not count unless the paragraph mentioning the subordinate behavior links it to the president.

[c] Number of criticisms contained in paragraphs mentioning name of president.

Newsmagazines analyzed: For Carter, articles in *Time* and *Newsweek* issues of May 5 and 12, 1980; for Reagan, *Time* and *Newsweek* of Oct. 31 and Nov. 7, 1983.

Carter's popular standing and professional effectiveness. The impact might have been less destructive if coverage had not linked Carter so closely to the event.[27]

The rescue mission could have generated widespread public approval. Even when the U.S. suffers a setback, presidents may enjoy rallying responses to crises.[28] Carter had in fact experienced an extraordinary upward lift from the original hostage seizure, when he did little more than talk. Though his failure to heed intelligence warnings arguably made the takeover possible in the first place, Carter's overall job approval rating zoomed from 32 to 61 percent during the first month of the crisis (November 1979).[29] Though unsuccessful, the rescue mission actively attempted to solve the problem and thus might have stimulated another rally. Yet approval of Carter's handling of the Iranian situation dropped from about 48 percent just before the raid to 40 percent a couple of weeks later, where it remained for the rest of his presidency.[30] His overall approval rating before the April 30, 1980, raid was 39 percent. After a statistically marginal rise (to 43 percent) the first few days after the raid, general approval sank to 32 percent by mid-June.[31]

In contrast, Reagan's general approval rating in October 1983 before the barracks bombing was 46 percent, and after, 53 percent.[32] The increase was probably due mostly to the Grenada mission, which came two days after the bombing. But public approval specifically of his handling of the Lebanon crisis did go up, by 15 points, after he spoke on TV about a Marine wounded in the attack who had scrawled the motto "Semper Fi" in the dirt while awaiting medical care.[33]

Comparison of news criticism also illustrates the negative slant Carter received. The coverage contained 84 critical assertions about the Carter administration's actions, of which 62 came in paragraphs mentioning Carter's name. The reporting connected the bad news from Iran with mistakes by President Carter. In contrast, the Reagan administration received 45 critical assertions, only 16 of them in paragraphs mentioning the president's name. Carter suffered four times the amount of this especially damaging form of criticism. Around three-fourths (62/84) of the criticisms of the Carter administration occurred in paragraphs containing his name, compared with one-third (16/45) of the

Reagan administration's. Reagan managed to create a larger gap between himself and criticism surrounding the crisis.[34]

One explanation of the gap could be that there was simply less coverage that mentioned Reagan at all; perhaps there was less criticism of Reagan because he was linked to the story less. Just so. Dimensions of news slant often reinforce each other.

The cover treatment of the events in *Time* and *Newsweek* graphically reveals the contrast in linkage. The *Time* cover (May 5, 1980) was headlined "Debacle in the Desert" and showed a forlorn Carter and a drawing of a ticker tape reading "Bulletin: An attempt to rescue the American hostages in Iran was aborted. . . . President Carter 'accepts full responsibility. . . .' " Another picture of a heavy-lidded, dejected Carter looking downward was a sort of logo for the coverage, repeated at the beginning of four separate stories.[35] The *Time* cover the next week showed former Senator Edmund Muskie (D.-Me.), who had just become Secretary of State after Cyrus Vance's resignation in protest of the rescue mission (an event harmful to Carter's power image). A corner insert included a picture tagged "The Rescue Mission: Aftershocks." The first *Newsweek* cover showed helicopter wreckage under the headline "Fiasco in Iran." The second had pictures of Carter, Muskie, and Vance, with the headline "Rescue Mission in Washington," referring to the "rescue" of Carter's foreign policy.

After Beirut, Reagan did not appear on either magazine's cover. The first *Time* cover showed pictures of servicemen in Grenada on the top half and in Beirut on the lower half. The headline said "Worth the Price? Tough Moves, Hard Questions; Rescue in Grenada, Sacrifice in Beirut." Note that the Grenada rescue was on top; note too Beirut was no fiasco or debacle but a (heroic) "sacrifice." The next issue of *Time* showed John F. Kennedy on the cover for a story unrelated to current events. A corner picture showed a soldier and the line "Grenada/The Pullout and the Payoff." The first *Newsweek* cover showed a serviceman in Grenada. The headline was "Americans at War" along with "Special Report: Grenada and Lebanon." The second cover featured a picture of Jesse Jackson. A corner picture included the tag "Lebanon/The Suicide Bombers."

Presidents attempt to manage newsmagazine covers and other

aspects of publicity by manipulating the forces behind news slant. They try to enhance journalists' perceptions of popularity and professional repute, to frame events to fit or clash with the production biases, and to convey the impression of involvement or distance.

Consider perceptions of presidential involvement. Carter actively inserted himself into the Iran rescue operation and aftermath, Reagan reacted passively and distanced himself from Beirut. Note, however, that while Carter's embrace of the media spotlight and Reagan's shrinking from it may largely explain the contrast in linkage, by itself Carter's media strategy cannot explain the much heavier degree of personal criticism he sustained.

The critical slant was as visible in the photographic images as in the text. *Time* and *Newsweek* published an identical picture of President Reagan, upon his return to the White House from a golfing weekend in Georgia, gravely making a statement to the press about the bombings. The photo showed Nancy Reagan at his side, holding his hand. Mrs. Reagan's presence personalized the story and conveyed important symbolism. When a pivotal development of state occurs, the president usually announces it alone, in an official setting, at a podium or desk. Having his wife there established the bombing as a personal concern more than a policy mishap. Her presence helped turn the Beirut events into a nonpartisan tragedy passively experienced by all Americans, along with their mournful but not contrite President. The caption underneath the photo in *Time* read "An anguished, angry Reagan on his return to Washington from Augusta, Ga." His statement said, in part, "I know there are no words to properly express our outrage and the outrage of all Americans at the despicable act. But I think we should all recognize that these deeds make so evident the bestial nature of those who would assume power if they could have their way and drive us out of that area."

Compare this to what Carter said. He personalized the event in a way damaging to himself, seizing blame for actively causing the Iran failure, and isolating himself from the American people. *Newsweek* quoted Carter as saying to members of Congress, "I have no right to ask you to be supportive [in the wake of the rescue failure], though if you're inclined to do so, it would be helpful." Such a statement fairly begs for disloyalty as it signals guilt and weakness to Congress and the media.

Carter's press tactics made the production and evaluation biases work against him, feeding negative news slant. Carter's *mea culpas* offered grist for reporting that singled him out as the simple cause. And it was because Carter helped to personalize the story by making the rescue disaster seem his own individual failure that the story came to symbolize the wide impression of Carter as incompetent. The implications of the rescue failure for Carter's popularity and effectiveness provided a major, explicit theme of the coverage. Reagan framed the Lebanon bombings as an act of evil, impersonal madness, certainly not the fault of any identifiable individual. The stories did not focus on doubts about Reagan's professional competence. The press strategy offered a clear villain other than Reagan, along with a simple, symbolic explanation matching familiar audience stereotypes: fanatical Middle Eastern terrorists.

Presidents can occasionally time events for a favorable event context; or sometimes they are just plain lucky. The original seizure of the Iranian hostages (November 1979) came at a perfect time for Carter's nascent renomination campaign. The hostage crisis stimulated a rallying response, just as Carter's chances for renomination seemed irredeemable. Approval of his handling of Iran was nearly 80 percent in the weeks after the embassy seizure, although it declined over the next several months.[36] As noted earlier, his overall job approval also rose nearly 30 points to 61 percent by the end of November 1979.[37] The context later turned against Carter. Although the rescue failure did not derail his renomination, it damaged his standing and in my view bolstered the negative impression of his effectiveness that made the press and the Washington elite so ready to pounce upon Billygate a few weeks later.[38]

In the Beirut case, Reagan's timing was quite fortunate. The 1983 barracks attack occurred before the re-election campaign had begun. More important, the bombing occurred only two days before the U.S. landing in Grenada, which the magazines depicted as a success. With the Iran rescue mission story, Carter endured two straight weeks of cover-featured news highlighting the Iran rescue mission failure. Reagan saw the patriotic surge around Grenada crowd out much of the follow-up on Lebanon.[39]

Reagan's perceived popularity and professional reputation helped to insulate him from assault in the press. Carter was vulnerable. His apparent unpopularity and ineffectiveness gave fellow Democrats, journalists, and Republicans the motivation and license to engage in stinging, negative evaluations. Paradoxically, the magnitude of the Lebanon loss may have helped Reagan. The death of so many Americans created a tragic atmosphere in which direct attacks on the policy of the man leading America's mourning, by Democrats or Republicans, would have seemed craven, even unpatriotic.

Reality and News Slant

The negative tilt against Carter may not have been as marked in most stories as it was in the cases of Billygate, Lance, and the Iran rescue. Even on these stories, message dimensions not measured might have treated Carter better than Reagan. The data analyzed here cannot prove (although they do support) the conventional wisdom that Reagan consistently enjoyed a much better press than Carter.[40] That is not my point. For Reagan as for all political actors, slant depends on the four forces described in the model. Even when a president enjoys high current popularity and respect as a powerful Washington player, a news event that significantly threatens his future standing can call forth negative slant. But unless party allies unleash sustained public attacks, and the other forces become unfavorable, negative slant tends to fade as the specific story becomes old news—and it usually does, rather quickly.

Some might trace the differences in coverage to significant contrasts in the actual events reported. Yet, reality is never strictly equivalent from case to case; it is always subject to varied readings. Journalists are charged with deciphering and purveying an interpretation that accommodates both their mirror and watchdog responsibilities.

Comparing interpretations of the scandals and crises from the perspective of accountability illustrates the point well. Consider the ways journalists might have interpreted the events in deciding how best to hold the presidents accountable for their scandals. One might suggest that Billygate was a trivial story for which the president was not responsible. He did not choose his wayward brother or ask him to perform official functions. On the other hand, Donovan served in the cabinet at the president's pleasure, and continued in office even after indictment. If one believes a president's choice of cabinet officers illuminates his character and leadership, Donovan provided the more important opportunities for accountability news.

On the other hand, one might argue that Jimmy Carter's inability to control his own brother was part of a larger pattern of ineptitude. Because the family symbolism is more compelling and comprehensible to audiences, one might say Billygate provided better accountability news than the more abstract data on the putatively shoddy ethics of a Reagan appointee. Indeed, Reagan's loyalty to his subordinate could be seen as an admirable defense of constitutional principles; no jury had ever convicted Donovan of anything. Thus the media's greater concentration on Billy would be natural and appropriate.

Either argument offers a cogent, defensible construction of journalism's watchdog responsibilities. A third plausible view might judge the two scandals worthy of equal treatment. It is possible to debate on normative grounds whether the networks' actual choices best served the accountability function. But network television did make it likely that more people weighed Billygate in evaluating Carter than used Donovan in assessing Reagan. We cannot assume that network news organizations reflected on their accountability missions when deciding to give great weight to Billygate and, some years later, to downplay Donovan; rather, the relative slant in these cases emerged from the interaction of forces described in the model.

The same general point applies to the crisis reporting. It might be argued that Carter personally commanded the risky Iran rescue, communicated directly with the military, and approved the details of the operation. In the Lebanon case, several layers of military bureaucracy separated Reagan from those responsible for flawed security at the barracks. By linking Carter but not Reagan quite closely with the crisis, one might argue, the media helped the public hold Carter to account for a dismal failure.

Another view would be that Carter acted properly in overseeing the details of the rescue attempt, while Reagan abdicated his responsibility for an equally hazardous policy. A car bomb attack on the U.S. embassy in Beirut the previous spring that killed over 60 persons including 17 Americans had highlighted the dangers. Given the known peril, the president had a duty to ensure that his subordinates were doing the right thing, one might assert, and his detachment was more damning than Carter's deep involvement in the Iran disaster.

In the final analysis, Reagan was as responsible for the policy decisions that made the Beirut bombing possible as Carter was for the choices that culminated in the rescue failure. Carter might still have endured (and deserved) stinging coverage on the Iran mission, but coverage of Reagan could have condemned him equally. The events themselves had comparable journalistic potential, but the slant of Carter's news was decidedly negative.

Slant is virtually inevitable because journalists have to make choices. *Time* and *Newsweek* could not simultaneously emphasize the Beirut bombing as an enormous personal failure for Reagan and as a distant, tragic incident that was not linked to him. The one precludes the other. The magazines could have explicitly discussed both interpretations, but that would itself be a third choice. That approach too does not portray reality more accurately or hold government to better account.[41] And such coverage would have to be self-critical and almost Brechtian, requiring innovations that would probably subvert news conventions and confuse audiences.

Journalists should not assert that, because they follow rules of objectivity, the news stands apart from and mirrors reality. Nor should critics demand that journalism cleanse itself of bias to become neutral. Both defenders and detractors of journalism accept the misleading metaphor of the reflecting mirror. They should recognize that journalism cannot help refracting rather than reflecting reality and thereby exerting political influence.

In a way, ideological bias is a comforting explanation for the ills and power of journalism. To trace news slant to journalists' ideological predilections is to assume that the uncontrolled power of the media might change, if only journalists would behave themselves. But neither journalists nor anybody else can fully control the complex interactions that produce news slant. This is the paradox of media power.

Autonomy and Accountability

The four forces I have discussed combine to shape coverage of any particular event. But I believe the evaluation biases are the most important. Reporting negatively on an unpopular or ineffective president might appear sensible to some. But news slant does not merely ratify the reality of the president's Washington power and national popularity. Journalists' judgments of power and popularity emerge from selective assumptions and manipulated perceptions. The chief job of presidential press officers is precisely to obtain positive news slant and deflect negative. Often news slant does not reflect even the imperfect empirical gauges readily available, such as Gallup polls or legislative success indexes. For example, Ronald Reagan's average Gallup approval rating for the first term was barely higher than Carter's, and neither averaged over 50 percent or majority approval. During Reagan's first two years, his rating was considerably lower, on average, than any of his predecessors. These data did not prevent the media from repeatedly asserting that Reagan was unusually popular.[42] In any case, the complicated quality of popularity defies simple summary. And although the evaluation biases assume that popularity gauges the success of presidents at representing the public will, history repeatedly shows that popular presidents do not necessarily pursue the public's policy desires; nor do unpopular ones inevitably disserve the national interest.

News that is filtered through the evaluation biases can hold government accountable only in a sporadic and haphazard fashion. The dependence of news slant on outside forces makes the flow of reliable information about government capricious. Ironically, although the evaluation biases should allow reporters to serve as watchdogs of government, the biases often work inadvertently to short-circuit citizenship and accountability.

Indeed, news slant is self-reinforcing. It feeds on itself through the impact of perceived public approval on journalists' evaluations, and on elites' activities in the political market. Negative news slant begets negative public opinion or at least perceptions of public disfavor, which stimulate further negative news.

Thus news slant can distort the process of representation by failing to distribute credit and blame properly. Even when a particular presidential policy enjoys or merits wide public support, news coverage may exhibit a negative slant because journalists regard the president as generally inept or unpopular. Or, merely because the chief executive appears generally popular and effective, reporting can obscure presidential responsibility for specific mishaps.

In the case of the Iran rescue, I believe, if Carter had seemed more popular and effective, adroit media manipulation might have turned the rescue attempt into a cathartic and unifying patriotic event. Just such an outcome occurred after the Mayaguez rescue effort, early in the Ford administration. Through a tragic mixup, fifteen U.S. servicemen died in fighting that began after the Cambodians had already released their thirty-nine American hostages (crewmen from the Mayaguez, a private cargo ship), and twenty-three airmen died in a helicopter crash on their way to the senseless combat.[43] Ford directed the attempt. Yet the *New York Times* called it "a domestic political triumph."[44]

It seems that the amount and nature of accountability news often depends on forces not directly connected to the "reality" itself or to the needs of the public for accountability. And lest we overgeneralize from the Carter-Reagan comparison, recall that the fickle flight of news slant can victimize a conservative president or allow a liberal free rein. The benign coverage Lyndon Johnson received in his Tonkin Gulf–Great Society heyday illustrates the point.

None of this is to deny that accountability news is almost always available somewhere, if a citizen knows where to look. Unfortunately, all too few do. Nor is it to suggest that the media serving mass audiences fail entirely to offer valuable accountability news. But the flow of such news is erratic, and journalists themselves exercise only partial control over its course.

Applying the evaluation biases to other subjects—interest

groups, ideas, unknown candidates—deepens the puzzle. A press that consistently tilts against the ideas or people it thinks unpopular or unlikely to have an impact cannot nourish the circulation of diverse ideas.[45] To a degree, media judgments are self-fulfilling. Just ask the "dark horse" presidential candidates who struggle without avail to attract sustained media attention.[46]

Yet if the evaluation biases yield flawed journalism, it is far from clear what standards of evaluation journalists ought to employ. Objectivity rules notwithstanding, they do need to select information about presidents which illuminates their performance. Similarly, the production biases may give us too much simplicity, personalization, and symbolism, but journalists cannot ignore the needs of the mass audience in composing the news. Indeed, these practices can be beneficial where they engage the audience's interest.

The standard solutions for such conundrums rely on market ideals. Markets are thought to yield diversity, so if this newspaper personalizes too much, that one will take the proper approach; if this network overestimates a president's popularity, another will assess it properly. Unfortunately, reliance on the market is a problematic response.

Only by consulting a variety of media that follow diverse rules for constituting news could audiences escape their dependence on journalists' judgments. For local news, most Americans have or exercise few such options. For national news, the competitive daily media and weekly newsmagazines offer surprisingly homogeneous coverage.[47] The average audience member does not regularly seek the more arcane media outlets. Certainly in the cases described here, the scandal coverage of the networks and crisis reporting of the newsmagazines were indistinguishable. In general, I would hypothesize that, as a story grows in importance, homogeneity among media rises. The bigger the story, I believe, the more similar the coverage across the national media—and the more powerful its impact on public opinion. Less important stories that appear on the back pages or only once or twice tend to be more diverse.[48] But precisely because other media fail to reinforce the message, the influence of such scattered individual stories on politics is slim.

Even if the media did vary widely in news slant and audiences could choose from a variety of news reports on the important stories, accountability would remain problematic. Only the people who happen to read or see the "correct" story receive accountability news. Those who do find the good story may not know it is the best version. Those who see an inferior version may not know it is wrong—especially where the "wrong" version, which "appears" in most media, is a failure to report anything at all. Ideally, people would compare several stories, argue among friends and family members who have seen other depictions, and somehow discern the best one. Most Americans do not appear to behave this way. Once again the deficiencies of the public, caused in part by the shortcomings of journalism, prevent the emergence of the informed citizen envisioned in free press ideals.

Reality and Slant in the Iran-Contra Affair

The Reagan administration's biggest media disaster, the Iran-contra affair, illustrates the way public dependence upon news slant can stymie accountability. Stories about Oliver North's activities for the Nicaraguan contras had appeared sporadically before November 1986, along with an occasional charge that the White House was running an extensive covert operation. According to David Ignatius, the *Christian Science Monitor, Los Angeles Times, Wall Street Journal, Miami Herald, New York Times,* and *Washington Post* all reported on North's doings in 1984 and 1985.[48] So did the television program "60 Minutes."[49] This provides further evidence of the significance of the four forces described in the model, not just reality, in shaping news slant. It also illustrates the primacy of the first dimension of slant, importance judgments; without repeated high-emphasis coverage, most stories disappear, leaving little trace on public or even elite consciousness.[50]

The reality of illegal contra aid not only existed for two years before the scandal broke, the news media had occasionally reported it. But the scattered reports made absolutely no difference to Reagan's political fortunes. Neither Republicans nor Democrats assailed the president or provided journalists with further information. News organizations did not independently pursue the matter. Without elite sources ready to spill some dirt, even the premier news organizations seem rarely to investigate a potential scandal, especially one involving an apparently popular and powerful president.[51]

The model laid out in this chapter offers insight into the emergence of the Iran-contra affair as Reagan's first full-blown media scandal. The *reality* of questionable arms shipments to Iran and violation of the congressional ban on aid to the Nicaraguan contras alone did not elevate this story. Rather, the media became more aggressive in linking Reagan to these actions after November 4, 1986, after the forces that shape news slant had changed.

1. *Evaluation biases: Popularity and power.* The first key event was the November 4 election. The GOP loss of the Senate, despite Reagan's vigorous campaigning, suggested deterioration in the president's popular appeal. His reputation for effectiveness in Washington may have waned after policy miscues such as the failed Iceland summit with Soviet leader Gorbachev. Elite support in Reagan's own party crumbled with the revelations of secret arms shipments to Iran and funding of the contras.[52] Partially due to the election results, GOP members of Congress may have felt freer to criticize Reagan. Some wanted to insert protective distance between themselves and a tarnished president's foreign policy blunders; others seized the opportunity to bludgeon unpopular Reagan aides such as Donald Regan. For the first time in six years, congressional Republicans, cabinet members, and White House staffers conducted sustained and critical public assaults upon Reagan and upon each other.

2. *Production biases: Congruence with media needs for simplicity, personalization, and symbolism.* Any merits in Reagan's complicated case for secret normalization of relations with Iran were difficult to convey. The simple thing for audiences to see was a president breaking his public word and aiding the detested Ayatollah. The scandal seemed to involve Reagan personally. In addition, the story was easy to report: for a time, Washington was full of sources keeping the issue hot. Because of this, major national media were willing to put more reporters and resources into the story, filling the pages and airwaves and heightening its importance.

3. *Event context.* For a change, Reagan's timing was unlucky.

The 1986 election had turned out badly. A string of mini-tempests had alerted reporters to possible administration confusion: a disinformation campaign about Libyan officials that had misled American media; the bungled Iceland summit;[53] and the capture of an American (Eugene Hasenfus) running guns to the contras in Nicaragua.

4. *Skill.* With the other three forces unfavorable, even Reagan's talented press team could not prevent the story from becoming a major scandal. As Carter's staff found out much earlier in his term, it is impossible to manage news slant successfully when major administration players and party leaders are not on the team. However, a few weeks after the scandal broke, skillful news management and renewed Republican loyalty allowed Reagan to contain the damaging publicity and limit his slide in the polls. This experience reveals again the media's heavy dependence upon presidents even as journalists probe into matters the White House would prefer ignored.

Consider two articles by David Broder published in the same edition of the *Washington Post,* the Sunday after President Reagan's major Iran-contra press conference (March 19, 1987). In the first, an excerpt from Broder's book, he wrote:

> [T]he White House propaganda machine has become an increasingly effective instrument. . . . It has enhanced the power of the communicator-in-chief. And it has raised to even greater importance the unmet challenge for the press to provide an alternative, non-propagandistic view of the presidency. That is a challenge we in the Washington press corps—and our editors and bosses—cannot afford to ignore.[54]

He warns journalists here against cooptation by adroit news manipulators and urges the press to resist manipulation.

Yet in his regular column the same day, Broder wrote:

> [T]he White House has repaired the damage from the Iran affair explosion and reopened for business. President Reagan's news conference on Thursday night provided the strongest evidence yet that the proprietor of the shop has regained a good measure of his emotional balance and is ready to reclaim his role at the center of gov-

ernment. The president did not change his story—or add much to it. But he showed the steadiness and confidence that had been so conspicuously missing in the final months of 1986. . . . Now Reagan can begin refocusing the nation's attention on his policy agenda without being accused of trying to avoid The Painful Subject.[55]

Not only was this conclusion questionable on its own grounds, but Reagan did not fully repair the damage with the public, where his approval ratings remained at about 50 percent for another year (down 20 points since the revelations). Even less did he recover among Washington elites, where his professional reputation was shot.[56]

More remarkable is that Broder admits Reagan revealed nothing new or important in the press conference. Substantively, then, Reagan did avoid the subject. But Broder takes a different measure, Reagan's demeanor, which he said seemed confident and relaxed compared with the president's previous press conference. The administration's news managers aimed above all else to convey the image of confidence and encouraged journalists to judge Reagan by that standard. Ignoring his own finding of the emptiness of Reagan's answers, Broder accepts image-making as the measure of success, and proclaims the scandal over and the administration ready to turn the nation's attention to other business. Broder falls into the trap he warns against on the same day in the same paper. The White House can manipulate even the best journalists, even those like Broder consciously on guard against news management.[57]

Any content study should acknowledge that media messages are complex and multilayered. Audiences are varied, their reactions to news still poorly understood. In no way would I claim this study "proves" Carter received more negative coverage than Reagan on every medium, along every message dimension, either generally or in these particular scandals and crises. Rarely are media messages totally one-sided. But the evidence suggests that in several important aspects of reporting, Carter fared worse than Reagan. Given what we know about the tendency of the national media to approach stories similarly, we would expect to find similar slant in media not studied here, although differences between Carter and Reagan might not be as marked, say, in the *New York Times* as on television or in newsmagazines.

Lacking complete quantitative data, this chapter is a first attempt rather than the last word on news slant. It seeks to begin the process of understanding how the media influence public opinion even while remaining dependent on elites and obedient to objectivity rules. Perhaps on a practical level, the model might assist journalists in developing more self-conscious insights into the nature, justification, and impacts of their news choices. An exploratory effort to push inquiry in a new direction, the model is not as fully developed and bolstered by quantitative evidence as would be, say, another study probing the effect of televised violence on children.

Consider this example of the difficulty of proposing a new conceptual model. While elite support is crucial to the model, there is no source of independent data on that variable. If we had continuous surveys that monitored changing elite opinions, better data to test my model and many other important hypotheses in social science would be available, but there are no such surveys.

Close analyses of language in the press itself might provide another source of data. As one example, since it is not merely elites' views but their willingness to voice them to reporters which controls news slant, the appearance of critical quotes with named rather than anonymous sources might index the shifting degree of fear or respect elites have for a president. These or other new measures require testing and refinement. To understand the sources and consequences of media messages, social scientists will simply have to conduct further research on elite thinking, language, and behavior. One response to the data problems would be to avoid offering a model like the one in this chapter until the data are available. But as Edelman says, constraining inquiry in this way would be to make social science into a practice akin to ". . . looking under the lamppost, where the light is good, for the quarter one dropped in a dark section of the street." I offer the model in hopes of shedding some light in a direction of value.[58]

Many previous analyses of what I call news slant—and others have termed spin, balance, or tone—imply that idiosyncratic forces produce the politically potent information contained in news reports. They fail to offer a general model explaining why in one case media portrayals would, say, blame the president for a foreign mishap while in another mostly blame his subordinates. The premise of this chapter is that news slant varies in regular and predictable ways amenable to scientific explanation. Moreover, most content analytical studies categorize stories or assertions in a global way as positive or negative, without offering an explicit theory of why the messages would tend to boost or diminish public support. The model discussed here yields a more detailed map of the influential information a story contains, based on social scientific understanding of public opinion.[59]

The model should apply to news of other officials, interest groups, and even policy proposals. I believe editors and reporters employ the evaluation biases, assessing the popularity of individuals, ideas and groups and their likelihood of having an impact on official Washington. I further believe production biases, event context, and news management also affect slant in most political reporting.[60] Although these must remain tentative hypotheses, not definitive conclusions, I shall assume the model does have some validity and draw the implications for democratic theory.

The Iran-contra scandal provides a clear example of the dilemma that the interdependence of government and the press poses for democracy: journalists rely heavily upon the very elites they are supposed to hold accountable, not only for legitimate facts but for political action and talk that can fuel coverage. Elite responses to news events heavily shape the journalist's agenda. If too few elites act in the political market to make an event big news, stories rarely push past the threshold of importance necessary to penetrate public consciousness. A story that receives unimportant treatment in turn seldom puts pressure on government, either through changing actual public opinion or through altering elites' perceptions of what the public wants. Thus the officials who are supposed to be held accountable in fact feel little need to change priorities or policies.[61]

Only if the Iran-contra affair had become an important story early on might the press exposure have changed the administration's course. A story here, a story there hinted something was amiss; but by itself the press could not enlarge the story. As the Iran-contra fiasco also suggests, the media are most effective at countering presidential news management when disunity racks the president's party.[62] When presidents maintain their own party's support and the opposition's quiescence, as Carter did in the month after the Iran hostage seizure, and Reagan in the two years before the Iran-contra affair broke open in November 1986, the media have trouble succeeding as watchdogs.

The closest any one group comes to controlling presidential news slant is when the political party in the White House is unified and skilled at news management, and the opposition is divided. Even under the best circumstances, however, presidents' control over news slant is limited. They remain at the mercy of the production biases, unexpected events, and unlucky timing, all of which can give the news a negative tilt. More important, they can select only among those news management tactics that accord with the media's needs and practices. For example, however skilled in press relations, and even if they evade negative slant, presidents have trouble breaking through the simplification bias to obtain positive coverage of complicated policy proposals. Thus winning the news slant game means playing by the rules journalism enforces, and that can limit a president's leadership options.

Journalists too are constrained by the rules they enforce. Their news decisions may be powerful, but individual reporters and editors have to decide in accordance with the legitimate (non-ideological) biases and standard operating procedures of American journalism. The best evidence for journalists' limited leeway is the tendency for news slant to be similar (though of course not identical) across the major national media. The implication is that journalists exert only weak control over the slant of the news—and over its ability to highlight information vital for accountability. We return to the sorry paradox of aggressiveness without accountability discussed in the book's introduction. The powerful media have helped undermine support of several presidents in succession, but too late to prevent policy mistakes from degenerating into policy debacles.

4

How the Media Affect What People Think—and Think They Think

Previous chapters assume that news slant significantly influences public opinion. This assumption clashes with the belief long dominant in the scholarly community: that news messages have "minimal consequences."[1] Many media scholars still endorse something close to this view.[2] Other scholars think media influence is significant but confined to shaping the problems the public considers most important—their agendas.[3] In some respects agenda research challenges the minimal consequences view, but the two approaches share a core postulate. Both assume the audience enjoys substantial autonomy.

During the 1980s, scholars have published research directly disputing the notion that media have minimal consequences or influence only agendas.[4] But analysts have still not developed a general theory that explicitly attacks the underlying logic of the assumption of audience autonomy. Continuing my critical stance on the idea that any participant in the news system operates autonomously, building instead on the theme of interdependence, this chapter shows that media messages significantly influence what the public and the elites think, by affecting what they perceive and think about.

The Research Tradition

The assumption that audiences are autonomous is the corollary of the assumption that journalists are independent; both notions pervade discussions about the marketplace of ideas. The audience autonomy assumption provides the basis for the minimal consequences position that audiences develop their political opinions in relative independence from the media. There are two somewhat distinct variants of this view. The first emphasizes that audiences think about communications selectively, screening out information they do not like.[5] The second holds that audiences pay so little attention and understand so little that the news cannot influence them.[6] In practice, both the selectivity hypothesis and the hypothesis of inattention and incomprehension (hereafter just "inattention") hold that media messages tend only to reinforce existing preferences rather than help to form new attitudes or change old ones. Thus the conclusion is that the media have little net impact on politics.

The central assumption of the more recent research on agenda setting has been that media do exert significant influence, but only in a narrow sphere. In this view, the news can affect what people think *about,* not what they think. The public's autonomy is not complete, but its susceptibility to media influence is limited to agendas. Agenda researchers almost always include a sentence like the following: "Although a 'minimal effects' model most accurately describes the media's ability to change opinions, recent research has shown that the media can play a much larger role in telling us what to think about, if not what to think. . . ."[7] Agenda scholarship does not provide a comprehensive theoretical explanation for why media influence is confined to agendas, but selectivity and inattention again seem to be key. In the agenda-setting view, the media can overcome these barriers in determining the issues people think about but not in shaping what they prefer to be done.[8]

The problem with the agenda-setting position is that the distinction between "what to think" and "what to think about" is misleading. Nobody, no force, can ever successfully "tell people what to think." Short of sophisticated torture or "brainwashing," no form of communication can compel anything more than feigned obeisance. The way to control attitudes is to provide a partial selection of information for a person to think about, or process. The only means of influencing what people think is precisely to control what they think about.

However, no matter what the message, whether conveyed through media or in person, control over others' thinking can never be complete. Influence can be exerted through selection of information, but conclusions cannot be dictated. If the media (or anyone) can affect what people think about—the information they process—the media (or anyone) can affect their attitudes. This perspective yields an assumption of interdependence: public opinion grows out of an interaction between media messages and what audiences make of them.

From here on I will refer to the minimal consequences and the agenda positions, which both endorse the audience autonomy assumption, as the "autonomy model." The burgeoning research that demonstrates the media do have significant influence—over attitudes, not just agendas—has not yet generated a competing theory to explain more fully the media's impact on public opinion. This, I believe, should be an "interdependence model."

Information Processing and Media Impacts

Combining a recognition of the interdependence of audiences and media with models of information processing may offer the best foundation for a new theory.[9] There is no consensus among the cognitive psychologists who study information processing. But their work provides a number of generalizations pertinent to the mass media's impacts.

Information processing research shows that people have cognitive structures, called "schemas," which organize their thinking.[10] A person's system of schemas stores substantive beliefs, attitudes, values, and preferences along with rules for linking different ideas.[11] The schemas ". . . direct attention to relevant information, guide its interpretation and evaluation, provide inferences when information is missing or ambiguous, and facilitate its retention."[12]

Schemas are not filters used to select out all unfamiliar or uncomfortable information. As Bennett writes, "[I]nformation processing constructs [i.e., schemas] like party identification and ideological categories should not be regarded as rigid cognitive frameworks that work in fixed ways to screen out unfamiliar information."[13] Certainly people fail to think about much of the news, but not necessarily because they choose only congruent messages, or because they inevitably misunderstand or deliberately ignore media reports. The autonomy model stresses selectivity and inattention, but that leaves us to explain why many citizens do think about a great deal of the new information they encounter. Information processing theory recognizes and helps explain how attitudes emerge from a dynamic interaction of new information with people's existing beliefs. In Bennett's words, political thought is "data-driven" by external information and "conceptually driven" by internal schemas.[14]

Information processing theory suggests that whether people ignore or pay attention to new information depends more on its salience, on whether it meshes with their interests, than on whether it conflicts with their existing beliefs.[15] While people may resist knowledge that challenges their fundamental values,[16] most can accommodate new information and even hold a set of specific beliefs that may appear dissonant, contradictory, or illogical to an outsider.[17]

The explicit model of thinking that cognitive psychologists have been putting together thus contradicts the implicit model upon which most media researchers have relied. Rather than resisting or ignoring most new or dissonant media reports, the information-processing view predicts, people may often respond more positively to media messages. In the information-processing perspective, a person first assesses a media report for salience. If salient, the person processes the news according to routines established in his or her schema system. Processing may lead the person either to store the information or to discard it; if stored, the information may stimulate new beliefs or change old beliefs.

So selectivity and inattention are not the whole story. Often people may select out information that contradicts their current views; but other times they think about disturbing reports they find relevant. The notion of an audience that resists all potentially conflicting information rests upon an assumption of involved and knowledgeable citizens, a vision that does not apply to most people.[18] Common sense suggests it takes more information and more time to change the minds of strong adherents than weak ones, but sometimes even loyalists change. When the implications are not obvious—for example when the information is contained in the often-subtle form of news slant—the probability increases that even ideologues will store conflicting information without experiencing any immediate dissonance.

And while it may take many repetitions of a media message to pierce the public's indubitable haze of neglect and distraction, this very same political indifference may enhance the likelihood that messages which penetrate will have an impact. Just because on most matters Americans have so little knowledge and such weakly anchored beliefs, the news reports they do notice can significantly shape their attitudes. Not only do the majority of Americans lack detailed, expert knowledge and strong opinions,[19] sometimes they have no old attitudes to defend. Many of the most significant political contests are played out over emerging issues or leaders; audiences have no set attitudes toward them. That clears the path for media influence.

Testing Media Influence

Identification as liberal, moderate, or conservative is a key component of the schema system that most people apply to political information. Ideological leanings affect responses to specific media reports; those who identify differently may read the same message differently. The interdependence model predicts that media influence varies according to the way each person processes specific news messages. Instead of treating ideology as a tool people use to filter out reports that conflict with their liberalism or conservatism, the model sees ideology as a schema that influences the use people make of media messages in more complicated ways.

The interaction between the attributes of the message and the schemas of the audience shapes the impact of the news. One component of this interaction is message salience. Stories that interest liberals may bore conservatives; items that intrigue ideologues on either side may not interest moderates, who have few strong preferences.

Another aspect of interaction is whether the message is relevant to peripheral or central attitudes. Centrality will differ for different groups, since liberals and conservatives appear to structure their ideas distinctively. Central to liberalism is attachment to ideals of change and equality; central to conservatism is attraction to capitalism.[20] The two groups probably process some media messages differently. This decidedly does not mean that liberals, say, screen out all material that challenges liberalism. Consider an editorial praising the ideal of capitalist markets and proposing to make the post office a private enterprise. While the message may conflict with some elements of liberal ideology, it does so only peripherally, since government ownership of public utilities is not fundamental to American liberalism. The message may not only bolster conservatism among conservatives but may weaken liberals' ties to liberalism, if only at the liberal margin.

Another point of interdependent interaction between media reports and the audiences' schema systems involves whether the media message comes from an editorial, with its overtly persuasive intent, or from a news story ostensibly designed merely to inform. Conservatives, for example, may be more likely to screen out liberal editorials than news slanted favorably to the left, since editorials are explicit while the slant of news is often subtle, and news stories appear to convey only factual information.

A final aspect of interdependence lies in how new or unfamiliar the reported topic is. All else being equal, the less familiar the object of the news, the less likely a person will respond by fitting the report into an established category and maintaining a set attitude. Where the subject of the news is unfamiliar to people across the ideological spectrum, all will be susceptible to media influence.

Four predictions emerge from this use of information processing theory to develop an interdependence model. These are not all the hypotheses that merit exploration, but they are the ones that can be tested with the available data, and they should provide support for the superiority of the new model.

Prediction 1: Editorials will affect those who identify with a particular ideology more than moderates. Those identifying themselves as liberals or conservatives are likely to find ideologically charged editorial messages salient. Those who eschew ideological commitments, the moderates, may not find ideological editorials relevant.

Prediction 2: Liberal editorials should exert a leftward push on those attitudes of conservatives not central to their ideology.

Prediction 3: Editorials have a stronger effect when coverage is of a new subject rather than a long-familiar one.

Prediction 4: News slant affects beliefs among liberals, moderates, and conservatives alike. Shaped by objectivity rules, news stories are designed to appear neutral to audiences.[21] We have seen how slant nonetheless enters into "objective" reports. Because of the appearance of neutrality, people probably screen out these messages less than editorials.

Findings and Implications

The data set combines a national survey on Americans' political attitudes from 1974 to 1976 with information on the political content of the newspapers read by respondents. I explored the significance of the habitual news slant of the papers using an index of news diversity, which measures perspective.[22] I tested the effect of newspaper content openly intended to persuade with an index of editorial-page liberalism. A full discussion of the data and statistical findings can be found in Appendix B. I confine the discussion in the rest of this chapter to the implications of the statistical results.

The data generally support my four predictions. The findings suggest that media messages can indeed move audiences in directions counter to their predominant dispositions. The influence of news stories and editorials that oppose existing dispositions or reinforce current beliefs varies depending upon the message, attitude, and schema involved. In particular, as Prediction 1 suggests, editorials have little impact on moderates, who may find them of little interest. But editorials do influence those who consider themselves liberals or conservatives. The influence does not hold across the board, however. As Prediction 2 hypothesizes, liberal editorials appear most influential in moving conservatives against their dispositions on matters not crucial to their identities as conservatives. But while the beliefs susceptible to influence may not be central to conservatives' ideological self-images, they may be significant to their political behavior. For example, the data show that conservatives who read liberal newspapers were significantly more likely than readers of conservative papers to vote for Jimmy Carter over Gerald Ford in 1976.

Testing the effect of liberal editorials on liberals suggests an important modification to the autonomy model, with its assertion that the media tend only to reinforce people's existing beliefs. The data indicate that where media content conforms to existing predilections, it does not always significantly reinforce those beliefs. Rather, left-leaning editorials seem to bolster only the more peripheral attitudes of liberals. This finding may have significance for election outcomes. In this particular case, liberal editorials did not heighten the tendency of liberals to vote for Carter, even though the editorials made conservatives more likely to vote for him. In an epoch of loose political loyalties, reinforcement is not as trivial or simple a media effect as the autonomy model seems to imply. More research is needed on the ways the media reinforce as well as change public opinion.

The data also support Prediction 3, that attitudes toward the unfamiliar are more susceptible to media influence than those toward the familiar. The most important evidence is that opinions toward the previously-unknown former governor Jimmy Carter were affected by editorials among conservatives, and even among moderates, who were otherwise immune to the impact of editorials. Finally, Prediction 4 receives considerable buttressing from the statistical analysis: news slant, measured as diversity in perspectives, appears to influence people in all three ideological groups. Selectivity and inattention seem to apply less when people read the news than when they read editorials. For example, the more diverse the news perspectives in a paper, the more likely were its conservative readers to evaluate liberal and poor groups positively. Lacking strong selectivity tendencies, moderates were most susceptible to news slant. For them, reading more diverse newspapers was associated with more liberal responses on five of seven opinion indexes.

This finding highlights a barrier that objectivity erects against any ideal marketplace of ideas. Free of the requirement to conform to objectivity rules or to play by the other rules of the political market, editorialists can take explicit stands and argue for truth. According to a number of researchers, newspaper editorials and columns often provide information and analysis that overtly challenge the claims of presidents or other elites who may be taking advantage of reporters' objectivity to manage the news.[23] Editorials and opinion pieces, at least in the print media, may contain more of the data readers need to make autonomous judgments than do news reports, whose important and powerful political implications are often subtle and unplanned. Yet, though editorial pages may be more likely than news pages to offer complex truths, they are labeled as opinion and lack the legitimizing mantle of objectivity, and they appear far from the front page. As the findings suggest, most of the time they probably exert less direct influence than news slant over the thinking of most audience members.

Perhaps we should amend the old phrase to read "The media do not control what people prefer; they influence public opinion by providing much of the information people think about and by shaping how they think about it." Americans exercise their varied dispositions as they ponder political news, but the media's selection of data makes a significant contribution to the outcome of each person's thinking.[24]

These conclusions need to be placed in a larger context of social scientific research. With the exception of voting for president, we simply do not know very much about how people develop and change their political beliefs and preferences. Social scientists have fashioned neither a general theory of the forces that shape political thinking nor a consensus understanding of cognitive psychology itself. Our store of findings is far too primitive to dismiss the specific role of the media. It is premature to conclude "the media do not tell people what to think" when we know so little about the forces that do determine their thoughts. To advance that understanding will require a deeper grasp of the part the media play in each individual's processing of political information.

Audience Autonomy Reconsidered

One might take the finding that conservatives, moderates, and liberals process news messages differently as an endorsement of the audience autonomy model. Rather, I believe the findings support the interdependence model. Indeed they suggest that the very way scholars have conceptualized media influence may need revision. Scholars have usually attempted to find evidence that the media are persuaders, deliberate causers of public thinking. It may be more realistic to think of the media as contributing to—but not controlling—the structure of publicly-available information that shapes the way people can and do think politically. Such a picture suggests an interdependent media and public, with neither one fully controlling the news or its effects. Three points bolster this revised view of media influence: the media's contribution to the orientations that people use in processing information, the sometimes hidden and often unintentional nature of media impact, and the media's effect on perceived public opinion.

The model of audience autonomy would require that people produce and apply their schema systems completely on their own. But members of the audience do not form and maintain the orientations they use to process information independently. Their partisan and ideological loyalties arise from socialization in a political culture transmitted, reinforced, and constantly altered by parents, teachers, leaders, friends, and colleagues—most of whom use the media.[25] Further, much of the nation's political dialogue takes place in the press, where the meaning of terms like "liberal" and "conservative" varies over time. Such ideas as a flat income tax, once "far right," entered the mainstream in the 1980s, as ideas like national health insurance departed for the "far left."

The information that comes from the media includes not only concrete data for cognitive processing but symbols that may engage little-understood emotional needs. Leaders often use the media to stimulate emotional responses. Recall, for example, the television scenes and newsmagazine photographs of the American medical students arriving safely in the U.S. after their Grenada ordeal, or of the flag-draped caskets of the Marines killed in the

Beirut barracks bombing (both in 1983).[26] If the schemas people employ in processing information are themselves influenced by media and other changing cultural forces, and if people can be moved by messages that operate at levels other than rational persuasion, determining ultimate control over "what people think" becomes too complicated for an assumption of audience autonomy to be accurate. The system is one of interdependency and connection, where the notion of autonomy finally does not make much sense.[27]

For example, the autonomy model tends to neglect a hidden aspect of media power exercised through news slant: exclusion of inferences. The autonomy model emphasizes two possibilities: Either readers accept interpretation "A," which news coverage emphasizes; or they keep thinking "B," as they did before. Yet by excluding or barely mentioning some information, the coverage may have a third effect: preventing audiences from thinking of "C," an entirely different reading. The media's discouragement of deductions that audiences might draw from political reality may be as important as encouraging inferences. While audiences can ignore any conclusion that bothers them and stick to their existing beliefs, it is harder for them to come up with an interpretation on their own, one for which the media do not make relevant information readily available.

So one neglected way that the media exert influence is by omitting or de-emphasizing information, by excluding data about an altered reality that might otherwise disrupt existing support. To continue an example from Chapter Three: if the press had linked the Beirut Marine barracks bombing more closely to the president, Ronald Reagan's popularity might have declined. Through their comparatively tame coverage, the media inadvertently bolstered existing attitudes toward Reagan. Such reinforcement via news slant is far from the trivial effect that the autonomy model implies. Holding support under adverse new conditions is a crucial goal in politics, not just winning over new supporters.

Finally, the autonomy perspective has searched for media influence in direct relationships between individuals' opinions and news messages. The impacts on perceived public opinion may be as important as those on actual public opinion. This unexplored facet of media influence helps explain the enormous gulf between elites and scholars on the question of media power. Elites think the media are the most powerful of all American institutions, despite many scholars' continued insistence that media influence is limited.[28] One reason may be that scholars define media influence as changing the average individual's actual opinions, while elites define media influence as affecting the behavior of other elites. At least intuitively, elites recognize the media's impact on perceived public opinion, and grasp the effect of these perceptions on government decisions. Elites know that they can act only on their perceptions of what the public wants, and that the media are primary sources for information on public sentiments.[29] Scholars have barely begun to study the media's role in elite decision making.[30]

Unfortunately, when conventional wisdom ascribes one central tendency to public opinion, it often cannot help but falsify actual public sentiments. The very notion of "public opinion" may be fanciful, because people have shifting, contradictory, and sometimes inchoate beliefs. Consider the case of the widely reported conservative mood of the 1970s and 1980s. In the words of Barry Sussman, "By the middle 1970s, despite abundant evidence to the contrary, it was an accepted part of the Washington dogma—for Republicans and Democrats—that the public had become more conservative. . . . [Yet a] wide variety of surveys showed that Americans in the 1970s and 80s were more liberal than at any time in the past on race relations, premarital sex, abortion, the role of women, and the question of whether the government should try to reduce the gap between the rich and the poor. . . ."[31]

The point is not that "public opinion" was "liberal," because again, any simple label misleads. Rather, although the public's actual policy preferences did not change appreciably, the media-fed perception that they had swung right influenced politics. The wide assumption of a conservative surge probably legitimized Republican conservatism, reinforced exaggerated claims of Reagan's popularity,[32] and distracted the media, the elites, and the public itself from the absence of majority support for many of the president's policy decisions. Because of the media's evaluation biases, the conservative mood notion may also have encouraged gentle coverage (what I would call positive slant) in reporting Reagan.

Since journalists' beliefs about the popularity of an idea or leader influence news slant, perceived public opinion is a valuable commodity in the political market. Journalists need simple symbols, and during the 1970s and 1980s the stereotype of a "conservative mood" helped journalists to explain complicated political developments to themselves and their audiences.[33] But the description was more a product of conservatives taking advantage of the evaluation and production biases than of actual public opinion. Similarly, during the 1960s, liberals probably benefited from exaggerated perceptions of public support for the Great Society.

This story of distorted perception reveals a further aspect of the public's failure to obtain the kind of accurate representation that a free press is supposed to ensure. At least in recent years, the public itself has enjoyed only slight control over perceived public opinion. Insights into the public's actual, complicated collective opinions available from surveys, election data, and scholarly analyses of voting patterns[34] rarely altered most journalists' portrayals of public sentiments as unambiguously conservative. Once again, simple symbols triumphed in the political market over a complicated reality.

So the media not only influence the actual preferences that members of the public use in voting and other forms of active participation. They also affect perceived public opinion. Since elites respond to the public sentiments they perceive, Americans passively "participate" through leaders' reactions to perceived public opinion.

These impacts should not be exaggerated. Scholars simply do not know very much about how and why ordinary or elite Americans develop their basic ideological orientations or their specific political attitudes. The forces that move actual and perceived public opinion remain complicated and mysterious, and the media fill in only part of the puzzle. While this chapter makes a strong case for taking the media's role seriously, it does not assert that the media are the only important source of information or influence.

Still, in a democracy, the public must and should rely in some measure on the mass media. The autonomy model takes the assumption that audiences resist media influence so far that it implicitly denies the press can enhance democracy at all. To participate effectively in politics, the public must remain responsive to the changing conditions portrayed (however imperfectly) in the news. The implication is clear: democracy in the United States is significantly affected by the performance and power of journalism.

II
IMPROVING JOURNALISM

5

Newspaper Competition and Free Press Ideals: Does Monopoly Matter?

The mourning that accompanies the death of newspaper competition in city after city offers a prime illustration of the great trust Americans place in economic competition. By the late 1980s, no more than twenty-seven cities enjoyed two or more completely separate, competitively owned daily newspapers.[1] Economies of scale in newspaper production and advertising, coupled with rising competition from television, apparently caused the demise of most of the papers.[2] Local newspaper monopoly appears to be a product of the very same economic market forces that putatively nourish free press ideals.

This point evokes a central contradiction between the logic of the economic market and the logic of the marketplace of ideas. Not only does competition in many cities tend to extinguish itself. Just as important is that publishers who follow the incentives and ethics of free enterprise by maximizing profits will (and should) provide the familiar and simple news their audiences and advertisers seem to want. This is the very kind of news that earns the least credit in the marketplace of ideas. Success in the economic market seems to contradict service to the idea market. Yet those who voice concern over the decline of daily newspaper competition seem to believe that the two markets coexist in happy harmony, and in particular that competition advances free press ideals.

The next two chapters probe and question the widely-held

notion that economic competition is the prime path to overcoming any deficiencies in American journalism. This chapter assesses the effect of the apparent decline in competition among daily newspapers; the next explores the impacts of the seeming rise in competition among broadcast media. These discussions pave the way for a concluding chapter which argues the need to transcend the economic market if we want to develop a more independent press serving a better-informed citizenry.

Economic Market Logic vs. The Marketplace of Ideas

The book has already discussed how economic competition limits the discretion of news organizations. The imperatives of keeping costs down and profits up affect the newsgathering procedures, content, and form of daily newspapers in every market. With rare exceptions, dailies must please large audiences consisting predominantly of people with little political interest or knowledge, and must rely on standard networks of legitimate elite sources. But once they meet the basic requirement of delivering a large audience to advertisers, publishers have some room for choice. The goals of the publisher and conditions in the market determine the degree of latitude owners enjoy. Many publishers of local papers appear to have flexibility in deciding whether and how to follow the objectivity norms prescribed by the national media. Some strive (with mixed success) to separate news decisions from editorials, others freely slant coverage to match the ideology of their editorial page. Publishers can select the mix of local, state, national, and international news the paper normally offers. It is these choices that this chapter explores: the amount of variation in newspaper content that can exist within the constraints common to virtually every mass medium.

Quite a few academic researchers have explored the impact of newspaper competition.[3] Different scholars define newspaper competition differently; some find that the absence of competition is harmful, others that it makes no clear difference. For example, Donohue and Glasser[4] suggest that greater use of wire copy, hence more homogeneous news, accompanies the decline of competition. Other scholars find an association between competition and content, but with more ambiguous implications for the marketplace of ideas. One study shows that competition increases the amount of local news and of (presumably low-quality) sensational or human interest stories.[5] But quite a few scholars find competition has little or no significant impact.[6]

The sum of the academic studies is a question mark.[7] The uncertainty is not surprising when we turn to the theories that seem to underlie this research. Scholars have not precisely explained why we should presume that economic competition enhances the contributions of newspapers to the metaphorical marketplace of ideas.[8] Many have assumed, without explanation, that economic incentives motivate newspaper publishers to purvey higher quality journalism.

In fact, the relation between economic competition and newspaper quality depends on a number of forces that vary from community to community. These include:

- the distribution of tastes for high-quality journalism among audiences;
- the competitive strategies of newspapers, for example, whether they target specific subgroups who care more about sports than political coverage;
- the desires of advertisers, for example, whether major retailers want to reach upscale audiences who seek higher quality news;
- newspaper management's knowledge of their audience's desires;
- whether satisfying audience tastes clashes with fulfilling other organizational needs, such as keeping powerful news sources or advertisers happy;
- the extent to which owners seeking such goals as community enlightenment, prestige, or political influence are willing and able to sacrifice profit; and
- what we mean by "quality."

Since the specific pressures, goals, and incentives operating in each media market may vary markedly, it is difficult to predict any consistent relationship between economic competition and newspaper content. Indeed, because newspaper markets are so idiosyncratic, directly contradictory predictions about the effects of competition are equally plausible. Competition might prod papers to include more detailed background and analysis of foreign trade, form subsidies, defense procurement, and other complex matters of interest to few readers. Or competition might encourage easily-digested, short and simple fare featuring gruesome crimes and happy life-styles. Competition might produce aggressive reporting, incisive editorializing, and daring investigative digging. Or competitive papers might skirt any controversy that could antagonize, in order to keep rivals from stealing their precious readers, advertisers, and sources.

In other words, it seems reasonable to hypothesize that competition stimulates both better and lesser "quality" newspapers. Indeed, logic might lead us to expect that monopoly, not competition, achieves the more desirable end—and precisely because monopoly papers do not have to cater quite so carefully to audience and advertiser tastes. In any case, the connection of market incentives and the news product is considerably more problematic than many discussions of media monopoly imply.

Abstracting from the literature and folklore in this field, it appears that four of the major alleged impacts of competition on newspaper quality are: (1) enhancement of the *"seriousness"* of newspapers, meaning more cosmopolitan, in-depth news and editorials; (2) provision of greater *diversity* of views on public issues; (3) encouragement of *fairness* or balance in presentation of political controversies; and (4) stimulation of greater *responsiveness* to the interests of the average person—providing stories and editorials that stimulate rational participation by ordinary readers. The prediction appears to be that papers facing competition will be higher quality: more serious, more diverse, fairer, and more responsive than monopoly papers.

These expectations can be explored with data from the University of Michigan Center for Political Studies's *CPS Media Content Analysis Study, 1974,* the same used in Chapter Four. Researchers coded all front page and editorial page items appearing in 96 newspapers during ten days in October and November 1974. This chapter uses data on 91 papers.[9] The papers were chosen to parallel the national survey that the CPS conducts each election year, so the newspaper sample should accurately represent the nation's daily press.

One group of papers in the study, numbering 32, faces genuine head-on competition from independently owned and operated papers in their local markets. At the opposite extreme, 26 sampled papers are monopolies facing no local newspaper competition at all. The rest of the sample, totaling 33, are "quasi-monopolies." These papers either share the market with a sister paper under the same ownership, or with a separately owned but jointly operated paper.

The Newspaper Preservation Act sanctions jointly operated papers. It provides an exemption from anti-trust laws, which allows separately owned papers to save money by sharing printing and other facilities. The stated basis for the policy is the belief that some newspapers would not be economically viable if forced to face real economic competition. The goal is to keep alive presumably diverse voices in the marketplace of ideas. Joint operation prevents two papers from having to operate expensive equipment like printing presses and delivery vans separately and thereby allows both to remain profitable. Some observers denounce the policy for encouraging the death of real competition and providing unnecessary subsidies to papers that would survive anyway.[10] Yet for many cities, it may be the vehicle that allows at least some competition to survive, because it permits two news organizations to share the benefits of economies of scale that otherwise would lead to full monopoly.

The Impact of Competition

The CPS study provides data pertinent to the four expectations of competition listed above: seriousness, diversity, fairness, and responsiveness.[11] For each trait, the data reveal whether economic competition and monopoly have the effects widely expected. Appendix C provides a detailed analysis of the statistics. Here I present the highlights.

Perhaps the most important element of the faith in competition is the notion that it stimulates diversity in ideas. To test that hypothesis, we can check for what I call *horizontal* diversity, that is, diversity in content between different papers in the same market. The more horizontal diversity, the more varied information and opinions are available from a community's newspapers. The question is whether there is more horizontal diversity where papers are in the hands of separate, competitive owners. (By definition, cities with only one paper cannot enjoy horizontal diversity, although they can have *vertical* diversity, that is, variety of content within an individual paper.) If so, the average pair of papers in genuine economic competition ought to be more different from each other than the average pair of papers owned or operated jointly.[12]

As detailed in Appendix C, the findings are inconsistent. On some measures the competitive markets have more horizontal diversity, meaning that the newspapers in genuine economic competition are more different from each other than the papers under common ownership or joint operation. On other measures though, the quasi-monopolistic papers (owned or operated jointly) are more distinct from each other than economically competitive papers. And on most measures competitive ownership makes no difference one way or the other.

A broader analysis was undertaken using regression techniques and encompassing all four of the desirable newspaper traits—seriousness, diversity, balance, and responsiveness. The regression data show that competition fails to exert much influence over newspaper content. The relationships are weak and scattered. Only two statistically significant though not terribly impressive findings emerge: competition seems to increase use of staff-generated as opposed to wire service copy (theoretically a measure of seriousness) but to decrease judgmental news (a measure of responsiveness), which I define as stories that contain overt criticism or praise. The import of even these two results is ambiguous. Stories written by a local paper's staff may often be inferior to those produced by the larger national wire organizations; and judgmental news may be seen not as guidance for readers but as manipulation. The statistical results may be read as evidence that competition marginally enhances or detracts from the marketplace of ideas, but the more accurate summary of the data would be that competition has no striking effects in either direction.[13]

Given the argument in Part I of the book, it might seem that competition would systematically lower quality. This is not the case. Within the narrow band of discretion allowed by the economic market, it is the priorities of the publisher and the specific preferences among audiences and advertisers—not degree of competition—that most directly shape newspaper quality.

Some observers might question the reliance upon data from 1974 for this conclusion. They would point to rising economic competition between urban and suburban dailies, and between large-scale chain papers extending their tentacles into each other's territory. They might also cite the rise of competition from television. If one could figure out more specific hypotheses to test with more current data, one might find stronger associations. But the logic behind hypotheses that competition invariably advances free-press ideals remains shaky. And the dilemma of American journalism, which appears to be cemented by economic competition, persists. Moreover, although the data are older than one might prefer, they are the most comprehensive available. Since they were collected, monopoly in the urban, daily newspaper market has actually spread, and newer though less extensive data support the conclusions reached here.[14] Assuming then that the findings are generally valid, I shall discuss the implications for normative reasoning about journalism and democracy.

Enriching the Marketplace of Ideas

Those who rely on economic competition assume first that it affects newspaper content and second that the impacts benefit democracy. The data suggest competition affects political news inconsistently and weakly, so there is little a priori reason to expect it to help fulfill free press goals. And even if economic competition does strongly shape newspaper content in ways untapped by these data, it will not necessarily yield news that comes closer to free press ideals. The specific effects of competition on the news depend upon consumer tastes and conditions in each market, including consumers' responsiveness to price changes; their willingness to spend time on news; the accessibility of untapped news sources;[15] advertisers' tastes; and availability of substitute products (e.g., TV news—and TV entertainment). It seems reasonable to conclude at the minimum that newspaper monopoly or quasi-monopoly may not be as harmful as often believed.

One reason that hopeful generalizations about competition often fail to depict reality is that newspaper managements responding to competition might not alter those elements of newspapers we care about, the political news and editorials. Publishers face uncertainty about the effect of their news choices on potential or current readers.[16] They do not know whether a boost in the amount of state or national or international news will attract more readers than it repels. They may not believe that large investments in improved quality would produce detectable profit increases—and they are probably right. As we have seen, the political interest and ideological sophistication of the average member of the public is not high. Most citizens rank political debate and policy issues low in their lives. Few fulfill the marketplace of ideas model of a vigilant readership surveying competing papers, detecting flaws in political content, switching newspaper loyalties, and so forth.[17]

Publishers do not even have good evidence that audiences perceive differences between competitive newspapers.[18] Nor can they be sure that, if they make perceptible changes, readers will break old habits and switch papers.[19] Many readers may choose papers for such features as comics, sports, film reviews, or the time of delivery. Management often responds to competition by sophisticated marketing efforts stressing non-news components of the product. As in many other forms of oligopolistic competition (beer, cereals, cigarettes), news manufacturers seek to build brand loyalty via ad campaigns emphasizing minor attributes: a columnist, comic strip, or lotto game.

Economic Markets and Publisher Power

The assumption that economic competition enhances a "marketplace of ideas" therefore requires reformulation. Although competition does not have broad impacts, it may in some circumstances incrementally enrich the diversity of ideas in a community. With two separate staffs scurrying about, scouring city offices and streets for news, markets served by two newspapers should have access to a marginally larger volume of data, at least about the local scene. Even assuming a good deal of content duplication in the two papers, the goals of the free press might potentially be better served. Although the editors and reporters of both city papers will tend to employ the same sources and highlight the same major angles of a story, overlap is not complete. Some of the tidbits unique to each paper may enlighten, even if most are trivial. The existence of a rival paper may stimulate competitive instincts that make reporters work harder and write better. When one paper has a scoop, the other may follow it up with new evidence, making more complete information available to the public.

But there is no clear reason these benefits could not be supplied by quasi-monopoly (jointly owned or operated) papers as well as by journals in genuine economic competition. The findings are compatible with the possibility that rivalry between staffs trying to please the same boss bolsters journalism as much as rivalry between employees working for different owners. The prestige and career incentives of individual reporters and editors may spur them to better performance regardless of who owns the paper. Moreover, the owners of quasi-monopolistic newspapers might have stronger economic incentives to enhance the marketplace of ideas than competitive owners. The profit-maximizing course for a firm that owns two papers may be to develop two distinct packages, appealing to any sizable minority with one paper while winning the majority with the other. Thus quasi-monopolistic markets might have more diverse journalism than competitive ones whose papers seek the least common denominator.[20]

On the other side of the ledger are the possible negative effects of competition. For one thing, competition may lead more to imitation than to differentiation; depending on the tastes of potential readers, duplication may be the most rational marketing strategy. Beyond this, the drive to attract readers may produce investigations of bogus scandals, hounding of public officials for minor trespasses, and jealousies—even sabotage—among competing reporters on the same beat. Reporters may spend their competitive energies in childish one-upsmanship, with each staff determined to mine the final nugget of trivia before its rival.[21]

Monopoly papers may be less likely to engage in this kind of distracting disservice. More important, enjoying monopoly status and revenues may allow a newspaper the freedom to report more extensively, innovatively, and fearlessly than it would under the threat competition poses of losing readers and advertisers. With deeper pockets, a monopoly publisher can afford to take chances. Of course, in other cases, enjoying a monopoly allows irresponsible publishers to gather lazy staffs to produce deliberately slanted or poor quality news. But there is no convincing evidence that competition necessarily precludes the same outcome.

Rather than predicting that competitive local papers will produce superior news and editorials, this perspective points to a force that might elude a scholar's quantitative categories: the philosophy of the owners. Within the constraints cited in this book, those who own the printing presses have substantial freedom to determine the quality of their newspapers.

Chain ownership introduces further complexities. Publishers of chain papers are employees of the larger organization, not individual entrepreneurs. Less rooted in the community, they may be more willing to shake up the local establishment. Or they may be less willing, depending on their interests and the amount of autonomy the parent corporation grants them. Many observers decry chain ownership as evidence of media concentration damaging to the marketplace of ideas.[22] However, as with local monopoly, the logic is too muddled, the forces too idiosyncratic to establish whether chain ownership encroaches upon free press ideals. A wealthy and responsible chain that buys a mediocre monopoly paper may invest in significant improvements; another chain may bleed it for even more profitability and dictate its editorial stands. There is no single pattern.

This observation brings up another ambiguity in normative visions of the marketplace of ideas. The purposes of competition become obscure if objectivity governs reporting. Under objectivity, news of similar events will look largely the same in different papers. Ownership will therefore matter little to the news. Only editorial pages, freed from the tyranny of objectivity, can contribute different ideas. Here separate ownership can make a difference. Cities that have only one newspaper publisher are vulnerable to the influence of editorial vendettas. Having an independent second voice may reduce the sway of one-sided editorial campaigns—although collusion or agreement between publishers can yield a monopoly-like grip on the political dialogue even in competitive markets.

This point suggests a more philosophical dimension to the monopoly problem, one not addressed simply by assessing a newspaper's content. Most newspaper owners exert considerable influence in their communities because of their sway over perceived and actual public opinion. When there is only one owner, community power is more concentrated than when there are two. Genuine, two-publisher competition may be beneficial less for its effects on news than for its potential leveling impact at the apex of the community power structure. Having two newspaper moguls in a town spreads out the power, although exactly how much depends on the circulation of each paper and the amount of respect it enjoys among elites, as much as on the diversity of content in the two papers.

Notice something else. Although competition may affect the distribution of power, it has no necessary impact on government accountability. As the data suggest, competition does not enhance the ability of journalists to act as independent investigative watchdogs; nor does competition necessarily improve reporting in other ways.

On balance, the wide concern with recent trends toward one-paper cities may be somewhat overdrawn. Consider the implications for the most important public policy that affects newspaper market structure, the Newspaper Preservation Act. The policy may not be as deleterious as critics believe.[23] The Act sometimes leads to provision of economically unjustifiable subsidies to newspapers that could earn reasonable profits if managed effectively. But judging by the findings of this chapter, the Act may do little harm to free press ideals. Even though it draws two owners into close operating relationships, we have no a priori reason to expect the seriousness, diversity, fairness, or responsiveness of the papers to deteriorate. There is even some reason to think two jointly operated and highly profitable papers produce the best journalism. The staffs of these outlets may develop a rivalry that spurs quality, since both owners, unlike those in full-blown competition, enjoy lower operating costs due to shared economies of scale. That may give each more economic leeway to fund investigative reporting and risk the wrath of advertisers.

The corollary to the fear of monopoly is the faith in competition. That devotion underlies recent policy decisions made by the Federal Communications Commission, to which I now turn.

6

Faith and Mystification in Broadcast Deregulation

During the 1980s, public policy toward broadcasting changed dramatically. The dominant trend was virtually to eliminate government regulation and to rely upon an enlarged, vigorously competitive economic market to protect and expand the "marketplace of ideas." Perhaps the most important and controversial case in point is the Federal Communications Commission's 1987 decision to abolish the broadcast Fairness Doctrine.[1] A direct attempt by government to foster diverse accountability news, the doctrine required that broadcasters devote time to controversial issues and air varied opposing views. The FCC's decision assumed that rising economic competition will provide a better means of attaining the original goals of the doctrine than regulation.

The FCC eliminated the doctrine in the belief that audiences and media behave in the real world as they do in the ideal marketplace of ideas.[2] The commission provided little evidence in support of this assumption. It neglected to probe the actual impacts of growing economic competition in television, to determine what an increasingly competitive market produced while it was still under fairness regulation. And it provided only the most optimistic of scenarios about what to expect with the removal of the doctrine.

Explaining the commission's vote to end the doctrine,[3] Chairman Dennis Patrick voiced his abiding faith in free press ideals and the marketplace of ideas:

Freedom of speech is democracy's crown jewel. Without it, government ceases to be a faithful instrument of the people's will, and, all too often, becomes an instrument of oppression. . . . The founding fathers . . . placed their faith in the people, upon the assumption that free men and women would be able to distinguish truth from falsehood, the authentic from the fraudulent, the statesman from the charlatan. . . . Faith in democracy entails a belief that political wisdom and virtue will sustain themselves in a free marketplace of ideas, without government intervention.[4]

The commission's decision cites two main specific arguments. The first is constitutional: television news ought to enjoy the same First Amendment protection from government interference as the printed press. By regulating broadcast content, the Fairness Doctrine violated constitutional guarantees and posed the peril of government intimidation. The second argument is policy-based: the threat of sanction for violating the fairness rules actually diminished the amount of high-quality and diverse news on television. (I limit my attention to TV, although radio was also covered.) To avoid fairness requirements that they give free time to opposing viewpoints on controversial issues, stations simply did not televise much controversy. Thus, the commission says, the doctrines's consequences were the opposite of those intended. Designed to promote diverse ideas on television, the doctrine discouraged them. By replacing regulation with competition, then, the commission sought to solve both the policy and the constitutional problems: to increase broadcasters' incentives to provide diverse news while enhancing their autonomy from unconstitutional government intrusion.

The constitutional issue I leave to others.[5] For First Amendment absolutists, the policy argument may not matter; for them, the doctrine intruded upon the free speech of broadcasters, an invasion outweighing any possible good.[6] I sympathize with that approach. But I believe that we need to reason about democracy rather than taking the First Amendment as the last word. Most First Amendment scholars acknowledge that some conditions justify restricting freedom of speech or press, for example, when national security, defendants' rights, or defamation are involved. The debate is whether current conditions justify the particular case of the Fairness Doctrine. Many policymakers seem to support this instance; majorities in Congress have voted to reinstate the doctrine and they may yet succeed.[7] But final resolution of the debate over constitutionality may be left to the Supreme Court.[8]

Most policy analysts endorsed abolition of the doctrine, taking the same leap of faith in economic markets as the FCC.[9] Similar reasoning energizes the commission's drive to rescind or restrict other broadcasting regulations.[10] All this backing illustrates a widespread faith in economic competition as the foundation for a genuine marketplace of ideas. The findings and analysis of this book suggest the dangers of basing public policy on the assumption that the economic market inevitably nourishes journalism's contributions to democratic citizenship. Decisions rooted in this premise, such as the FCC's elimination of the Fairness Doctrine, might actually retard progress toward a freer press and citizenry.

The Fairness Doctrine in Theory and Operation

Federal broadcast regulation has pursued two central goals. The positive goal is to provide diversity: a wide variety of facts and opinions on public issues so that Americans can discover truth and participate effectively in democracy. The second, defensive goal is to prevent the media (or the government through the media) from controlling public opinion by limiting the circulation of ideas. The two specific and closely related aims of broadcast policy, then, have been enhancing citizenship by enriching the diversity of ideas and constraining the power of the media over public opinion. The goals restate Americans' ambivalence toward the media: the desire to have a press that is powerful enough to rein in government, but not so powerful as to dominate public opinion.

The explicit requirements of the Fairness Doctrine were two:[11] that broadcast stations devote a reasonable percentage of time to the discussion of controversial issues of public importance and that they provide reasonable opportunities for presentation of contrasting views on these issues. The commission rarely enforced the first part of the doctrine. The second part, mandating some kind of balance and diversity, generated most of the complaints and commission attention.

The FCC did not intrude deeply into the editorial process. Licensees did not have to present the opposing views on the very same program or series of programs; nor did they have to provide an exactly equal balance of views. As the commission wrote, "[A]ll matters concerning the particular opposing views to be presented and the appropriate spokesmen and format for their presentation are left to the licensees' discretion subject only to a standard of reasonableness and good faith."[12]

In a typical year, the FCC received five to ten thousand fairness complaints (most informally phoned in) and issued six admonitions to stations. These consisted of a request to show how the station would offer contrasting views an opportunity for expression, or a notification that the commission would place a description of a fairness violation in the station's file and consider it at license renewal time.[13] Only one station (a radio outlet in suburban Philadelphia) ever lost its license on Fairness Doctrine grounds. That station allegedly purveyed one-sided anti-Semitic analyses of public issues.[14]

Despite this record of seemingly gentle enforcement, answering frivolous fairness complaints sometimes cost stations money.[15] Fear of such experiences, however rare, may have posed a disincentive to issue programming. In this sense, the FCC believed, the second part of the doctrine undermined the first. The Commission's decision to deregulate emphasized this "chilling" effect.[16]

Before the 1980s, the commission believed this effect to be minimal. As the commission said back then, "The purpose and foundation of the Fairness Doctrine is 'to preserve an uninhibited marketplace of ideas in which truth will undoubtedly prevail. . . .' "[17] The old FCC felt the economic market would not provide freewheeling diversity because of scarcity; broadcast frequencies, hence broadcasting outlets, were limited. The commission reasoned further that most audience members do not follow news assiduously, which led it to seek to induce *vertical diversity*, variety within each individual station's programming. The commission felt the doctrine would yield vertical diversity, thereby preventing each broadcaster from censoring or inhibiting the flow of ideas.[18]

During the 1980s, the commission redefined diversity as it redirected policy. An emphasis on horizontal diversity replaced traditional commission reliance upon vertical diversity. Horizontal diversity means a variety of ideas are available from a host of different media outlets. In the commission's view, by the 1980s, horizontal diversity existed almost everywhere in the United States; broadcast outlets were no longer scarce, making diverse news readily available. The commission assumes further that autonomous audience members will actively search among the competing media in fashioning their views on public issues: "Individuals . . . can be expected to consult a variety of sources in a wide array of media."[19] Thus the Commission's 1985 fairness report concludes that "the interest of the public in viewpoint diversity is *fully served* by the multiplicity of voices in the marketplace today. . . ."[20] The commission believes there is an active, independent citizenry that can obtain quality journalism through the mechanism of the competitive economic market.

Previous chapters have provided considerable reason to question any faith in horizontal diversity. Vertical diversity holds audiences and media to lower, perhaps more realistic standards. Under the old regulatory regime, even if they watched only one station, audiences could in theory receive an assortment of views, because each individual broadcaster would be required to provide them. Although the FCC asserts there is no longer any danger of having Americans "left uninformed on public issues,"[21] it fails to unearth evidence of a significant rise in political interest or knowledge among Americans. The reasoning unequivocally rests on market competition: "[T]he Commission should rely on the broadcasters' ability to determine the wants of their audiences through the normal mechanisms of the marketplace. The public's interest, then, defines the public interest."[22]

Competition's Benefits: New Supply, More Demand?

In essence, deregulation proponents argue both that economic competition brought about considerable diversity even under the Fairness Doctrine and that, freed of the doctrine, the market will further increase the supply of varied views on public issues. They emphasize changes of supply and demand in the new market-place, which now includes cable television services and many new broadcast stations. At the time of the *Red Lion* decision affirming the doctrine,[23] there were 6,595 radio and 837 TV stations; in 1987 there were 10,128 radio and 1,315 TV stations.[24] According to deregulation champions, the competition among this multitude of stations for viewer or listener attention will prevent the dominance of any media outlet as it expands the diversity of ideas. In this way, says the FCC, competition informs citizens and constrains media power—the economic market advances much more efficiently and constitutionally the same goals the Fairness Doctrine proclaimed but actually undermined.[25] If scarcity of broadcast spectrum once provided a rationale for FCC regulation, the explosive increase in TV outlets makes the justification obsolete.[26]

But the commission fails to probe what the audience is actually seeking from those new media. Because of this, it overlooks an important scarcity that persists despite the growth in TV stations: demand for news and public affairs programming. For the competitive marketplace of ideas to flower as envisioned by the FCC, the discerning, informed, interested citizen of free press ideals would have to be a reality.

The scarcity of audience attention, the limited demand for detailed, multifaceted news has not changed.[27] If anything, demand for the national evening news on TV has dwindled. In the 1980–81 season, 72 percent of households watching TV during the time the evening news is aired tuned in the networks. More recently, the figure has been 62 percent.[28] The paltry ratings of TV documentaries and news analyses playing against network entertainment provides a simple index to the shallowness of the mass audience's taste for public affairs programming.[29] The mass audience's inclinations may restrict information diversity even as competition and the number of producers expands.[30]

The mainstays of any American "marketplace of ideas" operate outside the normal economic market—and beyond the awareness of most Americans. The major sources of new ideas are magazines such as *The Nation, Harper's, The Public Interest,* and academic or quasi-academic journals such as *Foreign Policy* and *Regulation.* They tend to be non-profit or low-profit operations that get by on service to a small, select readership. Most of their revenue shortfalls are made up by charitable foundations and individuals, with an assist from postage and tax breaks.

Believers in market sovereignty might accept these outcomes: economic competition will produce the amount and level of diverse news that audiences seek. The mass media serve the mass audience, the specialized media handle the elites and intellectuals. Having two distinct market segments appears to be an economically efficient way to satisfy the most people at the least cost. Genuine market competition is usually superior to government regulation at achieving economic efficiency so defined. But leaving it at that substitutes economic efficiency for the original goals of fairness regulation. Economic efficiency may even work against these goals. The FCC says it still supports the original aims; it should analyze the possibility that efficient responsiveness to audience demands will undermine them.[31]

If we consider what the new TV outlets have actually supplied, presumably in response to audience tastes, it seems clear that most members of the audience seek something other than public affairs. Looking first at the national news market, Cable News Network (CNN) and Cable-Satellite Public Affairs Network (C-SPAN) are the main new suppliers. C-SPAN and CNN[32] do provide many more minutes of news and public affairs than the TV networks. And a study of CNN reveals that it does employ a slightly different range of news sources than ABC, CBS, and NBC.[33] But scholars have not probed whether CNN's sources express distinct notions rarely heard on the three broadcast networks. I do not gainsay the merit in these services. CNN's live coverage of major events like Supreme Court confirmation hearings or summit meetings certainly benefits the tiny portion of the public that watches. C-SPAN's relays of congressional hearings and debates probably offers more diversity to its even tinier audience than any other mass medium. C-SPAN, incidentally, is a non-profit organization; it exists outside the economic market.

Even assuming CNN and C-SPAN do offer views distinct from the broadcast networks, the low ratings for CNN and C-SPAN suggest the mass audience has little taste for diverse news. If large audiences were hungering for diversity, public affairs on cable would generate more robust ratings. One reason it does not is that these two admirable services are not even available to a majority of the nation's households.[34] Among TV households that have access, the ratings indicate under 1 percent watch either service during the evening. Similarly, the ratings of the evening news show on PBS, the "MacNeil/Lehrer NewsHour," also hover around 1 percent.[35] Although the ratings of the big three networks have declined by over 10 percentage points since 1980, they still draw many times more viewers than the cable or PBS alternatives.[36] The network evening news in a recent period received ratings of 11.3 (ABC), 11.2 (CBS), and 10.5 (NBC), meaning 33.0 percent of all television households had their sets tuned to one of the shows.[37] Given the low ratings of CNN and C-SPAN, most of the decline in network news ratings since 1980 must be caused by audiences tuning in entertainment or turning off their TVs. A few may be viewing news on independent, non-network broadcast stations. In sum, only a small fraction of the news audience has abandoned TV network news for news on cable or independent broadcast stations. The overwhelming majority of the audience for national TV news continues to rely on the same old networks. The power of ABC, CBS, and NBC in shaping actual and perceived public opinion on national issues is little diminished.[38]

However, individual stations may be offering a greater variety of views, or vertical diversity. "Nightline," "MacNeil/Lehrer NewsHour," "Donahue," and other shows provide some topical disputation on network TV. Their existence might enhance the variety of views available to audiences. But the FCC offers no empirical data on this possibility.[39] Nor does the commission ask whether the most influential programs, the evening news shows on ABC, CBS, and NBC, now cast a significantly wider net for sources and views. On balance there may be more vertical diversity than before on each national TV network. But as we have seen, there is no evidence the public knows, cares, or acts more in national politics than before, or that they have developed different views as a result of the alleged surge of new ideas on television.

The other area that concerns policymakers is the local media market. The commission tends to focus on the explosion of new stations, but this increase may not bolster the audience's ability to acquire more ideas about local issues. Scholarly research is meager, but it seems likely that, among local markets, supply and demand for political news varies widely. Not all markets have one-hour local TV news shows; some have half-hour shows, others no news at all.[40] The amount of news on local policy issues probably varies among markets as well, depending upon how many communities the market encompasses, the dispersion or concentration of population, and the like.[41] A station serving a large city like Washington, D.C. might address local policy issues when the bulk of its audience lives or works in the central city. But it would probably not address anything but the most extraordinary local issues of the suburban communities. Stations in markets such as Raleigh-Durham, N.C., serve no large population concentration. Broadcasting over a couple dozen separate city and county jurisdictions, the stations tend to report only unusual controversies in the politics of individual localities. Market pressures seem to encourage general human interest stories—accidents, sports, weather, and crime—that attract viewers throughout the station's viewing area, rather than news of any specific community's politics and policy issues.

While the FCC may believe apolitical local news was a by-product of the Fairness Doctrine's chilling effects, more likely producers were responding to audience tastes. If viewers had wanted a great deal more issue programming, the fairness rules provided plenty of latitude for the stations to air it. Indeed, even though national networks were subject to the doctrine too, they devoted a higher proportion of their evening news shows to issues.

To add some empirical substance to the suspicion that local TV news provides little political information, let alone accountability news, I conducted two content analyses. The first coded local news from the two dominant stations in the medium-sized Raleigh-Durham, N.C., market.[42] Table 3 reports the findings.

Reporting on local policy issues averaged under two minutes per half hour—perhaps 250 words. Reporting on national/international news rarely went beyond the material provided by networks or other news agencies. Total coverage of all substantive policy or political matters averaged about six minutes per broadcast. The stations devoted more time to sports and weather, and to commercials, banter, and previews. (Chatter among anchors and reporters, along with previews of upcoming stories, averaged

Table 3. Average Time Devoted to Nine News
Categories in Local Television News, 1986
(WRAL and WTVD)

Category	Week 1 (Oct.) (Min.:Sec.)	Week 2 (Nov.) (Min.:Sec.)
Local policy	1:12	1:45
Human interest	3:21	4:18
Disaster	2:38	1:42
National policy	1:47	2:03
State policy	2:37	2:18
Local economy	0:41	1:18
Weather	3:18	3:05
Sports	4:12	4:26
Mixed, ambiguous	0:16	0:00
Totals[a]	20:02	20:55

[a] The rest of the 30-minute period was devoted to commercials, happy talk banter among the anchors, previews
of upcoming stories, and credits.

nearly two minutes per program, a bit more than local policy
news.) The totals did not vary much between the two weeks, one
just before the 1986 election, one after.

To provide a flavor of the local policy news the stations did
cover, here is a complete list for both stations during the pre-
election week:

Day 1: Voters in Halifax County will decide on use of property
taxes for education (1 minute:30 seconds)
Shearon Harris nuclear plant coalition meeting (0:27)

Day 2: Shearon Harris plant emergency preparedness drill (2:15)
Sam Nunn campaigns for Congressional candidate David
Price (0:31)
Views of Price opponent Bill Cobey (0:24)
Strom Thurmond campaigns for Cobey (0:06)
Shearon Harris emergency drill (1:02)

Day 3: Redevelopment in downtown Durham (0:48)
United Way campaign in NC (0:16)
Bond issue in Durham (1:03)

Day 4: Third District Congressional race (1:54)

Day 5: Student group campaigns for SDI in Chapel Hill (1:12)
Glendale water company violates state regulations (0:29)

Notice that, during the week before the election, the closely contested race to represent Raleigh and Chapel Hill in Congress drew less than three minutes' coverage. State legislative races received no attention at all.

A second study, drawing from a separate research project on local news coverage during the week of the "Super Tuesday" primary elections, provided a sample of 36 local news shows for the single day of Thursday, March 10, 1988. The shows probably contained more political news than they would have on a random day outside the primary season, but by Thursday virtually all of the election results were in; it is as close to a "normal" day as the sample contained. While strictly speaking the sample was not randomly drawn, it does include large, medium, and small markets throughout the country.[43] The early evening news show was analyzed. Table 4 displays the average number of minutes per hour the shows devoted to politics and policy. These data suggest that local and state issues are far from the central concern of local TV news. Together, these categories comprise less than five minutes per local news hour, and much of that is devoted to the crime issue. Even if one assumes *all* of the time devoted to the presidential primary would have gone to state and local policy in a week without Super Tuesday, the total remains under eight minutes per hour, even though Fairness rules were gone.

Though I cannot vouch for the representativeness of these samples, I suspect the market forces that limit political and policy news are common to many stations. One study of the Mobile, Ala.–Pensacola, Fla. market came up with similar findings: news of "local and state government" or "politics and political campaigns" averaged about two minutes per show on each of the three stations; another study of Chicago yielded parallel results.[44] Readers can check against their own experiences of local TV. Given the well-known statistic that the entire script of a half-hour news show (including weather, sports, and the rest) would fit comfortably on a single page of a newspaper, it seems likely that even with the increase in stations, the amount of unique (i.e., unduplicated) local political news on TV and radio probably

Table 4. Average Policy or Political News per
Hour on 36 Local TV News Shows

Local:	
Local policy (non-crime)	1:36
Local policy (crime-related)	0:51
Local politics	0:07*
Total local	2:34
State:	
State policy (non-crime)	1:18
State policy (crime-related)	0:33
State politics	0:06
Total state	1:57
Other:	
Primary (presidential)	3:18*
Primary (state/local/referendum)	0:22
National policy	0:12
International policy issues	0:17
Total other	4:09
Mixed, ambiguous	1:37
Grand Total (Average minutes per hour)	10:17

* These two categories exclude the three network
affiliates in Chicago, which were extreme outliers.
Had they been left in, they would have accounted
for 82 percent of all local politics coverage in the
sample and 45 percent of all presidential primary
coverage. The Illinois primary was to be held the
week after Super Tuesday. With Chicago included,
the averages would have been 34 seconds and 4 minutes, 37 seconds, respectively.

comes to less in most markets than the amount in one newspaper.[45] And of course the ratings reveal that few people watch
more than one or two local news shows per night.[46]

The proponents of deregulation might argue that competition
has yielded little enhancement of local news because it operated
within the framework of the Fairness Doctrine; until late 1987,
the chill of regulation discouraged stations from increasing the
supply of diverse news as they and audiences would have liked.
Analyzing how a specific policy issue was addressed in the print
media provides one indirect test of that view, since the doctrine

does not cover them. I explored coverage of the Fairness Doctrine itself as a policy issue in a national sample of newspapers. If diversity of views flourishes in the absence of a Fairness Doctrine, newspapers ought to provide a wide variety of editorial positions on this and most issues.

I probed editorial comment on the FCC's August 4, 1987, decision to abolish the doctrine. I analyzed editorial pages in 39 newspapers, most with national or regional reputations.[47] Here was a policy issue of great importance to journalism. On the one hand, we might predict considerable variety in editorial views. In the commission's own words, "[T]he fairness doctrine remains a source of immense controversy, marked by the strong interest exhibited by Congress. . . . and the divergence in views expressed. . . . Accordingly, we anticipated . . . lively debate over the doctrine. . . ."[48] On the other hand, newspapers tend to take a self-interested, absolutist view of press freedom issues.[49] That might lead us to predict a one-sided approach to this issue, more so than for most.

Over the 11 days following the decision, the 39 papers ran a total of 23 editorials on the FCC's decision. Nineteen papers praised the decision. Three offered mixed assessments. One opposed abolition of the Fairness Doctrine (the *St. Louis Post-Dispatch*). The papers also ran 28 opinion columns on the action. Praising abolition were 25 columns, of which 23 were syndicated and two were by local writers. James Kirkpatrick wrote 12; Edwin Yoder, seven; and Daniel Brenner, four.[50] Two local columnists in other papers offered mixed views. One piece, a guest column by an academic in the *Denver Post,* opposed the decision (an editorial there had previously cheered it). So the total score in 51 expressions of views in a sample including some of the best papers in the country: 44 for abolition; five mixed; two opposed.

People seeking diverse views on the Fairness Doctrine as a policy issue would not have found them in most newspapers. Even if they were willing to read five or ten good papers, the odds are they would not have found a single analysis condemning the FCC's decision. On this issue, newspapers provided neither horizontal diversity across different papers nor vertical diversity within each paper. No doubt newspapers show more vertical and horizontal diversity on other issues. Still, the case study shows that diversity is hardly inevitable, even without a Fairness Doctrine, even in papers spanning the geographical and ideological breadth of the nation.

Removing the Doctrine to Enhance Autonomy

Beyond arguing that expunging the doctrine ends the chilling effect and frees stations to offer more diversity, the commission avers that fairness deregulation bolsters broadcasters' autonomy. Commissioners believe ending the government's Fairness-borne invasion of editorial decisions will free television journalism from the threat of government pressure, leading to better-informed, more independent citizenship. The commission neglects two major problems. First, the government plays an enormous role in shaping the content of all news, print and broadcast. This impact has nothing to do with the Fairness Doctrine. Second, by making broadcasters more autonomous from government, the FCC may be rendering them more vulnerable to the pressures of the economic market, which can diminish unadulterated free speech just as government regulation can.

Consider the actual role of the government in the manufacture of the news.[51] Government has always managed print and electronic news to some degree, and will continue to do so even without the Fairness Doctrine. Perhaps the most thoroughly documented of all findings by communications scholars is that government officials and quasi-official elite sources heavily shape many dimensions of the news.[52] Journalists do reformulate the information following rules of objectivity and the evaluation and production biases. But, as discussed in Chapter Three, elite sources still dominate the exchange. Government press officers can usually stage media events, withhold information, try to generate a positive slant on unfortunate developments, dissemble, or otherwise manage news coverage without generating criticism for violating the Constitution. There are even arguments that, given the power of the press, skillful news management serves the interests of democratic leadership.[53]

Evaluating the Fairness Doctrine requires a recognition of this government-press symbiosis, not an invocation of an ideal media autonomy. To be sure, nobody compels stations to accept the data from official sources, while the Fairness Doctrine involved some compulsion. But the doctrine compelled stations only to broadcast a variety of views, not to propagate some standard government line.

If media organizations chose to maximize autonomy over all other values, they could and would spend more money to escape dependence on government press officers and elite sources. That they do not suggests that audiences are not demanding autonomous news in enough numbers to make such investments of broadcasters' resources profitable. It also indicates profitability takes higher priority for broadcasters than values such as autonomy—which is as it should be in a competitive economic market. Of course other goals do shape news organizations' behavior besides profit. Whatever they are, they do not put a premium on autonomy from official and powerful sources.

This observation highlights a second logical tension in the FCC's reasoning about autonomy. According to the FCC, freed of fairness (and some other) rules, broadcasters will have to respond only to economic market signals. However, the economic market is hardly an arena of independence. Economic competition links the desires of consumers to the products of suppliers; in this case, it connects the demands of advertisers and audiences to the broadcasters' programming. Cementing such bonds is the central purpose of an economic market. The need to cater to these demands curtails what broadcasters can express. Increased competition may even tighten the constraints on expression. Only where station owners are willing and able to suffer economic losses are they truly independent of compulsion.

Economic competition forces broadcasters to minimize unnecessary costs and to invest in the most profitable programming. These pressures may yield reductions in spending on less profitable news and public affairs programming. Far from raising television's investment in covering public affairs, competition could reduce news budgets. In fact, by the logic of the economic market, news budgets ought to shrink if consumers prefer entertainment.

Some indirect evidence suggests competition (mostly from cable and VCRs) is diminishing network news quality. In the latter 1980s, each network eliminated many positions from news divisions that had registered large losses during the decade.[54] Fewer reporters and researchers can mean more use of the simple story, the routine handout and photo opportunity—less autonomy from the blandishments of news managers in the political market. Sacrifice of lengthy investigative projects that may not turn up usable stories seems likely, along with elimination of longer stories that might bore audiences. Competitive pressure could also lead to flashier, more superficial news in efforts to win back audiences.[55] This points again to the possibility of a direct conflict between the economic market and free press ideals. Competition may be changing the kinds of information emphasized, diminishing the availability of news that fosters citizenship. If public tastes run toward entertainment and away from hard news, increasing competition may yield more entertaining, "softer" news. As was true of newspapers (see Chapter Five), so with broadcasters: analysts should not equate economic competition with better or more diverse journalism.

In order to discover whether the focus of network news has been changing along with economic competition, I conducted an analysis of the major categories of news for four randomly selected months in 1975 and 1986, using news summaries in the *Vanderbilt Television News Archive Indexes*. I sought to determine whether the networks have de-emphasized news of U.S. government policy issues in favor of other categories of news less likely to enhance accountability.

The categories were federal domestic policy; U.S. foreign policy; policy-related developments in foreign countries; state and local policy issues and decisions; terrorist attacks; and human interest, defined as stories about people involved in situations not linked to public policy or political issues.[56]

Table 5 reports the results. Several changes are considerable, especially in reporting on federal domestic policy, U.S. foreign policy, and human interest. While domestic policy coverage decreased by 37 percent, from 13,717 seconds in 1975 to 8,448 seconds in 1986, human interest stories rose by over 50 percent (from about 4,000 seconds per month in 1975 to 6,200 in 1986). Foreign policy reporting grew 50 percent (from about 5,096 seconds to 7,720). The total of 4,800 seconds added to foreign policy and human interest just about accounts for the drop in domestic

Table 5. Total Seconds of Network Coverage in Six Categories, 1975 and 1986*

	HUMAN	FEDDOM	USFOR	FOREIGN	STLOC	TERROR
June 1975						
ABC	3890	13760	5000	2390	1520	440
CBS	3570	14040	6280	3310	530	810
NBC	4160	14370	5100	2670	1000	420
Network avg.	3873	14057	5460	2457	1017	557
October 1975						
ABC	4210	12520	4400	3415	1500	780
CBS	4060	13550	4810	4230	1210	1270
NBC	4270	14060	4990	3125	1100	1010
Network avg.	4180	13377	4733	3590	1270	1020
Two-month avg. for 1975	4026	13717	5096	3023	1143	788
January 1986						
ABC	3880	9740	6780	2140	1590	3400
CBS	6400	10680	6910	1430	1410	1290
NBC	5540	8840	7640	2240	1050	720
Network avg.	5273	9753	7110	1937	1350	1803
May 1986						
ABC	7040	7430	9050	1820	420	1450
CBS	7210	7550	8430	2220	1350	1290
NBC	7350	6450	7510	2830	620	1880
Network avg.	7200	7143	8330	2290	797	1540
Two-month avg. for 1986	6236	8448	7720	2113	1073	1671

* Categories:
HUMAN Human interest, non-policy, and non-political stories
FEDDOM Domestic policy, U.S. federal government
USFOR U.S. foreign policy
FOREIGN Policy-related developments in foreign nations
STLOC State and local government policy issues and decisions

policy reporting. Human interest stories add little if anything to accountability. And while the foreign policy coverage may increase the public's knowledge, international reporting is notoriously susceptible to one-sided symbolic manipulation by the U.S. government. The hurly-burly of domestic partisan conflict that normally ensures a degree of diversity in domestic policy coverage often vanishes in news of American foreign policy.[57] In the meantime, TV audiences may be learning less and less about those domestic policies of their government and ever more about heartwarming or poignant events of emotional gratification but little political meaning.[58] Thus, these data further support the hypothesis that growing economic competition may enhance neither the broadcasters' autonomy nor their contributions to government accountability.[59]

Life Without Fairness: The Uncertain Future

Let us put aside the reasoning about autonomy and accept the FCC's belief that deregulation will at least bring a manifold increase in television's attention to issues. What else will the demise of the Fairness Doctrine offer the nation? The metaphor of the idea marketplace assumes the interests of idea purveyors and idea-consuming citizens harmonize rather than conflict. Yet even though owners of broadcast stations are now freer to slant news deliberately and conduct one-sided editorial and advertising campaigns, their gain is not necessarily the public's. Increasing broadcasters' freedom might not yield a better-informed citizenry or one more able to resist manipulation by powerful media or government officials.[60]

Unlike what the FCC appears to believe, it is difficult to predict the effects of ending the doctrine. At the national level, the end of the Fairness Doctrine could allow the three networks to collude and push a common political line. But it seems more likely that each network will feel freer to editorialize openly, to slant news choices, and to accept issue advocacy commercials. It is a matter of pure conjecture whether ABC's choices will balance CBS's, and CBS's, NBC's. With only three important suppliers, even one can exercise quite a bit of power over public opinion if it decides to pump up a policy option or ignore an issue.[61] It is also possible that all the networks will continue to abjure controversial issue programs, editorials, and ads in order to avoid offending any substantial segment of the vast and varied national audience.

On the local level, ending the doctrine will have different results in different communities. As one cannot know in advance the effect of newspaper competition on journalistic quality, so one cannot predict the impact of exposing broadcasters to economic competition without the Fairness Doctrine. Unregulated local competition can affect both of the original goals of fairness regulation. The questions are whether unregulated competition will increase or decrease the amount and diversity of TV's coverage of local politics and policy, and whether it will moderate or heighten broadcasters' power and inclination to manipulate public opinion.

In some communities, competition for ratings may spur broadcasters, freed of the threat of fairness complaints, to devote more time to policy issues. Elsewhere, the ratings race may encourage broadcasters to reduce issue coverage substantially. Since many stations felt no strong compulsion to implement the doctrine's requirements, abolition may actually have no discernable effect. The impacts of competition on diversity in policy and political reporting depends on the tastes of audiences and desires of station owners.

Perhaps more important and predictable are the effects on television's ability to sway public opinion. It is likely to increase. Even if the average station continues to devote only a few minutes in its newscast to local politics and policy, television's power to manipulate public opinion could grow. In pluralistic cities with well-organized pressure groups and healthy party competition, fear of one-sided editorial campaigns or censorship of major viewpoints may be unfounded. In such markets, groups might protest and viewers might tune out obviously crusading stations. Yet even if broadcasters cannot get away with a year-round comprehensive political slant, in most markets they may be able to push one or two key issues around election time. And in homogeneous communities, broadcasters may feel free to propagate their own views exclusively.

It would be impossible for the FCC to inventory conditions in every local market to see if more communities will benefit than lose without a Fairness Doctrine. That might not even be a good basis for decision. In any case, making predictions on the local level is as hazardous as for the national market. Advocates of abolition ought to admit the uncertainties and risks rather than sketch one-sided rosy scenarios.

Whether the amount and diversity of local policy coverage grows or not, it does seem reasonable to hypothesize that local stations' political leverage will increase. There may be reasons to prefer otherwise. Television seems to have inherent limitations as a provider of cognitive information. With its penchant for rousing visual symbols, it may enjoy advantages over print as a stimulator of emotions. TV exerts stronger control over the flow of the narrative and juxtaposition of stories; one cannot reread or clip as with a newspaper story. Print requires more active work and for many persons may impart less pleasure; TV may be more seductive. The majority of the public also finds television more believable than print news.[62] Given these qualities, a public more exposed to issue-oriented, advocacy journalism on TV is not necessarily better-informed. Indeed, some research suggests those who rely upon print know more.[63]

If the Fairness Doctrine reduced the amount of issue programming on television, that may have even been on balance a benefit to democracy. By reducing slant and advocacy on TV, the doctrine controlled the medium's power to define and influence preferences on public issues, and reinforced the relative power of more informative and sober newspapers and magazines.[64] The FCC avoided considering such subtle normative issues. The commission seems to prefer leaving such enigmas to the economic market. But the commission ought at least to acknowledge this kind of complexity and potential cost of deregulation.

Let us probe the possible benefits of the Fairness Doctrine a bit further. News slant already existed within the confines of fairness rules; without the doctrine it will probably multiply. There will be more deliberate manipulation of news content on

TV, as there already is in many newspapers.[65] The benefits of an increase in deliberately slanted television news are obvious only if one assumes the public actively and autonomously searches in a marketplace of ideas for the truth among conflicting views. Of course this is just what the commission presumes: "[W]hile some stations would likely be biased toward one side of an issue, other stations would likely favor the other. . . . [O]pposing points of view would in all likelihood still be available to the citizen on other stations or from other media."[66] The question remains whether openness will be the rule,[67] whether the average audience member will detect slant, and whether audiences will seek and easily find alternative views on most matters.

Beyond news are editorials and ads. Without a Fairness Doctrine, more stations are likely to editorialize. As noted in Chapter Four, the public can benefit from editorials. The editorial pages of newspapers sometimes do offer more independent analytical data than the news pages, and thereby serve the public's need for truth. But the editorial practices of most television stations are likely to differ from those of newspapers. Editorial pages normally offer more text than an entire half-hour news show, and they usually publish not only the owners' views but those of letter writers and columnists. Given the value of television time, many TV stations seem likely to offer less editorial diversity. They are more likely to air short, oversimplified editorials that promote only the views of the station owners. As an example, broadcasters can now air one-sided editorials endorsing abortion, placing an emotional issue on the agenda and putting a "pro-life" candidate on the defensive while enhancing the chances of a "pro-choice" politician. (Under regulations still in force stations cannot attack one candidate by name without giving the opponent some opportunity to reply.) Again the public benefits are unclear.

Finally, perhaps the most important likely source of one-sided messages will be not owners but the wealthy organized interests that can afford commercial time. The Fairness Doctrine covered advertising. Abolition will tighten the link between idea production and money. Such a connection violates the spirit of free press ideals as it heightens television's political power.[68]

Releasing stations and networks from fairness obligations portends the burgeoning of one-sided ads unanswered by poorer opponents.[69] One might expect this during election campaigns. Although the FCC regulation requiring stations to provide equal time to candidates remains in effect, advertisers can run commercials that promote a candidacy by stressing issues that help the favored candidate and hurt the other side. Referendum campaigns are particularly vulnerable to the power of television advertising. The Fairness Doctrine provided some limited ability for the poor side in a referendum to answer the organized interests on such issues as smoking bans or nuclear power safety; that lever is no longer available.[70] Freed of fairness restrictions, broadcasters can decide to accept only pro-smoking ads during a referendum on making public buildings smoke free. They can refuse even to sell time to anti-smoking forces, let alone to provide free reply opportunities.

In some markets, this may not be a problem; broadcasters and advertisers may disagree with each other and fill the air with clashing editorials and commercials discussing key issues. In other markets, however, those who control advocacy on TV may see things largely the same way. Certainly many viewers will disregard and even protest open attempts to persuade via commercials and editorials, but others may respond positively to such campaigns.[71] In any case, money will have more of an impact in shaping public discourse. Those who have the wealth to own stations or buy time on them will dominate television's contributions to issue discussion.

Some would classify the problem of money controlling the flow of ideas as one of income distribution, not communications policy. They would argue that, if Americans want more equal income and wealth distribution in order to enhance equality of idea distribution, they should seek public policies that redistribute income and wealth. But the point is precisely that linking idea production to money may distort political dialogue, preventing the emergence or fair discussion of issues like income redistribution.[72] Communications policy decisions can affect the nation's political dialogue. That is why the Fairness Doctrine and other communications policy choices are so significant to democracy.

If truth is the goal, the merit of an idea ought to guide its circulation and acceptance by the public, not money. To some small extent, the Fairness Doctrine probably helped diminish the role of money by limiting the amount of one-sided issue coverage, editorializing, and advertising on television.

Critics of regulatory agencies like the FCC typically charge that they are "captured," meaning that they follow the wishes of the special interests they are supposed to regulate. In this case, the FCC is no captive of broadcasters; it abolished the doctrine for reasons it felt compelling. The commission's decision raises deeper dilemmas: it reveals the power of cultural values, even myth, in the analysis of communications policy. The FCC's reasoning founders upon its faith that economic competition inevitably serves free press ideals.

Even though the Fairness Doctrine may have discouraged broadcasters from airing diverse coverage of policy issues, the economic market may not provide many incentives for stations to reverse course.[73] The evidence points to a future where growing economic competition could impel networks and local stations to air even less news of public policy than they did when the doctrine was in force.[74] Accompanying the diminished news may be an increase in editorials by station owners and issue advertisements by wealthy organizations. While in some communities this material might supplement the ideas conveyed in the daily newspaper, in others it will simply bolster television's power to sway public opinion, an outcome that may not enhance democracy.

All this suggests that neither traditional forms of regulation nor burgeoning economic competition can produce the diverse "marketplace of ideas" and independent citizenry envisioned by the FCC and so many other observers of American journalism. However competitive broadcasting becomes and whether the Fairness Doctrine is reinstated or not, elevating citizenship beyond its current depressed level is likely to remain outside the reach of television as it now operates. Transcending the dilemma of journalism requires a new approach.

7

Improving Journalism by Enhancing Citizenship

Pressures from the political, economic, and idea markets combine and collide to yield news that frustrates all sides. Elites face a ceaseless threat of oversimplification and stereotype from opponents taking advantage of the volatile combination of aggressive reporting and uninformed public opinion. Under these conditions they have no choice but to engage in news management. For their part, journalists must endure the manipulative efforts of their sources while coping with conflicting pressures to generate accountability, remain objective, and contribute to the bottom line of their employers. As a result, journalists' sincere and energetic attempts to illuminate the powerful often yield coverage that serves the long-term interests of nobody: neither the manipulators nor the media, and certainly not the general public. No single rational force guides the media's focus and slant. This threatening situation redoubles politicians' anxiety and determination to evade or manipulate reporters, which in turn dampens the autonomy of the press and the public. As we have seen, increasing economic competition offers little hope of escaping these dilemmas. This chapter explores alternative paths of deliverance.

Demagoguery and the Dilemmas of Interdependence

Bluntly speaking, the media now provide an overwhelming temptation for politicians and other political figures to engage in demagoguery—a term that has gone out of fashion even as the practice has been virtually institutionalized. Other forces besides the media create incentives for political opportunism. But demagoguery does feed on the biases of the news for the simple and symbolic, for the appearance of power and popularity and against any sign of ineffectiveness or public disfavor.

Recent election campaigns are rife with examples of media-borne campaign ploys that smacked of the demagogic—but worked. In 1976, the Democrats exploited Gerald Ford's clumsy analysis of Russia's inability to dominate the Polish spirit (as if the conservative, hawkish President were soft on communism). In 1980, the Republicans hammered Jimmy Carter for the U.S.'s humiliation in Iran (without proposing to let the hostages die to save face). In 1982, Democrats pounded the Republicans for proposing reductions in Social Security (neglecting their own asserted devotion to helping the poor and working classes, whose education and health programs suffered larger cuts because of the taboo against touching Social Security). In 1984, the GOP damned Walter Mondale for his realistic recommendation of tax increases (without presenting a practical plan for curing deficits).

As the examples suggest, the media's vulnerability to manipulation winds up discouraging leaders from telling the public complex or painful truths. If officials speak those truths, the media usually fail to explain them well and political enemies often succeed in fomenting negative news. The sad irony is the media foster this environment through their laudable attempts to enhance democracy by applying the evaluation and production biases. Public officials face a no-win choice. If they manage the news, they will almost inevitably oversimplify and mislead. But if they do not self-consciously play to the media's biases and limitations, their opponents will; and journalists seeking to hold officials accountable in the only way they can—by quoting those opponents—will inadvertently penalize public servants who fail to manage news skillfully.

While political manipulation, hypocrisy, deception, and timidity are nothing new, the media have altered the conditions under which political bargaining and decision making take place in Washington. In the old days, politicians did not face quite the same intense demand to legitimize their acts through the media.

Success did not require them to meet the standards of the evaluation and production biases, to demonstrate public support to journalists and other elites. As David Broder writes: "[I]n reality, the play of public opinion, as reported and magnified by the press, has grown so powerful in the United States that it has become the near-preoccupation of government. . . . [W]hen a president loses popularity, he also loses the ability to govern, whatever the Constitution may say."[1]

Because of the media, elites may be more attentive than ever to what they perceive as public opinion. Before the television age, back when political parties held more power, a president's image beyond the Potomac could be less favorable than his professional reputation in Washington, and he could still dominate the Washington power game.[2] Now, maintaining that separation is more difficult. Now, even if the public is not always tuned in, politicians behave as if they are. Managing media impressions to bolster perceived and actual public support has become one of the central tasks of presidents and other politicians. As Samuel Kernell suggests, "What presidents say to the public, and what others say to the public about them, matters more today than ever before . . ."[3]—and most of what they say comes through the media.[4]

Arguably, in the days before the glaring concentration of intrusive and judgmental news coverage on the political game in Washington, the president and Congress together enjoyed more autonomy. Without the extra strategic complexity imposed by media coverage, they could generate a decision on difficult matters internally, within the Washington system. Presidents and legislators could concentrate more on selling the party elite and local activists, who understood the complexity of policy choice and resisted demagogic manipulation by the opposing party. Public opinion (perceived and actual) would tag along or not. Now, with the media ever eager to obtain evidence that presidents are losing power or popularity, opponents have constant opportunities and incentives to use the media for strategic gain whenever a president makes a decision that might antagonize or disappoint one group or another. Yet, of course, leadership demands that such choices be made.

Beyond the many veto points in the congressional process,

beyond the presidential veto, media coverage now offers another lever of opposition in politics. The mere threat of using the media to clobber the other side with a negative symbol (as with the issue of tax increases in the 1980s) is a potent weapon. Candidates for office have always had incentives to be vague;[5] now they find even more reason to disdain specifics. Any detailed proposal can create an enticing target for opponents. The other side needs only to publicize an oversimplified version of the proposal and attack the straw man. Often, proponents can defend themselves only by providing the detail and context that media often cannot handle.

The media feed a spiral of demagoguery, diminished rationality in policymaking, heightened tendency toward symbolic reassurance and nostalgic evasion of concrete choices, and ultimately misrepresentation of the public. Not only is this unintentional; the conscious goal of the national press is precisely the opposite, to make government accountable.[6] Nor is it fair to blame officials for managing the news. The alternative is for politicians to ignore the clear incentives that media practices present, as the Carter administration often did, with woeful impacts on its ability to lead.[7] In this sense, the media force presidents to engage in news management, even as journalists depend reluctantly but heavily on images the administration manufactures.

This negative and compulsive media-elite interdependency means no single rational intelligence consistently guides the press's powerful messages. Rather, as we have seen, news slant emerges from journalists' application of their institutional biases and practices, under constant and contradictory pressure from contending elites, to ever-shifting and often unpredictable events. Observers usually define political power as acting deliberately to induce someone else to do what the actor prefers.[8] With the rise of media clout, a new form of unintentional political power has entered the equation. Now political power can be exercised by the process of journalism, through the inadvertent news slant the process creates.

In some cases, the thinking and behavior of elites and ordinary members of the public is shaped or modified not because some person or group necessarily prefers an outcome, but because news slant stimulates it. An example would be the media's neglect of the Iran-contra scandal until it surfaced virulently to damage the stature of the Reagan administration and the credibility of the nation's foreign policy.

If the media performed as ideally as they should, if they actually served an informed and interested citizenry, democracy might more closely approximate its ideal. Instead, democracy has gained little from the rise of media power. Ironically, even as politicians' consuming attention to public opinion has grown since John Kennedy, the first modern media president, the majority of Americans have become cynical about politicians and government. Even as politicians bend over every which way to please the public through the media, bombarding them with images of caring and wise public policy, most Americans have come to distrust them.[9] One reason may be the erratic deployment of the media's spotlight, which encourages elite responsiveness to apparent public opinion more than to the public's actual preferences or needs. Indeed, the final irony is that before the mass media played as much of a role, back when party and group allegiance seemed to determine public opinion and voting, Americans were at least as knowledgeable politically as they are now, and they voted more regularly.

The Supply and Demand Sides of Journalism's Dilemma

The centrality of journalism to modern democracy makes the public policy issues surrounding the press more important than ever. If we abandon unquestioned faith in a marketplace of ideas nourished by economic competition, we can ask exactly what journalism might do to escape or diminish its dilemma of interdependence.

The two basic sources of the problem are inadequate supply of high quality, independent reporting, and paltry demand for such news. Increasing supply will be difficult. Competition and the reliance upon elites will stymie many potential improvements, although paths to enhancement do exist. Driving up demand for accountability news may be even harder, but for democracy to improve, the bottom line is that the public must begin craving better journalism.

Journalists could act unilaterally to improve supply, as critics have often urged. They could craft stories to "make reality interesting."[10] and render news more comprehensible.[11] News organizations could show more creativity in defining and conveying news, without spending more money. But they do not. It seems the elites' compulsion to manage the news, engendered by competition in the political market, has its counterpart in the media managers' seemingly compulsive refusal to reform journalism, which is engendered by their competition in the economic market. The question remains why economic incentives do not lead news organizations to undertake active attempts to mold the tastes of their consumers. If news companies want to offer higher quality journalism, why do most of them fail to innovate and market improvements energetically? The rigidity of many news operations may actually reduce their profitability. Consider, for example, the tiresome redundancy of presidential campaign news, with all networks featuring the same basic stories of the day's doings, strategic manipulations, and predictions. A series of biographical explorations of the characters and records of candidates might give a network the ratings edge. But the networks rarely deviate from the well-worn standard.

One explanation may lie back in the political market, in the environment of political tension and pressure that surrounds the commercial activities of news organizations. The relationships among firms, suppliers, and consumers of goods such as cereals or soft drinks, where there are no political byproducts, differ from those endured by news companies. When a cereal company starts adding raisins to the corn flakes, nobody's political interests are threatened, but if a news organization were to let reporters write in the first person, it could affect political power. The safest course for organizations faced with a web of conflicting pressures from clashing groups and individuals may be to stand still. Enduring self-imposed paralysis and sticking to familiar practices allows news firms to play contending factions against each other by invoking their continued adherence to "neutral and objective" journalism. Any move off this point could threaten the delicate balance.

One option posing minimal danger is for media to cooperate in sharing information. New information technologies could aid the public indirectly by making data more available to news producers. News organizations could sponsor dial-up computer databases managed and run for all media. The Associated Press wire service, a cooperative owned jointly by many media organizations, provides a model. For example, a database with results from public opinion polls could tell journalists about actual public opinion (as imperfectly measured by surveys). Reporters could dial up poll data and challenge news manipulators to justify their claims about the public mood. Common and instant access to databases would reduce news organizations' dependence upon elite information without requiring enormous expenditures.[12]

Another path to improving supply is changing the expectations, assertiveness, and sophistication of individual journalists. By demanding their full rights as professionals, editors and reporters who understand journalism and its current limitations in a more sophisticated way could help counterbalance the other pressures on media owners from advertisers, sources, and audiences. Journalism schools could become significant forces for positive change by altering their undergraduate curricula and aggressively promoting mid-career seminars that inculcate theoretical insights into the nature of mass communication. There remains the question of how much individual autonomy news organizations can afford to allow journalists; this issue deserves more scholarly research.[13] Any change here might conflict with the commitment to objectivity, a norm that serves many important needs of news organizations.

A third supply-side option is for the national media to reduce their cynical and suspicious approach to politicians. News organizations could eliminate their tendency to assume that politicians act purely on self-interest and desire actively to manipulate the public and withhold information. They should understand that their own news practices partly cause politicians' wariness and Machiavellianism. If journalists would exhibit less cynicism, elites might allow reporters more leeway to resist and undermine symbolic manipulation without pouncing on them for violating objectivity. Honesty and trust just might grow on both sides.

This point suggests another possibility: that elites themselves might decide to change their news managing ways. Elites could come to a tacit understanding that altering the focus of journalism would be in everyone's best interests. One sign of a desire for more substantive news may be in the many debates candidates agreed to hold during the 1988 campaign for the presidential nominations. Widely covered by the press, they focused some attention on the candidates' issue stands and perceptions. By themselves the debates did not alter daily campaign news, let alone the rest of political journalism. As an index of discontent, however, they suggested the potential for elites to inspire positive changes in journalism.

Coverage of presidential campaigns offers an opportunity to try another option that takes advantage of the possible yearning for change among elites. Reporting of incumbent officials is necessarily bound to specific sites and processes of decision, to real world events. But a campaign is a less structured story.[14] It features only one indisputably important happening: Election day in November. In covering campaigns, the national media could free themselves from the dominion of staged visual events and horse-race trivia. Until Election Day, the media could impose more of their own order on the campaign. The real campaign is not the numbing succession of predictable speeches and rallies. It is the struggle to construct reality for the public and build a coalition of elite and interest group support. News organizations could move most of the "boys on the bus"[15] off the bus, off the campaign plane, and onto investigations of candidates' careers, records, characters, alliances, and perceptions of reality.[16] One advantage to candidates is that they could talk more freely without having to worry about a gaffe landing on the network news. They could also stop spending so much time and money on staging events for television. On the other hand, they might not appreciate reporters snooping into their records. They might well prefer the horse-race/hoopla focus, with all its frustrations.

The most common proposal for increasing supply is expanding network news to an hour. This would allow longer and more diverse stories. The networks have long complained of their "inability" to do this. Local affiliates have refused to give up their lucrative early evening quiz shows and reruns. In fact, the networks *could* offer a news hour. There is some finite amount of money the networks could give the local stations to make up for the ad revenues the locals would lose by ceding the time slot over to more national news. The networks must believe that the expanded national news would garner lower ratings than the entertainment programming it would replace, so that remunerating their local affiliates would cost more than they could earn from the added advertising on an hour-long news show. The evening news remains at thirty minutes. The economic market is yielding responsiveness by the networks to consumer tastes and a weighing of additional costs versus profits: just what the market is supposed to do. Only if mass audiences were to start yearning more for longer evening news than for syndicated entertainment would the news slot likely increase.

As the networks' failure to lengthen the evening news suggests, merely urging the media to enhance the supply of accountability news is not enough. If it were, news organizations, which employ many intelligent and concerned people, would have changed already. For example, CBS engaged in searing self-criticism of its horse race-oriented, symbol-saturated campaign coverage of 1976, only to find itself following the same basic course in 1980 and 1984.[17] The network could not tear itself away from the stunning visuals, and the horse-race analysis. The forces that originally created these patterns have not changed. Major innovations that fail can threaten the jobs and fortunes of media owners and managers. Whatever their advance resolutions, as they come to work each day they face pressures to conform with competitors and do what worked in the past.

National news organizations have developed one common innovation in response to their inability to alter fundamental news practices. They have begun highlighting the manipulative nature of their own coverage. A striking example of this new self-consciousness appeared on the networks immediately after the 1988 debates between the presidential candidates. First, network correspondents briefly conveyed their own instant impressions of "who won." This is misleading, since by winning, the reporters mean "who gained the most support because of the debate?" That question cannot be answered without data the networks do not have: results from a representative national panel surveyed before and after the debate. The shows then switched to a self-conscious depiction of the candidates' "spin doctors." The sole aim of these campaign spokespersons, the networks told us, was to manipulate the media's, and hence the public's, impressions of "who won." Although they told the viewers that spin doctors were not credible, the networks proceeded to put some of them on the air to claim victory.

This strategy is common in the networks' presidential campaign coverage. The technique rejects responsibility as it denies the networks' power: it is the politicians who are to blame for media manipulation, the coverage says, and journalists are doing the only thing they can. They have to cover each campaign's manufactured media events and self-serving assertions, but at least they are warning viewers to be on guard. The underlying message, unfortunately, may well reinforce political cynicism. The implication of this self-conscious new tack is that the public can trust neither the politicians, who are only interested in election, nor television news, which is powerless to do anything but caution against trusting the very politicians to whom the networks grant so much time. In these circumstances, where network correspondents virtually announce their own exasperated inability to supply believable information, it should be no surprise that many Americans withdraw from politics. However laudable in motive, the new narrative strategy is not the innovation needed to stimulate citizenship.

By reducing the worry that change will advantage competitors, reduce revenues, or stir up a political reaction, we might encourage more innovative boldness among media executives. The best way to reduce news organizations' anxiety about innovation is to encourage the public to read, see, and think more about politics. The more interested and informed Americans become, the more freedom and confidence news organizations will have to enhance journalism without fear of losing money; the more secure their financial bases, the less likely news companies will feel vulnerable to any political tempest—the more independent they will become.

But the first step to lasting improvements in journalism is isolating some outlets from the economic market altogether; the boost to their autonomy would allow them in turn gradually to raise the supply and augment the mass public's taste for accountability news. The goal is genuine diversity and richness in ideas, a scenario in which media, audiences, and governing elites participate more often in mutually beneficial democratic debate.

The colloquy might actually focus on the merits of ideas and candidates. If this seems too idealistic, we can at least hope for a reduction in the perversities now imposed by media coverage, and an increase in the availability of accountability news.

There are two major options for expanding journalism that operates more independently of economic pressure. One is augmenting public broadcasting, the other creating publicly subsidized private media. The Public Broadcasting Service and National Public Radio both offer arguably the highest quality daily public affairs programming in the form of PBS's "MacNeil/Lehrer NewsHour" and NPR's "All Things Considered" and "Morning Edition." This is no accident; these programs do not seek to maximize the size of their audiences. But their biggest problem is precisely the small audience and meager impact on perceived and actual public opinion. Their very weakness protects the budgets of PBS and NPR from political attack by the commercial networks. In addition, the public broadcasters must maintain cordial relations with the politicians, foundations, and corporations that fund most programming. Only imperfectly insulated from political and economic pressures, sometimes too scrupulously balanced to provide their audiences with clues to truth, they are far from autonomous.

This suggests the option of combining guaranteed, irrevocable, and large tax subsidies for expanded news with a structure that would better protect the autonomy of public broadcasting. If these organizations could mount a news effort funded at the level of the commercial networks (say $250 million a year), it might well alter the course of electronic journalism. With this money they could offer frequent documentaries, investigative projects, and essayists like Bill Moyers doing more topical commentary. The Fairness Doctrine would cover their activities. In these hands the doctrine would generate considerable diversity on issues of public importance. While audience size might never reach that of the big three networks, if PBS and NPR could generate enough creatively packaged new information, it would significantly supplement and prod the three commercial networks, and even the print media.[18]

Some propose that subsidies for public broadcasting come from a tax on commercial station revenues. The tax would be a fair trade for the de facto perpetual monopoly on their frequencies that stations now enjoy.[19] But such a tax guarantees opposition from an intense organized interest, the broadcast industry. Reformers would do better to obtain the money from general revenue.[20]

The political fate of this proposal would be uncertain. A rich and autonomous public news service could inflict pain on all established institutions. Members of Congress might see a powerful new voice conveying accountability news as a threat to their political interests and oppose any significant change. The commercial networks might not look kindly on a proposal to strengthen PBS and NPR news operations. As discussed in Chapter Six, the news divisions of the big three experienced hard times in the 1980s and would not appreciate subsidized competition. Others would raise First Amendment fears. Assuaging those doubts would require ingenious mechanisms for insulating PBS from political manipulation.

Beyond the politically difficult option of strengthening public broadcasting lies the possibility that political parties—and the public's interest in politics—could be invigorated through public subsidies for partisan media. Serious constitutional difficulties and political opposition would confront any move in this direction. If a new policy passed those hurdles, the most likely outcome would be failure to transcend the dilemma of journalism. I offer the following ideas in a spirit of cautious though realistic hope.

I propose to create national news organizations run by the major parties and subsidized by the government. Financial security would increase the autonomy of the organizations. The long-term goal is more analytical information, more diversity, more readily accessible ideas. The targeted audience would be not just the public but other news organizations. The new media might at least stimulate the old to deeper insight.

To be sure, blind party loyalty is no necessary improvement over what we have now. If parties merely reinforced partisanship through manipulative propaganda, citizenship might even deteriorate. But parties appear to be the best vehicle for enhancing the public's inclination and ability to seek and process political information in a more sophisticated way.[21] Party newspapers or television channels might encourage a move toward a system of mass membership and loyalty more akin to the European democracies. Parties might sell newspaper subscriptions as part of membership, providing a selective incentive to join.[22] Partisan papers and TV shows might well contain entertainment features, reviews, and other cultural content along with news and commentary. Their existence might bolster party identification in the public, which in turn seems likely to boost participation.[23] The decline of participation in the U.S. has historically paralleled the dwindling of the partisan press and the rise of objectivity; perhaps an injection of party media would reverse the trend.

If successful, these new media would provide a competitive challenge to the rest of the press by publicizing hearings and other congressional work and exposing bureaucratic activities occurring beyond the normal news net. C-SPAN does this to some extent, but in a haphazard way limited by tiny budgets and a desire for objectivity. The journalists working for the party organs would be free to analyze and evaluate substantively, constructing arguments about truth woven into news narratives.

To free their staffs from the drudgery of covering the standard beats, party newspapers might employ wire services for routine news. They could devote their major resources to building specialists in editorial, policy analytical, and investigative journalism. Ideally, the staffs of the party outlets would constantly uncover new facts, hidden implications, and problems with current policy. They would publicize the findings of congressional investigations, they would mine the hearing records the way I. F. Stone once did to highlight information usually known only by self-interested experts in the policy arena. These revelations might in turn inspire the commercial media to cover the same things or strike out into related territory.

The party newspapers might employ the new technologies of distribution, like *USA Today* transmitting copy by satellite to printing plants around the country. The party television outlets would probably use cable; parties might also put together syndicated shows that commercial stations could broadcast.

These novel news organizations would have partisan and ideological biases; they would also develop considerable dependence upon their own party elites. But the party would have to promote the paper or TV programming, to the public and to the rest of journalism. Blatant distortion and predictable diatribes would render the medium virtually useless for the party. So the hope would be that the new media could serve citizenship, not serve up party propaganda.

Still, potential drawbacks abound. One party might develop a much more effective operation than the other. That would be not only a problem for the weaker party but a dilemma for democracy. Severe imbalance in the effectiveness of the two parties' operations would not energize knowledgeable participation. Another danger is that party leaders might engage in struggles over the content of the party organs. Determining who runs the show could turn into a divisive internal issue. One would hope party media could develop a life of semi-independence from party organizations, as appears true in some European democracies. But one can envision a scenario in which both parties produce either bland material carefully balanced to avoid offense to constituencies or constantly changing biases to placate shifting dominant factions. If this occurs, the new party media would become largely irrelevant. Only if they offer a different and respectable product would they receive attention from wide audiences and other journalists.

Another major but surmountable obstacle is funding. Precedent suggests several mechanisms for establishing a subsidy. The government could offer a tax credit for contributions designated to party media funds. A tax check-off might provide support, as it already does for the presidential campaign. The government would prohibit the print or TV outlets from accepting advertising, in order to limit the intrusion of economic market pressures and to prevent vast inequality of resources among the party organs.

An unresolved problem is how to deal with minor parties. On the one hand, the danger of limiting the subsidy to the two big parties would be narrowing the flow of ideas even more by tightening the hold of Democrats and Republicans on the political dialogue. On the other, it is impractical to fund any other party as generously as the big two. A compromise might be to channel publication subsidies to all other parties in proportion to the number of votes they receive in presidential and congressional elections and to allow minor parties to accept advertising in their media. This practice might give more people who sympathize with third parties an incentive to vote for them in order to bolster their media budgets, even if they are sure to lose an election. With richer media, more parties might become viable forces.[24]

Beyond subsidized party media, other forms of government intervention in the news industry are common in Europe, including grants, loans, aid by parties, price regulation, and funding for news agencies.[25] All would be controversial here. Americans would probably look on such proposals skeptically because of the First Amendment and the deep-seated fear of media-government collusion. In addition, owners of private news organizations dread subsidized competitors. They would mount considerable political opposition to my proposal, based on their economic interests; they and others would also cite the danger to ideals of the free press. So the political process would present serious barriers to the party media proposal.

Apart from revivifying the parties through new media, and leaving aside the improved contributions to citizenship that the public schools and other civic institutions must make, the most promising—and more politically feasible—mechanism for enhancing demand for accountability news would be simply to make voting easier. Registration laws in the U.S., among the most stringent in the world, demonstrably diminish voting and confer no obvious social benefits.[26] Reforming registration would increase voting significantly, and that might increase political interest and knowledge. Many politicians seem to prefer to keep the electorate smaller, perhaps more manageable. On the other hand, party organizations might gain from mobilizing new voters, and the media themselves might reap larger audiences if more people cared about public affairs. Hence a coalition to pass a federal law encouraging easy registration is at least conceivable. Surely that idea comports with the fundamental ideals of democracy. Of all the options proposed in this chapter, easing registration seems the most politically feasible and least questionable on other grounds. But it is also the most indirect means of enhancing journalism.

Acknowledging Intractability

Despite years of pleas by journalism critics and scholars, and despite occasional attempts at reform, news practices resist change. News coverage cannot transcend the limitations and interests of media audiences. Nor can journalists entirely escape their links to political elites. Any solutions to the dilemma of American journalism remain problematic. We can make progress at least by admitting the real state of citizenship, acknowledging the limits on journalism, and understanding the implications of both for the health of American democracy. The dilemma only deepens when we assume and invoke a mythical marketplace of ideas.

Beyond this, the notion that good journalism can yield government accountability may be exaggerated. Merely presenting enough information might not make government responsive and responsible to the public. Mechanisms that relate public opinion to the behavior of policy makers, such as elections and interest groups, might fail in enforcing government responsiveness even to an enlightened public. In other words, even if we enjoyed a more autonomous press and a more interested, perceptive public, democratic accountability might not closely resemble the ideal portrait. But improving journalism would at least give democracy a better chance.

Appendix A

Citizenship and Opinions: Data and Statistical Analysis

Chapter One discusses the differences in belief between high- and low-knowledge voters and nonvoters. This appendix reports statistical tests of the differences. The results of t-tests are displayed in Table A-1. Full details on the composition of the attitude indexes can be found in Appendix B.

The top half of the table shows average scores on the attitude measures. The first column in the bottom half of Table A-1 reports the significance level of t-tests for the differences between the average attitude of high-knowledge voters and high-knowledge nonvoters. (T-tests are two-tailed using separate variance estimates.) By convention, .050 is the cutoff for statistical significance, which means that in only 50 times out of 1000 would the difference between the sampled groups be this large by chance. We can have considerable confidence that the difference indicated in the sample is real, not due to chance, when this value is .050 or lower. The entry for the Liberal Feelings index is .016, which means that the t-test indicates a difference this large could be expected by chance only 16 times out of 1000; it is therefore judged statistically significant. Entries of .000 mean that the significance is even greater than .001.

Lending further credence are some statistics that those familiar with regression analysis will find significant. Leadership knowledge was entered as an independent variable into the regressions displayed in Table B-1 (located in Appendix B). The regressions included age, education, income, party and ideological identifi-

Table A-1. Average Attitudes and Differences Between
Citizenship Groups

A. Average scores on attitude indexes

	Nonvoters		Voters	
	Low knowledge	High knowledge	High knowledge	Low knowledge
Feeling Thermometer Indexes				
Liberal	282.3	289.9	273.4	270.4
Radical	14.4	46.7	7.6	6.6
Poor	83.3	101.1	91.7	87.3
Conservative	180.1	170.3	177.8	184.3
Republican	159.8	136.2	154.9	164.8
Policy Preferences Index	25.2	23.7	26.2	27.8

B. Probabilities of significant difference by t-test

	High-knowledge nonvoters vs. high-knowledge voters	Low-knowledge nonvoters vs. high-knowledge nonvoters	High-knowledge nonvoters vs. low-knowledge voters
Feeling Thermometer Indexes			
Liberal	.016	.123	.000
Radical	.000	.000	.000
Poor	.010	.000	.000
Conservative	.089	.006	.000
Republican	.000	.000	.000
Policy Preferences Index	.000	.006	.000

Notes:

"Low-knowledge" means low scores on leadership knowledge index (0–6 correct); "high knowledge" means high scores (7–14 correct).

For the *italicized* attitude indexes, higher scores are more liberal; for non-italicized indexes, higher scores are more conservative.

Source: 1974 national survey, Center for Political Studies, University of Michigan. See University of Michigan Institute for Social Research, 1979.

cation, and other independent variables. Even with these controls, leadership knowledge had impacts of high statistical significance on four of the six attitude indexes. In each case, knowledge increased liberalism. The results suggest again that researchers need to take account of political knowledge before they rest easy about representation in the United States.

Appendix B

Public Opinion Impacts: Data and Statistical Analysis

Chapter Four offers a model of media impacts on public opinion. The discussion is based on empirical analysis of the 1974 Michigan Content Analysis Study, which provides extensive information on the front-page news and editorial-page content of 92 newspapers throughout the country. The total number of news and editorial items employed here is nearly 18,000.[1] The content information[2] is matched to data from a representative national survey, the University of Michigan Center for Political Studies poll of 1974, with a weighted sample size of 2,523 persons.[3] The sample analyzed consists of those who read one of the 92 newspapers included in the Content Analysis Study, a total of 1,292 persons in the weighted sample. Excluded were those who did not read a paper (approximately 30 percent) or who read papers for which no data were collected.[4]

The content data were gathered for ten days during October and November 1974. Even though the data were obtained over short time periods, a check suggests they accurately reflect the typical stands of the papers. For example, among the 92 newspapers, the *Washington Post* scores higher in editorial liberalism than the (defunct) *Washington Star;* the New York *Daily News* scores to the right of the *New York Times,* and so forth.[5] In any case, while far from perfect, the data set is the most comprehensive collection linking media content to people's attitudes.

One measure of media content taps *liberalism in editorials,* the other, *diversity in news stories.*[6] I expect both aspects of the newspaper's message to encourage opinions to move toward more sympathy with liberal politicians, groups, and ideas. The basis for predicting that news diversity moves audiences leftward is that the majority of local newspapers, which tend not to be diverse, appear to promote a generally Republican and conservative perspective.[7] The editorial context they create does not favor liberalism. All else being equal, I believe those papers with higher diversity probably provide more information that challenges the conservative editorial baseline.

In addition, the mere presence of conflicting views in the news may convey an awareness of the diversity of the country, including its variety of races, economic classes, and viewpoints. Such consciousness may promote tolerance of change and empathy for positions or groups that challenge the status quo.[8] Diversity may also undermine authority by conveying the impression that a range of ideas is plausible, that the existing distribution of power, wealth, and status is not immutable. As for editorials, while many readers no doubt skip the opinion pages, Bagdikian shows that the editorial perspective tends to be mirrored in news slant. The editorial liberalism index may reflect not only the tone in the editorial columns but, indirectly, the political tendency of news coverage.[9]

The survey included "feeling thermometer" questions. Interviewers asked respondents to express their feelings toward several well-known groups and politicians. Respondents chose numbers ranging from "0" for the coldest feelings through "100" for the warmest, with "50" meaning neutral or mixed feelings. I constructed five attitude indexes using a statistical technique called factor analysis. The Liberal Feelings Index combined ratings of Edward Kennedy, Hubert Humphrey, liberals, Democrats, and unions. The Radical Feelings Index consisted of thermometer ratings of radical students, black militants, civil rights leaders, and policemen. The Poor Feelings Index tapped thermometers of poor people, blacks, and George Wallace. The Republican Feelings Index was created from ratings of Gerald Ford, Richard Nixon, and Republicans. Finally, the Conservative Feelings Index rated big business, the military, and conservatives.[10]

The Michigan survey also asked respondents for their stands on government-guaranteed jobs; dealing with urban unrest by solving the problems of unemployment and poverty; protecting legal rights of those accused of crimes; busing to achieve racial balance; the Equal Rights Amendment; integration of schools; government aid to minorities; and self-placement on the liberal-conservative spectrum.[11] Using factor analysis again, all but one of the responses (to the ERA) were associated together and became the Policy Preferences Index.

Two final variables come from readers of sampled papers who participated in surveys during both 1974 and 1976. Their responses in 1976 provide an opportunity to check for media impacts on the feelings toward a previously unknown presidential candidate, Jimmy Carter (Carter Feelings Index), and on presidential vote (Vote 76). Testing the four predicted media effects requires probing for impacts of editorial liberalism and news diversity on the seven attitude indexes and on presidential vote.

Findings

A statistical technique called regression analysis enables us to see whether, with all else equal, readers of more liberal or diverse papers have more liberal attitudes and voting behavior. Editorial liberalism taps the persuasive element of the newspaper, or, in agenda-setting terms, the aspect of the paper that attempts to "tell people what to think." News diversity taps the putatively informational element that only "tells people what to think about." The interdependence model holds that both editorials and news provide information to think about and thereby influence attitudes. If selectivity or inattention preclude media influence, or if the effect is limited to agendas, these regression statistics should reveal no significant associations between attitudes and newspaper content. The regression equations include the following additional variables to control for forces that might also influence attitudes: urban-rural place of residence; age; years of education; family income; race; region; party identification; and ideological self-identification.[12] Incorporating these other explanatory variables helps to ensure that we do not mistakenly attribute differences in attitudes to newspaper content when they are really caused by differences in income, education, or other variables.[13]

Table B-1 summarizes regression results for the impacts of newspaper content on the beliefs of the entire sample of readers. It is possible for readers untrained in statistics to explore the data for themselves. Regression analysis attempts to show whether various independent, explanatory variables have a significant statistical impact on a dependent variable of interest. Here the dependent variables are the political attitudes described above, and the independent variables of prime interest measure newspaper content: editorial liberalism and news diversity. In order to reduce clutter and conserve space, the tables include only the effects of the content variables.

In the tables, where an independent variable has a significant statistical impact on an attitude, an asterisk appears beside the regression coefficient that measures the impact. The coefficients are arrayed in columns. The more asterisks, the larger the statistical effect and the more confidence that the relationship is real, that it did not occur by chance. There is always some possibility that any relationship between two variables occurred by chance in a particular sampling. If one conducted other studies it might not appear. When $p \le .05$, it means the probability of the relationship being due to chance is less than or equal to one in twenty; $p \le .01$, less than or equal to one in 100; and so forth.

The feeling thermometers are coded from 0 to 100 so that higher scores are warmer (more favorable). The higher the policy preferences score, the more conservative the responses. Vote 76 is 1 for Carter, 0 for Ford, so higher scores indicate voting for Carter. The impacts of the non-media variables in the regressions (not shown in Table B-1) follow expectations, bolstering confidence in the validity of the attitude measures. Multicollinearity (overly close relationships) among the independent variables is not a problem. Of the 45 intercorrelations, only three exceed .20. The strongest was between education and income ($r = .357$).

As an example of how to read the table, the first numerical column in Table B-1 is headed "Liberal." This column summarizes the results of the regression that explains variation in respondents' attitudes on the Liberal Feelings Index. The higher their scores on this index, the warmer they are toward such liberal icons as Ted Kennedy. The independent variables attempt to explain why some people are warmer than others toward liberals. The column in the left margin of the table lists the independent variables measuring the two media content traits. The first column to the right lists the regression coefficients. There are two asterisks next to the first regression coefficient of 2.1 for editorial liberalism, suggesting it has a statistically significant effect on respondents' Liberal Feelings responses. The interpretation is that, controlling for all the other independent variables, for each percentage point increase in editorial liberalism, readers on average are 2.1 degrees warmer on the feeling thermometer toward liberals. By controlling we mean that, if two respondents are identical in all other respects except the paper they read, we would confidently predict the reader of a paper with more liberal editorials to be warmer toward liberals. An effect of this size, with a probability of .01 or less, is likely to be due to chance no more than one in a hundred times.

Table B-1 shows that the more editorially liberal the paper, the more warmly their readers respond on the Liberal Feelings Index. This relationship suggests that editorial liberalism influences the public's evaluations of key leaders and groups associated with the liberal coalition, in this case, Hubert Humphrey, Edward Kennedy, Democrats, unions, and liberals. Editorial liberalism is also significantly associated with less conservative policy stands among its readers,[14] with warmth toward Jimmy Carter,[15] and with voting for him.[16] (Below I consider the possibility that liberals choose more liberal papers, rather than that liberal papers cause more liberal attitudes.) The findings on Carter accord with Prediction 3, that editorial persuasion about formerly unknown people or other new topics is most likely to influence public opinion, since people do not have established attitudes. The relationship of opinions and news diversity is significant in four cases, and consistently in the liberal direction.[17]

These significant associations suggest that reading different papers makes a difference to the audience's attitudes. The influence probably comes from repeated exposure to a particular paper with its habitual level of news diversity and editorial liberalism. It is unclear how much of this influence involves altering

Table B-1. Regressions of Feeling Thermometer and Policy Preference Indexes (Entire Sample)

	Liberal	Radical	Poor	Republican	Conservative	Policy Pref.	Carter	Vote 76
Independent variables								
Editorial lib.	2.1**	.3	.2	.4	.1	−.2**	1.3*****	.02*****
News diversity	.1	.8**	.3	−1.2*****	−.7**	−.1**	−.2	−.00
Adjusted R^2	.38	.41	.23	.20	.32	.36	.25	.43
N	1056	1113	1071	1147	1055	813	785	601

Significance of regression coefficient: * $p \leq .05$; ** $p \leq .01$; *** $p \leq .001$; **** $p \leq .0001$.
All R^2 yield F significant $< .0001$.

Explanation of coding of variables: Editorial liberalism: See text. News diversity: See text. Policy Preference Index: 6 = most liberal; 42 = most conservative.

Note: Other independent variables entered but not shown in the table are age, region, income, party identification, urbanization, race, ideological identification, education, and (for Carter and Vote 76) rating of the economy.

existing attitudes, and how much forming new ones. In any case, in the real-world flux of politics, it is often difficult to distinguish between developing new and changing old attitudes; the one often begets or blends into the other.

Further evidence of significant media impacts emerges from separate analyses of each ideological group. Findings, displayed in Table B-2, largely accord with expectations.

Conservatives. The impacts on conservatives provide the most persuasive evidence against the assumption that selectivity prevents media impacts. For those on the right, editorial liberalism increases warmth toward liberals, the poor, and Jimmy Carter. It also makes conservatives significantly more likely to vote for Carter rather than Ford. While liberal editorials do not move conservatives on dimensions central to their identification—the Republican and Conservative Feelings Indexes—news diversity does. Diverse news also produces warmer feelings toward those all the way on the other side, the radicals.

No doubt, some conservatives screen out all liberal editorials, and others ignore news diversity. Still, these findings show that reading different newspapers does make a difference among citizens who identify as conservative. With all else equal, if you have two persons calling themselves conservative, the one who reads a paper with more liberal editorial pages or diverse news is likely to have less conservative attitudes and show more willingness to vote Democratic. Liberal editorials appear most influential in moving conservatives against their dispositions on matters not crucial to their identities as conservatives. But while the beliefs susceptible to influence may not be central to conservatives' political self-images, they are not trivial, as suggested by the significant impact on likelihood to vote for Jimmy Carter.

Liberals. For those identifying on the left, reading liberal editorials is associated with more favorable feelings toward radicals and with less conservatism on the Policy Preferences Index. News diversity also strengthens liberalism by diminishing esteem of the opposing side—making liberals cooler on the Republican and Conservative feelings indexes. Conservatives tend to dislike liberals more than liberals dislike conservatives,[18] so when the media heighten liberals' animosity toward conservatives, significant political consequences may follow. In the absence of such media

Table B-2. Regressions of Feeling Thermometers, Policy Preferences, and 1976 Vote For Liberals, Moderates, and Conservatives Separately

Newspaper content	Liberal	Radical	Poor	Repub.	Consv.	Pol. Pref.	Carter	Vote 76
1. Liberals (n = 291)							(n = 188)	(n = 138)
Edit. liberalism	.8	3.4**	−1.4	−1.1	.1	−.3*	.3	.00
News diversity	.1	.7	.2	−1.2*	−1.5	−.03	−.3	.03*
2. Moderates (n = 634)							(n = 447)	(n = 237)
Edit. liberalism	1.0	−.8	.6	.7	.1	.1	1.1**	.01
News diversity	1.3*	1.0*	.6*	−1.0**	−.3	−.2****	−.1	−.00
3. Conservatives (n = 367)							(n = 248)	(n = 226)
Edit. liberalism	4.2***	.1	1.5*	.9	.3	−.1	2.0****	.03****
News diversity	−.6	.9*	.4	−1.3**	−.8*	.1	−.4	1.5

Significance of regression coefficient: *p ≤ .05; **p ≤ .01; ***p ≤ .001; ****p ≤ .0001.

Notes:
1. All other independent variables in the regressions are the same as for Table B-1, except for ideological identification.
2. Moderates include the responses of don't know, haven't thought much about it, and not ascertained.
3. Numbers of cases for each regression vary slightly due to missing answers to opinion questions.

bolstering, for example, liberals may be more likely to stray toward a vote for conservative Republicans.

This finding suggests that reinforcement by the media is both more complicated and more important than previous researchers acknowledge. Further supporting that point, the regressions show that editorial liberalism does *not* boost warmth on the Liberal, Poor, or Carter feelings indexes. The reason that liberal editorials do not intensify liberals' feelings on the Liberal and Poor indexes may be that most people calling themselves liberal already share warm emotions toward major symbols like Ted Kennedy, Hubert Humphrey, and poor people. Liberals agree less and have less firmly established beliefs about radicals or policy issues;[19] thus opinions toward radicals and policy among self-identified liberals may be more open to media influence. As for warmth toward Carter among liberals, he did not define himself in ideological terms, and those already on the left did not judge him by ideological standards.[20] Even though some aspects of liberalism were reinforced by left-leaning newspapers, liberal readers may not have applied any revivified liberal feelings when judging the ideologically-fuzzy Jimmy Carter.[21]

Moderates. As predicted, editorials do not affect moderates much. Among the three groups, moderates may be the most immune to the influence of overt editorial persuasion. The imperviousness comes not from selectivity but from a failure to find editorial information salient. On the other hand, news diversity does have a consistent influence on moderates. The impact on five of the seven attitudes is significant, all in the predicted leftward direction.[22]

Alternative Explanation: Selective Exposure

There are two interpretations of the statistically significant impacts of editorial liberalism and news diversity among moderates and conservatives. The one emphasized here is that reading relatively liberal and diverse newspapers helps to loosen attraction to conservatism or engender more sympathy toward liberalism. The other interpretation is a variant of the selectivity hypothesis: selective exposure.

This view holds that people choose the newspaper most likely to conform to their existing opinions. To explain the findings described here, this perspective would assume not that newspapers affect attitudes but that the more liberal-leaning among self-styled conservatives and moderates simply choose the more liberal newspapers available to them. But selective exposure cannot be the whole story, even if some of the statistical correlation is caused by readers who selectively choose newspapers based on their editorial stands.

For one thing, research raises doubts about the prevalence of selective exposure.[23] While those with deep and consistent ideological feelings may seek and know how to find congruent media, most Americans are neither consistent ideologically nor sophisticated politically. Most Americans do not screen out all information contrary to their ideological leanings, because they just do not have strong enough inclinations.[24] The low level of citizenship creates conditions conducive to media influence.

The statistical findings themselves contradict a selective exposure explanation. If selective exposure were the dominant explanation, significant relationships would have arisen among all three ideological groups, as, across the board, liberals chose the most liberal paper and conservatives the most conservative. The variation in media impacts, which largely accord with the four predictions generated by information processing theory and the interdependence model, belie the selective exposure interpretation.[25]

In any case, a selective exposure hypothesis cannot explain the significant impacts upon moderates, who fail to identify themselves with a consistent left or right orientation. Adherents to the selective exposure position might predict that more liberal-leaning moderates would choose the more liberal of the papers available, and conservative-leaning moderates, the more conservative. But judging by the results, moderates are not selective in this way. The editorials did not influence them much; they probably have neither the information nor the inclination to select a newspaper on the basis of editorials. If moderates selected for editorial policy, the index of editorial liberalism would have shown significant relationships with their attitudes. The significant associations that did arise among moderates were between news diversity and more liberal opinions. These linkages could mean that right-leaning moderates selectively choose less diverse papers and left-leaning moderates more diverse. But it is difficult to imagine many moderates taking the time or having the ability to evaluate news diversity. Besides, if anything, given the open-minded self-image of moderates, we might expect them all to opt selectively for the more diverse papers; but if that were true no significant associations to attitudes would have arisen.

Extending selective exposure to conservatives multiplies the problems. The hypothesis would have to be that hardline conservatives choose papers farther to the right while less dogmatic conservatives choose more liberal papers. Curiously, then, selective exposure would assert that some conservatives deliberately choose to read the more liberal of two papers on ideological grounds. This becomes even more curious when recalling the prediction selective exposure made for moderates, which was that some right-leaning moderates choose conservative papers for ideological reasons. Applying the selective exposure hypothesis therefore requires forecasting that moderates often choose a more conservative paper than conservatives. A prediction that moderates act more conservative than conservatives renders the ideological terms virtually meaningless. It seems more reasonable to hypothesize that conservatives will selectively choose a conservative paper. Yet the findings deny that prediction.

Another explanation would be that people do not have a good sense of their actual beliefs when they apply ideological labels to themselves,[26] so that many persons who identify themselves as conservatives actually have liberal or moderate beliefs. This view would hold that people do experience cognitive tension when their actual beliefs are challenged by the news. So, unconsciously, they seek the more comfortable outlet even if it clashes with their professed ideologies. There is clearly some validity in this view. But analyzing the data reported here with respect to party identification, another measure of political schema orientation, rather than ideology, reveals similar findings, and party identification might be a more accurate reflection of attitudes than ideology.[27] Moreover, selective exposure is supposed to be a deliberate process of seeking out comforting information. If people select on the basis of anything, it ought to be their conscious ideological or party identifications. If selective exposure is perverse, with a lot of people who think of themselves as conservative actually holding liberal views and choosing more liberal papers, it becomes at best only a partial basis for a theory of media effects.

Not only the findings but the sober facts of the marketplace make selective exposure a difficult hypothesis: most readers do not have a clear choice between newspapers offering distinct and obvious ideological approaches in their editorial or news columns. As Chapter Five discusses, most local markets in any case offer only one newspaper publisher.

The data allow an empirical test of the selective exposure hypothesis. The sample was split into two groups. One included respondents living in newspaper markets that offer ideological diversity, the other respondents living in markets offering ideologically homogeneous papers, or only one paper.[28] If selective exposure explains the relationships between newspaper content and attitudes, those associations should be stronger for the group of respondents who have a significant ideological choice among papers than for the group that does not. If this were to prove true, it would suggest that the relationships shown in Tables B-1 and B-2 may be attributable largely to selective exposure among those who have an ideological choice among papers. Table B-3 displays results of regressions run separately for the two groups. The independent variables are the same as for the regressions in Table 1, except they include only editorial liberalism as the measure of media content, since it is unlikely respondents would engage in selective exposure based on news diversity.[29] There is no discernable pattern in Table B-3, with two significant coefficients for those in diverse markets and three for those in homogeneous markets. This finding suggests that selective exposure is not the primary reason for the relationship of attitudes and newspaper content.

As this discussion indicates, even if selective exposure has a longer tradition and falls comfortably within the autonomy model, it enjoys neither more inherent logical justification nor more empirical support than the interdependence model.[30] At least as much data and logic support a conclusion that newspaper content shapes audience attitudes as support the idea that audiences select newspapers they agree with. The small minority of

Table B-3. Opinion Impacts on Readers in Ideologically Diverse and Ideologically Similar Markets

	Lib.	Rad.	Poor	Rep.	Bus.	Pol. Pref.	Carter	Vote 76
1. Ideologically diverse markets								
Editorial liberalism	3.6**	1.9	.77	-2.1*	-.42	-.18	.56	.01
2. Ideologically homogeneous markets								
Editorial liberalism	3.0**	-.26	-.22	.46	.19	-.06	1.7****	.03*****

Significance: *p ≤ .05; **p ≤ .01; ****p ≤ .001; *****p ≤ .0001.

Note: The regressions that yielded the results displayed here included the same independent variables as the regressions summarized in Table B-1, except news diversity.

attentive Americans with strong ideological identities probably engage in selective exposure. Some of those who are less attentive and committed probably do too, at least on some issues. But many others do not. At a minimum, the selective exposure hypothesis requires considerably more refinement and testing before it is enshrined as the major reason for correlations between media content and public opinion.

Appendix C

Newspaper Competition: Data and Statistical Analysis

Chapter Five develops an analysis of the negligible effects of economic market competition on newspaper quality based on a data set that provides information measuring competition's effect upon each of the four desirable traits: seriousness, diversity, fairness, and responsiveness. Two measures show whether competition enhances seriousness. *Staff reliance* is the percentage of stories written by staff members of the paper, not supplied by wire services. Often conceived as an indicator of a publisher's commitment to quality, amount of staff-generated copy at least reveals the publisher's willingness to spend money and thereby stands for other elements of seriousness not measured here. *National and international focus* is the amount of news focusing on national or international problems. In the traditional view, competition should produce serious papers that are less parochial and offer more national and international coverage.[1]

Diversity has two dimensions. The first is *vertical* diversity, which refers to diverse content within a single paper. The *few actors* index codes how many different persons or actors (such as an interest group) a story mentions. The higher the score on this measure, the fewer actors mentioned by a paper and presumably the less diversity of views it offers. The *conflict* index codes the presence of disagreement among the actors quoted in a story. The higher the score, the more clashes the stories report, hence the more diversity in views. If the faith in competition is correct, competitive papers should have more stories with clashing views. Horizontal diversity is discussed shortly.

Two measures tap *fairness,* one for news, the other for editorials. *Partisan imbalance (news)* measures the net balance of criticism of Republicans and Democrats in front-page news stories. *Partisan imbalance (editorial)* taps the same dimension for the editorial page.[2] In both cases, the traditional expectation would be that competition yields roughly equal criticism of both parties—less imbalance or more fairness.

There are three measures of *responsiveness. Liberal stands in editorials* measures the amount of endorsement of liberal policy ideas. The index helps reveal whether competitive pressures cause more editorial responsiveness to the larger group of readers, the "have nots," who are presumably more benefited by liberal policies.[3] *Focus on economic problems* taps the amount of coverage focusing on economic problems, chiefly inflation and unemployment. Elections often hinge on economic matters; in peacetime, surveys usually find economic issues the most important to citizens. Economic news ought to be of particular assistance to citizenship, and papers that run more of it theoretically respond better to their readers' needs. *Praise or criticism* taps the amount of praise or criticism of politicians, positions, actions, or policies a paper offers. This index reflects the extent to which stories provide explicit guides to evaluation for readers. If competition aids responsiveness, it should be associated with higher scores on each of these measures.

Results

The first two columns of Table C-1 show averages (means) and standard deviations for all 91 papers. The standard deviations provide a sense of the dispersion or variation among the 91 papers for each index. A large standard deviation means papers vary widely on a measure, a smaller one means most papers are about the same. This column gives a general sense of the political coverage.

The other columns of Table C-1 display the means and standard deviations on the indexes for the 26 monopoly papers, 33

Table C-1. Average Scores on Nine Content Measures for All Papers, Pure Monopolies, Quasi-Monopolies, and Pure Competitive Newspapers

	All		*Monopoly*		*Quasi-monopoly*		*Competitive*	
	x̄	s.d.	x̄	s.d.	x̄	s.d.	x̄	s.d.
Staff reliance	.41	.20	.35	.18	.50	.21	.39	.18
National/international	.42	.12	.38	.14	.42	.12	.44	.09
Few actors	.62	.10	.62	.11	.64	.10	.61	.10
Conflict	.09	.06	.09	.06	.08	.06	.11	.06
Partisan imbalance (news)	.08	.03	.04	.04	.03	.03	.05	.03
Partisan imbalance (editorial)	0.8	.04	.08	.04	.09	.04	.07	.03
Liberalism	0.4	.02	.04	.03	.06	.02	.05	.03
Economic news	.14	.05	.13	.06	.13	.05	.14	.04
Praise/criticism	.16	.08	.16	.07	.14	.07	.18	.07

quasi-monopolies, and 32 competitive papers. On their face, the average content scores for the three groups do not appear strikingly different and raise immediate doubts about the impact of competition. Statistical tests described elsewhere confirm those doubts.[4] The differences between monopoly and other papers do not show any clear pattern.

One important issue is whether competition stimulates horizontal diversity. Table C-2 offers data on variation in content between two different papers. If competition increases horizontal diversity, the average pair of papers run by rival owners ought to differ from each other more than the average pair run by the same person. Comparing the content scores of each paper in cities that have two papers provides a check of this expectation. A city where two papers have markedly different scores on the nine content indexes offers more horizontal diversity than a city where the two papers have similar scores. Table C-2 displays the average differences between pairs of newspapers on each of the content indexes. The first column shows the average difference between competitively owned papers, the second, the average difference

Table C-2. Average Differences between Pairs of Newspapers
on Nine Content Measures

	Competitive[a]	*Quasi-monopoly*[b]
Staff reliance	.216	.158
National/international	.095	.078
Few actors	.081	.081
Conflict	.028	.074
Partisan imbalance (news)	.023	.030
Partisan imbalance (editorial)	.058	.025
Liberalism	.019	.024
Economic news	.059	.054
Praise/criticism	.067[c]	.080

[a] Includes the *Chicago Daily News/Chicago Tribune* pair.

[b] Includes the *Chicago Daily News/Chicago Sun-Times* pair.

[c] Distorted by unusually large difference between *New York Times* and *Daily News;* excluding it, the average difference between pairs of competitive newspapers was .048.

between quasi-monopoly papers, those not in economic competition. The findings show no consistent pattern. Sometimes the competitive papers are more different from each other, sometimes the quasi-monopolies are more distinct, but most often there is about as much difference between the competitive pairs as between the quasi-monopolistic pairs.

Linear regression offers a more rigorous way to probe any association of competition and content. This method provides controls against attributing differences in newspaper content to competition by mistake. For example, competition is itself associated with city population (correlation r = .39, a moderately strong linkage). Some differences that analysts attribute to competition might actually reflect differences between large and small cities.[5] Thus the regressions include as controls five other variables that might explain newspaper content apart from competition.[6]

Two variables measure competitive conditions. *Newspaper competition* is coded 0 for papers in cities where there is no other newspaper or where the only other paper is commonly owned or operated under a joint agreement, and 1 where there is at least one other newspaper in the market not commonly owned or operated. Fifty-nine papers are coded 0, 32 are coded 1.[7] *Electronic competition* taps the number of radio and television stations serving the market in 1974. The larger the number of stations, presumably, the more competitive pressure for the audience's time and the advertiser's dollars. In more active media markets too one might expect greater numbers of suburban dailies and weeklies that compete for some readers.[8]

Table C-3 reports the results of the three regressions that showed significant relationships between competition and newspaper content. The regressions for the six other content indexes (not displayed) revealed no significant relationship to competition. Since the overall regression F statistic is insignificant for the partisan imbalance equation, it is not discussed.

As in Appendix B, the asterisks are guides to understanding. The more asterisks next to a "t" or "F" statistic, the more statistically significant is the association between that independent or explanatory variable and the dependent variable we are trying to explain. The first regression measures whether different degrees of staff reliance (stories written by the paper's own staff) go with the traits measured by the independent variables. Looking across the top row, electoral conservatism and electronic competition have "t" scores with single asterisks. These two are the only independent variables in the regression that are significantly associated with staff reliance. Newspaper competition, population, college-educated population, per capita income, and voting participation all fail to have any statistically significant association with staff reliance. The two asterisks next to the F statistic of 4.36 show that this regression equation explains a statistically significant amount of the variation among papers in staff reliance. The R^2 of .21 means that these seven independent variables explain 21 percent of the variation in staff reliance among the papers. The rest of the variation in staff reliance (79 percent of it) must be due to other forces that the regression does not measure.

The interpretation of these results is that the more conservative the area and the more electronic media in the market, the more the newspaper uses copy written by its own staff. The associations are significant at .05, meaning the chances that the statistics falsely show a relationship are around one in twenty. Whether

Table C-3. Regressions of Content Measures on Seven Market, Demographic, and Political Traits

	Independent variables														
	Newspaper competition		Population		Electoral conservatism		College Educated		Per capita income		Electronic competition		Voting participation		Adjusted R^2	F
	b	t	b	t	b	t	b	t	b	t	b	t	b	t		
Dependent variables																
Staff reliance	.004	.03	−.020	−.19	−.280	−2.60*	.010	.11	.020	.15	.290	2.50*	.170	1.40	.21	4.36**
Partisan imbalance (news)	−.280	−2.00*	.160	1.10	−.250	−2.10*	.170	1.50	.080	.74	.050	.36	−.170	−1.30	.05	1.70
Praise/criticism	−.360	−2.70**	.090	.64	−.200	−1.70	.070	.62	.150	1.40	.180	1.40	−.220	−1.70	.08	2.13*

* For t or F significant at <.05.
** For t or F significant at <.01.

papers that rely more heavily on their own staffs are more serious is unclear; the quality of national news from the New York Times or other wire services might be higher than most local staffs could produce.

A second significant relationship emerged between newspaper competition and the praise/criticism index. Competitive papers had less judgmental coverage. Whether that finding accords with faith in competition is not clear. This measure was supposed to tap a newspaper's responsiveness to readers' needs, under the assumption that explicit guides to judgment aid citizenship. If the assumption holds, competition diminishes responsiveness to readers' *needs*. But some readers might find judgments manipulative or distracting and prefer non-judgmental news. If so, this finding suggests competition does increase responsiveness—but to readers' *tastes*, another matter altogether. Here as elsewhere normative expectations of competition are confused, and one's conclusion may be positive or negative depending on whether one assumes newspapers should respond to the audience's tastes or needs.

Notes

Introduction

1. See Federal Communications Commission, 1985. The number of daily newspapers has shrunk a bit. Chapter Five shows this development is not necessarily damaging to any marketplace of ideas.

2. I use "press" in this book as a synonym for news media. The term encompasses both print and electronic journalism.

3. Barber, 1987; cf. Bennett and Edelman, 1985; Bennett, 1983; Hart, 1987; Parenti, 1985; Klapp, 1982; Habermas, 1970; Edelman, 1988.

4. For Johnson, Nixon, and Carter (and Ford), there should be no controversy on this judgment. For characterizations of Reagan's effectiveness as mortally wounded, cf. Schneider, 1987; Phillips, 1987; Broder, 1987b. Horowitz, 1987, judges every one of these presidents a failure.

5. In this account I leave out the dozens of problematic decisions made by successive Congresses and administrations that in my view merited more thorough and independent highlighting by the press. For accounts of two in the foreign policy realm, see Herman, 1985; Dorman and Farhang, 1987.

6. Gerald Ford's reign was so brief and his legitimacy so fragile (as the disgraced Nixon's own appointee) that it may be inappropriate to include him. But his greatest single mistake, according to scholarly studies (W. Miller and A. Miller, 1977; cf. Horowitz, 1987; Lang and Lang, 1983: Chap. 9), may have been his pardon of Richard Nixon; in other words, Ford was in large part a casualty of Watergate too.

7. Hallin, 1986.

8. Braestrup, 1977; cf. Hallin, 1986.

9. See also Entman and Paletz, 1982; cf. Lichty, 1973.

10. Lang and Lang, 1983: 33. See Paletz and Entman, 1981: 158–66,

for evidence that television coverage consistently played down the possibility of Nixon's involvement. Lang and Lang, and Bagdikian, 1973, show how this resulted in part from the administration's clever media strategy.

11. Lang and Lang, 1983: 28; cf. Bagdikian, 1973; Woodward and Bernstein, 1974.

12. Lang and Lang, 1983: 309.

13. Chapter Three discusses "Billygate" in detail.

14. In the words of ABC's Ted Koppel (quoted by Schram, 1987: 301): "It was President Jimmy Carter, facing what he believed would be a tough primary campaign against Ted Kennedy, who resorted to the famous Rose Garden strategy, refusing to leave the White House because the hostage crisis was too important, too all-encompassing. It was, said President Carter, the first thing he thought about in the morning, the last thing he thought about at night." Larson (1986: 122) shows that, in 1980, one-third of all foreign coverage on the network evening news focused on Iran, an average for each network of 27 minutes per week. On average, then, each network devoted the equivalent of more than one entire newscast to Iran every week.

15. Altheide, 1985: 71–95, esp. 72.

16. Boot, 1987; Cornfield, 1988; Ignatius, 1986; Randolph, 1987.

17. Among the sources of such critiques are Gans, 1979; Gitlin, 1980; Paletz and Entman, 1981; Parenti, 1985; and Sigal, 1973.

18. For criticism from journalists themselves: Broder, 1987a; Crouse, 1973; Halberstam, 1979; Schorr, 1977; and Schram, 1987.

19. Cf. Kernell, 1986; Linsky, 1986; Horowitz, 1987.

20. While most of this book concerns national journalism, where appropriate, local journalism enters as well. In some respects, the two operate quite differently.

21. Cf. Edelman, 1988; Lindblom, 1977; Page and Shapiro 1988.

22. Research suggests that only a minority of citizens exercise this form of rationality. For example, political scientists have developed considerable evidence that symbols and perceptions of conditions in the society at large (such as crime and inflation) often override individuals' personal experiences and interests in determining their votes; see, for example, Kinder and Sears, 1985.

23. Cf. Schudson, 1983.

24. Orren and Polsby, 1987; Bartels, 1985; Patterson, 1980; Keeter and Zukin, 1983; Adams, 1984. Cf. Arterton, 1984. This pattern persisted in the networks' coverage of Iowa in 1988, according to Langley, 1988. Note that media-perceived winners are often not the literal top finishers in the balloting.

25. See Broder, 1987a; Crouse, 1973; Orren and Polsby, 1987; Schram, 1987.

1. *The Dilemma of Journalism*

1. Barber, 1985.

2. Although independent, detailed information about government and policy may be available in intellectual magazines and scholarly journals, and this material may reach elites, I do not define it as news. Most Americans do not read specialized journals, and the information they offer has no impact on their political thinking or behavior unless it enters the mass media.

3. See, e.g., Sigal, 1973, 1987; Gans, 1979; Paletz and Entman, 1981; Brown *et al.*, 1987.

4. On the importance of peers as a reference group: Crouse, 1973; Gans, 1979.

5. *USA Today* comes closest of any of the new media to redefining news. It consciously strives to offer a perspective less dominated by Washington elites; it plays positive developments more prominently than the bad news that dominates most papers; and it gives much more space than most to coverage of personalities, consumer and investment tips, sports, and weather. It is also famous for keeping stories, no matter what the topic, brief and straightforward. While its style has apparently influenced many newspapers, it has not diminished most journalists' reliance upon elites for hard news. And whether the *USA Today* approach is not merely an innovation but an improvement in journalism and a boon to citizenship is problematic. But there is a possibility that new information technologies, especially those involving computer databases, will allow journalists to develop ideas and facts more independently of elites at an affordable cost. See the concluding chapter for further discussion of the barriers to innovation in journalism.

6. Cf. Altheide and Snow, 1979; Hart, 1987.

7. Cf. Linsky, 1986; Entman, 1981.

8. Schram, 1987.

9. See, e.g., Graber, 1984a; Patterson, 1980; Goldenberg and Traugott, 1984; Clarke and Evans, 1983; Keeter and Zukin, 1983; Grossman and Kumar, 1981; Lemert, 1981; Orren and Polsby, 1987; but cf. Robinson and Sheehan, 1983. Goldenberg and Traugott (1984: 139, 147–48; cf. Entman, 1982; Graber, 1984a: 210) reveal that where the media do pay a lot of attention to incumbents and challengers, the public knows and cares significantly more about their U.S. House election. However, these scholars also suggest that economic barriers prevent more than

minimal attention to the bulk of congressional races in the daily press. Newspapers serving the majority of Americans cover several districts. They find it unprofitable to report multiple congressional races in much depth. Coverage of campaigns for state office may be even more barren.

10. Paletz and Entman, 1981: 238. Some might argue campaign ads take up the slack from the news. This may be correct in some places. But most ads are self-serving and simplistic; they do not provide a sufficient basis for informed voting.

11. Cf. Bennett, 1983; Nimmo and Combs, 1983; Parenti, 1985.

12. Funkhouser, 1973; cf. Hallin, 1986; Entman and Paletz, 1982.

13. Fishman, 1978.

14. Entman and Koenig, 1976; Entman and Paletz, 1980; Ferguson and Rogers, 1986; Smith and Hogan, 1987.

15. Cf. Schudson, 1983.

16. For examples of statements of the ideal by journalists themselves, see, e.g., Epstein, 1973: 13–14; Altschull, 1984. Also see writings of communications policy attorneys and analysts, where the First Amendment receives special reverence (FCC, 1985; cf. Van Alstyne, 1984; Emerson, 1970). Cf. Owen, 1975: 6–7 and *passim.*

17. Cf. Cohen and Young, 1981; Fishman, 1980; Altschull, 1984.

18. For critiques of objectivity, see Tuchman, 1978; Gans, 1979; Gitlin, 1980; Bayley, 1981; Parenti, 1985; Hallin, 1986; Schiller, 1981.

19. Standard news practices usually make it difficult for reporters to provide historical context. But analyzing what presidents or other officials have done or said earlier is more likely to yield accurate data than analyzing what they have said they will do, or just did (cf. Barber, 1985). Probing the past offers an opportunity to go beyond news management, because reporters do not have to rely on self-serving plans and claims. They can trace facts on the historical record. Unfortunately, such reporting requires large investments of time, money, and manpower, and goes against standard news values which stress the timely. Beyond the regular (though *not* constant) exceptions in *New York Times, Washington Post,* and a handful of other fine newspapers, contextual reporting is rare in daily journalism.

20. For both sets of four questions, the choices were frequently, sometimes, rarely, and never. Weighted "n" of the 1974 cross section sample is 2,523. The variables used in the indexes are 2028, 2030, 2031, and 2033 (TV) and 2050, 2051, 2053, and 2056 (newspaper). Descriptions can be found in University of Michigan Institute for Social Research, 1979.

21. This is illustrated by studies that show many persons tell polltakers they voted in the last election, when they did not (e.g., Katosh and Traugott, 1981).

22. The question wording and answer choices are different, so the comparison assumes "frequently" in the 1974 poll is equivalent to at least five days a week in the 1984 survey. The data for 1984 come from variables 110, 113, 114, and 115 as described in University of Michigan Institute for Social Research, 1986.

23. Related evidence comes from studies of media use cited by Graber, 1984a: Chap. 5; also see J. Robinson and Levy, 1986; Neuman, 1986; and Lichty, 1982. Most of the time Americans spend on media is for entertainment television. Exposure to newspapers does raise levels of knowledge and participation. See, e.g., McCleod and McDonald, 1985. Exposure to television may or may not. Clarke and Fredin (1978) and Becker and Whitney (1980) indicate no; data analyzed but not reported for the present study indicate yes (cf. Reese and Miller, 1981). On balance, media contact does appear to contribute to political knowledge. But this does not mean that the media-based learning is sufficient to approximate ideal or even effective citizenship for most Americans (cf. Keeter and Zukin, 1983; Graber, 1984a, 1984b).

24. Some respondents also may use weekly magazines and opinion journals to keep up, so the estimate of 15 percent fulfilling the ideal role could be low, at least for national news. On the other hand, some respondents no doubt exaggerated their news habits, which might balance any underestimate.

25. Erikson, Luttbeg, and Tedin, 1980; Keeter and Zukin, 1983; Neuman, 1986; Graber, 1984a; Converse and Markus, 1979; Converse, 1964; Dahl, 1961.

26. Burnham, 1981a; Wolfinger and Rosenstone, 1980; Patterson and Caldeira, 1983; Powell, 1986; cf. Glass, Squire, and Wolfinger, 1984.

27. The 1974 vote validation data are coded as variables 5014 and 5016 in the 1974 study.

28. Voting is but one form of participation, and perhaps one of the least effective at influencing office-holders directly (Verba and Nie, 1972; Entman, 1983). If one probes other forms of participation, even fewer Americans meet the standards of ideal citizenship. Relatively few people organize, petition, demonstrate, and so forth but fail to vote (Verba and Nie, 1972). Voting seems the most forgiving and inclusive criterion of citizenship.

29. Having stable or constrained attitudes of the sort much debated by political scientists since Converse (1964) is less relevant to citizenship than knowledge. However consistent and stable your beliefs, if you do not know where candidates stand, you are playing roulette when you vote. Cf. Lodge and Hamill (1983).

30. The 1974 survey asked respondents to rate the positions of these politicians on several seven-point scales ranging from most liberal to

most conservative. The variables were, for Ford, guaranteed jobs (2266); urban unrest and poverty (2274); aid to minority groups (2297); and liberal-conservative ideology (2306). For Nixon: guaranteed jobs (2268); urban unrest and poverty (2276); busing (2291); aid to minority groups (2299); and liberal-conservative ideology (2308). For Wallace: guaranteed jobs (2267); urban unrest and poverty (2275); busing (2290); aid to minorities (2298); and liberal-conservative ideology (2307). The following responses on the seven point scale (1 = most liberal, 4 = middle of road, 7 = most conservative) were coded as correct and scored 1 on the index:

Issue	Ford	Nixon	Wallace
Jobs	5,6,7	5,6,7	5,6,7
Urban unrest	4,5,6,7	4,5,6,7	6,7
Busing	Omitted	5,6,7	6,7
Aid to minorities	5,6,7	5,6,7	6,7
Liberal-conserv.	5,6,7	5,6,7	5,6,7

All other responses, including "haven't thought much about it" and "don't know" were coded 0, for incorrect.

31. The CPS item asking for ratings of candidates' stands on rights of the accused was omitted because the question wording, policy issue, and candidate stands were all too ambiguous. Ford's stand on busing was also omitted as being unclear, at least at the time of the survey.

32. Since more people vote in presidential elections, I ran the same analysis on the same sample but used the 1972 vote instead of the 1974. Knowledgeable voters comprised about the same proportion of the sample: 12.7 percent.

33. Also see Kinder and Sears, 1985: 662–63; Graber, 1984a; Erikson, Luttbeg, and Tedin, 1980: 19–33.

34. Markus, 1982.

35. The incorrect answers to variable 371 rating Reagan in the 1984 cross-sectional surveys of the University of Michigan Center for Political Studies were: extremely liberal, 3.1 percent; liberal, 7.2 percent; slightly liberal, 7.2 percent; moderate, 9.3 percent; don't know, 7.3 percent; and haven't thought much about liberal-conservative matters, 10.4 percent. The codebook is University of Michigan, 1986.

36. Based on variables 1006, 1007, 1008, and 1009.

37. Neuman, 1986: 16.

38. Computed from the 1984 CPS Survey, variables 741 and 745.

39. Knowledge seems to rise when leaders talk about issues or engage in clear ideological debates (cf. Page, 1978; Kinder and Sears, 1985; Sussman, 1986b). So any trend toward more ignorance (or even a pla-

teau of ignorance) may be due to leaders' behavior rather than the public's insufficiencies. But the further point is that the media encourage leaders to obscure the issues, and even when leaders differ, the news often fails to convey the distinctions clearly. More on this interdependence in Chapters Two and Three.

40. Wolfinger and Rosenstone, 1980; Ranney, 1983b; Ladd, 1980; Miller, Wattenberg, and Malenchuk, 1986; Neuman, 1986; cf. Burnham, 1981a: 5,37; Kleppner, 1982: 160–61; Kritzer, 1977. The authors of those studies are not against higher voting participation; for example, Glass, Squire, and Wolfinger, 1984, and Ranney, 1983b, support reforms to encourage voting; Burnham has long decried low participation. But they do not expect such reforms to alter election results.

41. Wolfinger and Rosenstone, 1980.

42. Since those who now vote knowledgeably are the most conservative group, some might predict that current nonvoters would become more conservative as they moved into knowledgeable citizenship. However, we simply do not know enough about the relationships between knowledge, participation, and preferences to predict. Neuman, 1986: 74–81, argues that the relationship between what he defines as political sophistication and liberal-conservative opinions depends on exactly which policy issues are chosen. For further evidence of a link between knowledge and liberalism, see Sussman, 1986a, and Clymer, 1983.

43. Comparing the simple distributions of two groups' opinions also ignores differences in intensity. The comparison also neglects other complexities of representation, majority rule, aggregating preferences, and similar problems of public choice.

44. Burnham (1981a: 4) notes that voting participation is closely related to socioeconomic status in the United States but not in western Europe. For example, 90 percent of Italians with less than five years of education vote, compared with 8 percent of Americans. Among the reasons he suggests are low levels of information and deficiencies in the American party system at mobilizing the lower classes. The class bias of participation in America receives its most elegant treatment in Verba and Nie, 1972.

45. Kelley, 1983: 46–57; Brady and Sniderman, 1985; Miller, Wattenberg, and Malanchuk, 1986; cf. Mann and Wolfinger, 1980.

46. Brady and Sniderman, 1985.

47. Reinforcing these questions about voters' rationality is the repeated finding that symbolic or "sociotropic" thinking dominates the public. Issue positions may not reflect knowledgeable calculation of self-interest or even assessment of personal conditions so much as symbols manipulated through the media by elites who seek to mobilize public support (cf. Edelman, 1988; Lindblom, 1977; Sears and Lau, 1983; Sears, Lau, Tyler, and Allen, 1980; Sears, Hensler, and Speer,

1979; Schlozman and Verba, 1979; Rosenstone, 1982; Feldman, 1982; Kernell, 1986).

48. They would also have to know exactly how their own representative voted, since he or she might have bucked the party leadership. Then again, they could decide to vote strategically against a minority party member even if he or she voted with the majority party, in order to strengthen the majority's hold on the legislature. And there are other options, but all require sophisticated knowledge.

49. Some scholars (e.g., Berelson, Lazarsfeld, and McPhee, 1954) believe the public is inevitably ignorant and subject to dangerous arousal by demagoguery. Others emphasize government's incapability of responding to an overload of conflicting demands from an active, informed citizenry (Huntington, 1975). These theorists believe a division of labor between a small active stratum and a passive mass public preserves democratic stability. They would argue American democracy is better off with its dearth of citizenship. From this perspective, a more sophisticated version of the marketplace of ideas might acknowledge the mass news media do not approach the ideals. But a thriving specialized market does serve the informed minority. Even if most Americans fail to seek complicated media accounts of complex government issues, attentive citizens desire and find diverse, detailed accountability news in a few important newspapers and a plethora of magazines. These are the active citizens and they represent the inert masses. For a recent statement of the view that the media adequately inform the members of the stratified public, which gets reasonable representation, see Neuman, 1986. Verba and Nie, 1972, are among the scholars who would tend to disagree with that view.

2. Objectivity, Bias, and Slant in the News

1. The best studies include Bagdikian, 1974; Stevenson and Greene, 1980; Merron and Gaddy, 1986; Frank, 1973; Hofstetter, 1976; M. Robinson and Sheehan, 1983; Gans, 1985. Studies that take exception to these conclusions include: Rothman and Lichter, 1987; Lichter, Rothman, and Lichter, 1986; Adams, 1985; cf. Clancey and Robinson, 1985.

2. Cf. M. Robinson and Sheehan, 1983; Tuchman, 1972; Gans, 1979; Molotch and Lester, 1974.

3. Journalists often violate objectivity in covering foreign governments and unconventional political activity (e.g., protest marches). In these cases, journalists tend to assume a consensus among audiences and elites in support of U.S. national security as defined by the president and in disapproval of political disruption. See Hallin, 1986; Gitlin,

1980. This book focuses on media coverage of conventional, non-disruptive, American politics and policy.

4. Robinson and Sheehan, 1983; Robinson and Kohut, 1986.

5. E.g., Berger and Luckmann, 1967; Fish, 1980; Molotch and Boden, 1985.

6. The term is Clay Steinman's.

7. See especially Lichter, Rothman, and Lichter, 1986; Rothman and Lichter, 1987.

8. Cf. Halberstam, 1979; Parenti, 1985; Gans, 1985.

9. Rothman and Lichter, 1984; Lichter, Rothman, and Lichter, 1986; Rothman and Lichter, 1987. Cf. Wildavsky, 1987; Rusher, 1988.

10. Data on the sample of journalists comes from Lichter, 1982: 75.

11. Wilhoit, Weaver, and Gray, 1985; Graber, 1984a; Gans 1985; cf. Schneider and Lewis, 1985; Robinson and Kohut, 1986.

12. Cf. Breed, 1955; Halberstam, 1979.

13. Cf. Bagdikian, 1974; Radolf, 1984; Thimmesch, 1984.

14. As the data to be discussed, from Clancey and Robinson, 1985, reveal, obeying the creed of balance may not assure or even enhance accuracy. Strict balance means citing each side in a dispute without offering information needed to assess veracity. Such stories may convey claims about a phenomenon when the evidence is almost entirely absent; crude objectivity requires reporters to treat liars and know-nothings the same as saints and experts. See Bayley, 1981, on the ways objectivity assisted Senator Joseph McCarthy's crusades. In other words, objectivity, though designed to guarantee mirroring of reality, may work against it.

15. Perhaps Reagan's bad news depressed his victory margin, though it is difficult to imagine a more sweeping triumph. Social scientific understanding is not sufficient to prove that the news the authors classify as bad actually was bad for him. Another strong possibility is that an accumulation of good press about Reagan and bad about Mondale over the months preceding the fall campaign established most people's opinions. These views could not be shaken by new information during the final weeks of the campaign, when the data were collected (September–November).

16. Behr and Iyengar, 1985.

17. The smallest variations in communication can markedly alter perceptions and reactions. Loftus (1979: 77–78) shows that changing a single word in a description of an accident from cars that "hit" each other to cars that "smash" each other alters responses; cf. Smith and Hogan, 1987 (on vast variations in responses to polling questions with subtle wording differences).

18. Buell, 1987: 80.

19. These norms and interests are analyzed thoroughly elsewhere:

Bennett, 1983; Epstein, 1973; Gans, 1979; Graber, 1984a; Paletz and Entman, 1981; Sigal, 1973; Tuchman, 1978.

20. This point is not cynical. The politicians manipulating the press usually do so to advance goals they believe benefit the public interest. If full and open disclosure serves the goal, the political figure may disgorge all he or she knows. Even then, the skilled politician will seek to frame the comprehensive coverage in the way that seems most advantageous. Selective disclosure is usually more helpful.

3. *Straight Talk on Slanted News*

1. Miller, Wattenberg, and Malenchuk, 1986.

2. Ostrom and Simon, 1985.

3. Cf. Haight and Brody, 1977; Grossman and Kumar, 1981; Entman, 1981; Weatherford, 1983; MacKuen, 1983; Hart *et al.*, 1984.

4. MacKuen, 1983; cf. Weatherford, 1983; Sigelman and Knight, 1985.

5. Sometimes the public rallies around presidents in times of crisis, but sometimes it does not, and media coverage seems to be one key to the difference (cf. Brody and Shapiro, 1987).

6. Cf. Broder, 1987a: 98–114.

7. See Tuchman, 1978; Gans, 1979; Paletz and Entman, 1981; Bennett, 1983; Parenti, 1985.

8. Diversity becomes particularly important for Chapter Four, in exploring media impacts on public opinion. Since diversity is a necessary component of accountability news, it is also vital to the normative and policy analyses of Part II.

9. All data were compiled from the Vanderbilt Television News Archives Indexes. While index volumes may contain some inaccuracies, the enormous disparity in the coverage of the scandals ensures that small errors will not affect the results significantly. In each case, the scandal period analyzed extended from the first week during which all three networks covered the story on at least two days, to the week when there was no day during which all three networks covered it. For the Lance story, there was a brief flurry of attention during July, when the networks devoted 27 minutes to the growing controversy, but by these criteria the full-fledged scandal did not begin until August 15, 1977. In addition, since the Vanderbilt Archives did not consistently record the networks' weekend news shows in 1977, the total minutes of coverage may be somewhat underestimated for the Lance affair; but this difference does not affect the conclusions.

10. Behr and Iyengar, 1985.

11. I am not in any way suggesting Donovan had anything to do with

any crime or unethical behavior. The special prosecutor cleared him, and later a jury found him innocent. I am saying these occurrences were dramatic and unusual; it is surprising they did not receive more coverage.

12. The survey took place over the period July 14–25, which coincided with the first two weeks of Billygate reporting. Polls on voting intentions also suggest Carter's steep fall. Harris polls showed 35 percent planned to vote for Carter in June. The figure dropped to 27 percent a few days after Billygate broke in mid-July (*Public Opinion* (October/November 1980): 21). The 27 percent figure is unusually low for an incumbent president. But approval in August was back up to 32 percent (*Public Opinion* (February/March 1986): 38; see also Gallup, 1981). And intention to vote for Carter increased to 39 percent by early September. The Billygate reporting may have caused only a temporary sharp dip in support of Carter. He simply faced a welter of bad news from the time of the Iran hostage rescue failure through Billygate, and we shall probably never know which specific events or messages caused potential supporters to peel off to other candidates.

13. As I suggest in my discussion of bias in Chapter Two, we would have to show that messages hypothesized to be slanted caused predicted effects on audiences to confirm the slant. This chapter offers only general poll results that cannot show exactly why members of the public changed or maintained their evaluations of Presidents Carter and Reagan. For a complete theory and documentation of news slant, such an explanation would be necessary. At this stage, demanding such data would proscribe all inquiry, because scholarly understanding of the effects of media messages and the data sets available are so limited. For clarity and brevity, I refrain from using "hypothesized" every time I mention "news slant"; but readers should infer its presence.

14. Cf. Zaresky, 1986, for a similar research assumption, and see the written credos discussed in Lambeth, 1986. Scholars have established that journalists gather and write news according to norms they may not articulate; see especially Tuchman, 1978, on objectivity, and Gans, 1979, on "enduring values." Journalism as an institution encourages individual reporters and editors to report in certain ways; "journalism" may prefer something that individual journalists do not.

15. Entman, 1981; cf. Ranney, 1983a; Gans, 1979; Weaver, 1972; Schudson, 1982.

16. Eugene Patterson, former managing editor of the *Washington Post* and publisher of the *St. Petersburg Times,* emphasized this point in a public talk explaining what he thought had been gentle coverage of President Reagan. (Duke University, November 14, 1986.)

17. Neustadt, 1980, coined this term; cf. Kernell, 1986.

18. An explanation related to the evaluation biases might be a "zeitgeist" effect. In this view, Carter simply had the bad luck to be the first elected president after Watergate, when the journalistic mood was especially suspicious and hostile. By the time Reagan ascended, journalists realized they had gone too far with Carter and decided the country would benefit from giving the affable Californian the benefit of the doubt. While this explanation is plausible (though cf. Nacos, 1988), it probably credits journalists with too much autonomy. Journalists cannot unilaterally alter news slant when their own moods change. Indispensable to changing the news was a likely shift in thinking among elites. Washington leaders appeared much less interested in publicizing scandals during the 1980s than the latter 1970s, when Carter was president. Besides the explanations already cited, it may be that, during the immediate post-Watergate years, Democrats as the party in power felt obliged to risk damaging their own president in order to distance themselves from any appearance of impropriety. This need may have become less compelling when the Republicans took power in 1981, by which time Watergate memories were fading.

19. Compaine, 1982.

20. Cf. Molotch and Boden, 1985.

21. Here and throughout I use "ideological" as a label for the liberal-conservative spectrum in conventional American politics. In another sense, the news is pregnant with ideological bias that favors American culture (individualism, private property, and the like; Lindblom, 1977). Yet contradictions often reside within the pro-system messages as well (Hall, 1977; Paletz and Entman, 1981).

22. Cf. Graber, 1984b: 90, 105; Edelman, 1988.

23. Linsky, 1986; Linsky *et al.*, 1986: 254–305.

24. A simple explanation of the findings might emphasize event context alone: the fewer competing newsworthy events at the time, the more importance a story will achieve. The explanation for all the fuss over Billy could be that nothing of much importance was happening during the period Billygate reigned, while a lot was going on when Donovan's problems surfaced.

In order to test this possibility, I totaled the number of network news stories about all topics that appeared among the first three reports each evening during the Billygate and Donovan affairs. Billygate took place in the midst of the presidential renominations, and there were 73 stories on Campaign '80 during the seven weeks of the scandal. There were also 23 stories on Iran and 18 on the Solidarity strike in Poland. Other things were going on; it was not a slow period for big news. Even if it was slow part of the time, it is highly unlikely nothing else of importance would occur during a seven-week period.

During the 1984 phase (September 24–October 8) of the Donovan scandal, Campaign '84 was covered by 26 stories, and no other major event took place. The networks had plenty of time to report on the first-ever indictment of a sitting cabinet member. In the Donovan case, big events were competing for media attention, but no more so than for Billygate.

25. *Public Opinion* (February/March 1986): 36. At the time of Lance's resignation it fell to 59 percent and a month later to 51 percent. Reagan's popularity was unaffected by the Meese scandal (see *ibid.*). Cf. Altheide and Snow, 1979: Chap. 5, for a detailed discussion of Lance that supports the conclusions offered here.

26. While Jimmy Carter and his Attorney General embroiled themselves in Billygate, and some opponents charged a coverup was occurring, the Donovan story could also have brought Reagan in, by asking, How much did he know about Donovan when he was appointed? What about those other charges against Donovan (in 1982); did Reagan or his Attorney General probe them fully? Who were Donovan's associates? Did Reagan attempt to find out who was threatening congressional staffers investigating Donovan? In a sense was Reagan passively covering up by not directing Donovan to cooperate fully with investigators? Again, I am not suggesting any particular answers to these questions or even saying these are questions that journalists should have asked. My point is simply that the questions are plausible ones similar to those asked Carter, and might have damaged Reagan had they been featured prominently in the news.

27. On Iran coverage, cf. Altheide, 1983; Larson, 1986.

28. Cf. Brody and Shapiro, 1987.

29. *Public Opinion* (February/March 1980): 29.

30. *Public Opinion* (December/January 1981): 27.

31. Gallup, 1981: 159.

32. *Public Opinion* (April/May 1984): 39.

33. Kraus, 1985: 321.

34. The key to the influence is probably the absolute volume of personal criticism, not the proportion. But recalling a point made in Chapter Two, the precise criticisms in the two stories could have varied in salience to the audience. If attacks on Carter were for minor missteps while those on Reagan were for major trespasses, Reagan might have suffered more even if criticized less. However, if Reagan's criticisms had been more severe, personal, and of higher concern to audiences, the press would have devoted more space to attacks on him. Again, the dimensions of news slant often reinforce one another. Although in theory Reagan's fewer criticisms could have been more telling than Carter's many, in fact public approval of Reagan's Lebanon policy *increased*

after the bombing. By definition, the attacks on Reagan could not have been more damaging than those on Carter, since approval of Carter's Iran policy decreased by eight points after the rescue failure (*Public Opinion* (December/January 1981): 27).

35. I realize my judgments of Carter's expressions are subjective. All I can do is suggest readers check the magazine for themselves.

36. *Public Opinion* (December/January 1981): 27.

37. *Public Opinion* (February/March 1980): 29.

38. The final blow was the coincidence of Election Day 1980 with the first anniversary of the still-unresolved hostage affair. By this time, approval of Iran policy was down to 40 percent (*Public Opinion* (December/January 1981): 27). The anniversary cemented the image of American and presidential impotence that had replaced the rallying response of a year earlier. Carter's overall job rating was about 34 percent. This, the only Gallup reading, was taken in December, after Carter's defeat. The closest previous reading, from August, was 32 percent (*Public Opinion* (February/March 1986): 38).

39. Of course deadlines for the daily press differ, so Reagan's daily news coverage might have been more negative. But the point is ultimately the public reaction, which rewarded Reagan for the Grenada policy and (after the "Semper Fi" speech) even for Beirut. This suggests that the slant on Reagan in the daily press was not negative compared with that of Carter.

40. E.g., Broder, 1987a.

41. In theory, *Time* could offer one slant and *Newsweek* another, and the public could decide the truth. But it is far from clear how readers could evaluate the versions; in any case *Time* and *Newsweek* did not differ significantly on the Iran mission, and rarely diverge markedly on national news. Vigorous competition in the political and economic markets leads them (and the TV networks) to converge upon similar political stories and themes. The failure of competition to yield diversity is a major theme of Part II.

42. For the data see *Public Opinion* (February/March 1986: 36) and King and Schudson, 1987. In addition, many journalists attributed Reagan's electoral success to a conservative swing in public opinion that political scientists have repeatedly shown did not occur (e.g., Entman and Paletz, 1980; W. Miller and Shanks, 1982).

43. On casualties, see "23 died in copter crash related to the Mayaguez," *New York Times*, May 22, 1975, pp. 1, 4.

44. See "Praise for the President," *New York Times*, May 16, 1975, pp. 1, 15, according to which, "By nearly every measure President Ford's military venture in the Gulf of Siam was being evaluated here as a diplomatic and domestic political triumph" (p. 15).

45. Cf. Gitlin, 1980; Domhoff, 1978; Lindblom, 1977; Parenti, 1985.

46. Cf. Buell, 1987.

47. E.g., Foote and Steele, 1986; Delli Carpini and Williams, 1987; also Lemert, 1981.

48. For an essay that lends support to this hypothesis see Manoff, 1987.

49. Ignatius, 1986; Boot, 1987; cf. Corn, 1987; Cornfield, 1988; Randolph, 1987.

50. This section suggests another impact of slant: on the evolution of the collective memory of the society, the stock of symbols and myths that inform Americans' historical self-understanding. Through the slant the media imparted to the hostage crisis and rescue mission, reporting helped turn Iran into an emotional symbol of purported U.S. weakness and humiliation. The shared understanding of Iran probably made sending arms to Iran more damaging to Ronald Reagan than sending them to Syria or Iraq would have been. Iran's involvement revved up the emotions of elites, journalists, and public alike.

There were differences between Carter's Iran and Reagan's Lebanon. Still, the media could have turned the Beirut barracks bombing, the subsequent pullout of the rest of America's forces, and the inability to free American hostages still held there into another symbol of American impotence. Elites did not promote Lebanon as a symbol, so the media did not. That establishes a different context for U.S. policy-making in Lebanon, different pressures on government, than would exist if Lebanon too had become a symbol for American consciousness.

51. Cf. Woodward and Bernstein, 1974; Lang and Lang, 1983.

52. Cf. Brody and Shapiro, 1987.

53. *Ibid.*

54. "How press secrecy backfired on Reagan," *Washington Post,* March 22, 1987, p. C4, an exerpt from Broder, 1987a.

55. "Sudden Change," *Washington Post,* March 22, 1987, p. C7, Broder's regular column.

56. According, e.g., to Horowitz, 1987 and Phillips, 1987. The *professional power reputation* probably suffered more than it might have because the administration's strategy for stanching the slide in Reagan's *public popularity* was to criticize deliberately his competence as a manager, admitting he did not supervise his subordinates properly. The only other choice was to concede Reagan had personal knowledge of all aspects of the scandal.

57. However, Reagan's slide to lower public approval and the damage to his reputation as a Washington power wielder probably made for somewhat more negative slant in reporting after the Iran-contra affair than before.

58. Edelman, 1988: 5. Another way to measure elite support might be to assess the president's success in getting bills through Congress. But that method would not be valid if the president has already accomplished the most important goals on his agenda. Congressional support for low-priority new proposals designed to appeal to the president's core ideological constituency may be low, but challenge in word and deed to the major decisions already in place may be low as well. This roughly characterizes the situation Reagan faced after his first year.

59. Cf. Boynton and Deissenberg, 1987.

60. Evidence for the tendency of the press to slant negatively against political actors and ideas journalists consider unpopular and unlikely to have an impact can be found throughout the scholarship on campaign reporting (e.g., Patterson, 1980; Orren and Polsby, 1987) and on coverage of unconventional political movements (Tuchman, 1978; Gitlin, 1980).

61. However, if a normally obscure agency receives sudden prominence, say on "60 Minutes" or in the *New York Times,* the intrusion can affect the agency's operations significantly (Linsky, 1986).

62. Given the Democrats' chronic disunity as a party, they may suffer a consistent structural disadvantage in managing news slant.

4. *How the Media Affect What People Think*

1. See Katz and Lazarsfeld, 1955; Klapper, 1960.

2. Cf. McGuire, 1985; Gans, n.d.; Neuman, 1986; also M. Robinson and Sheehan, 1983.

3. McCombs and Shaw, 1972.

4. See, e.g., the pioneering yet disparate work of such authors as Bartels, 1985; Patterson, 1980; Gerbner, Gross, Morgan, and Signorielli, 1982; Iyengar and Kinder, 1987; Page, Shapiro, and Dempsey, 1987; Page and Shapiro, 1988. DeFleur and Ball-Rokeach's "dependency theory" (1982) describes an important theoretical alternative to the autonomy assumption, but that work predates most of the recent surge in empirical evidence.

5. Klapper, 1960; cf. McGuire, 1985.

6. Neuman, 1986; cf. MacKuen, 1984. Neuman (1986: Chap. 6) grounds his argument in the lack of evidence that media can teach specific information or enhance political sophistication. This chapter explores political evaluations and preferences, which do not require much information—often a simple emotional response will do (cf. Abelson *et al.,* 1982). A related argument cites the public's inability to recall specific stories. But the influence of a single news story or show is rarely

of interest. The primary concern is the effect of repeated news messages over time (cf. Graber, 1984b).

7. Lau and Erber, 1985: 60; almost identical assertions appear throughout the literature, e.g., McCombs and Shaw, 1972; MacKuen, 1984: 372, 386; and even radical critiques such as Parenti, 1985: 23; also see MacKuen and Combs, 1981; Behr and Iyengar, 1985; Erbring, Goldenberg, and Miller, 1980. But cf. Iyengar and Kinder, 1987, for agenda-setting research which reveals that, when the media influence agendas, they also shape the criteria of judgment people use in thinking about political officials and Protess *et al.*, 1987, for evidence of impacts on officials' behavior. Also cf. Blumler and Katz, 1974; Weaver, 1984.

8. MacKuen, 1984, offers the most explicit discussion.

9. Cf. Graber, 1984b; Kraus and Perloff, 1985.

10. Scholars have used many other terms, including "scripts," "inferential sets," "frames," and "prototypes." While there are some subtle differences among them, they need not concern us here. The term schema is as good as any, and for clarity's sake I use the English plural "schemas" instead of the awkward "schemata."

11. Cf. Rokeach, 1973.

12. Fiske and Kinder, 1981: 173.

13. Bennett, 1981: 91.

14. Bennett, 1981: 92.

15. Markus and Zajonc, 1985: 162 and *passim;* Kinder and Sears, 1985: 710–12.

16. Axelrod, 1973.

17. Cf. Lane, 1962.

18. E.g., Converse and Markus, 1979; Kinder and Sears, 1985.

19. Cf. Fiske, Kinder and Larter, 1983.

20. Conover and Feldman, 1981.

21. E.g., Schudson, 1978; Tuchman, 1978; Molotch and Boden, 1985.

22. Readers will recall that perspective is the fourth dimension of news slant. The others (importance, linkage, and criticism) were explored in Chapter Three.

23. See, for example, Hallin, 1986; Entman, 1987a; Dorman and Farhang, 1987.

24. This point is bolstered by the findings that television news can "prime" the public as it sets their agendas; for example, when the news emphasizes defense issues, those issues become more important to the public's judgments of a president. See Iyengar and Kinder, 1987.

25. Cf. Chaffee, 1982.

26. On the media and emotional needs see Edelman, 1988.

27. Cf. Lindblom, 1977; Chaps. 15, 16. This is one of the reasons the paper does not attempt to construct a system of structural equa-

tions employing two-stage least-squares regression analysis or other sophisticated techniques. Given the data available, I do not believe such statistical approaches would illuminate the interdependencies better than the simpler statistics employed here. Combined with the limited nature of the data, the simplifying assumptions required by the advanced techniques could distort the complex intertwining of forces that produce public opinion. The process is a series of interactions among media content and many other cultural and personal forces that socialize, reinforce, and challenge thinking, including generational events, parents, teachers, and peers. Employing two-stage least-squares regression with the cross-sectional data available here could give a misleading picture of the influence paths. Thus, for example, the causal path from personal belief system to a newspaper's editorial liberalism might indicate substantial selectivity. But the model could not reveal whether the personal beliefs were formed by a set of influences from parents, teachers, and peers who were all swayed themselves by the newspaper. There is also a feedback loop between newspaper content and the dominant political culture of an area (as embodied in the values of parents and the others); establishing which is causally prior, the culture or the paper's stands, appears highly problematic. Research over considerable periods of time, perhaps following audience members from early adolescence, would help unravel the causal linkages. For another view of the need to reconceptualize and complicate the research paradigm, cf. Chaffee and Hockheimer, 1985.

28. Kelman, 1987: 33–34; cf. Linsky, 1986: 84–88.

29. One source of elites' readings of public opinion is their judgments of likely public reactions to stories. Whether most members of the public actually respond the way elites think may be less important than that elites believe the public does.

30. See Linsky, 1986; Hess, 1986.

31. Sussman, 1987. I first wrote of this misperception of public opinion in Entman and Koenig, 1976; cf. Entman and Paletz, 1980; W. Miller and Petrocik, 1987; Ferguson and Rogers, 1986. At least three distinguished scholars frequently associated with the American Enterprise Institute, a conservative think tank, come to similar conclusions: Lipset and Schneider, 1983: 342–51; Ladd, 1978. These latter writings also support my assertion that the media perpetuated the conventional wisdom by describing the public's mood as conservative. Cf. Noelle-Neuman, 1977.

T. Smith (1985) offers a "time series" analysis of changing trends over time and discovers: "Overall, 59 percent of the time series showed some shift in the liberal direction, 27 percent had a conservative tilt, and the remaining 14 percent were either constant or bounded around showing no net direction" (p. 246). He concludes that overall there has been a liberal shift since World War II, but that the rate of change leftward slowed down in the 1970s—that public opinion reached a "liberal plateau," not that the public moved right.

32. King and Schudson, 1987.

33. For example, the "tax revolt" of the late 1970s (Lipset and Schneider, 1983: 349–50) or Ronald Reagan's victories (cf. W. Miller and Shanks, 1982; W. Miller and Petrocik, 1987; Kelley, 1983).

34. E.g., Kelley, 1983, or W. Miller and Petrocik, 1987.

5. *Newspaper Competition and Free Press Ideals*

1. Randolph and Behr, 1986: 12.

2. Cf. Compaine, 1982: Chap. 2.

3. This chapter does not consider effects of monopoly and competition on advertising rates. Previous studies show mixed results (Compaine, 1982: 58–62). This chapter also passes over differences between chain and independent ownership. While the impact of increasing national newspaper concentration may be of great significance, the sample of newspapers employed here contains too few independents to allow meaningful comparisons with chain papers. In addition, discussion of chains repeats some of the problematic reasoning associated with discussion of local newspaper monopoly, so the findings and analysis of this chapter may apply.

4. Donohue and Glasser, 1978; cf. Gormley, 1980; Hicks and Featherston, 1978; Johannson and Wiklund, 1980.

5. Rarick and Hartman, 1966.

6. Bigman, 1948; Schweitzer and Goldman, 1975; Weaver and Mullins, 1975; and McCombs, 1987, for example.

7. Some economists have also entered the debate, arguing that, far from disappearing, competition between newspapers in larger metropolitan areas continues to thrive. They say that suburban and satellite city dailies compete for readers with central city papers. However, the economic studies only describe competition in theory; they offer no empirical data on newspaper content. See Rosse and Dertouzos, 1978; Owen, 1975. There are also anecdotal accounts of heightening competition in metropolitan areas. For example, according to the *Wall Street Journal* ("Read all about it—papers fight over turf," February 16, 1988, p. 39), "Newspaper wars are rumbling across Florida as major chains scramble for pieces of a lucrative market." It describes circulation battles involving the *Miami Herald, St. Petersburg Times,* and other papers. The anecdotes do not provide much evidence about the effects of

the competition on achievement of free press ideals. Cf. Patterson, 1987.

8. Though cf. Owen, 1975.

9. For four papers, the researchers coded either the front or the editorial page only. Along with the unique non-local *Wall Street Journal*, these four papers were excluded from analysis to give a sample of 91 papers. Readers interested in details about the data set should refer to the study codebook and to previous papers using the same data (e.g., Erbring, Goldenberg, and Miller, 1980).

10. Barnett, 1988; 1980; 1978.

11. Specifics on the formation of each measure are available from the author.

12. The relationship between competitive pressure and differentiation is not straightforward. Much depends on the tastes of the audience. As illustrated by the example of television entertainment, competition can lead to homogeneous products targeting the least common denominator rather than a diversity of products appealing to differentiated audiences (cf. Owen, Beebe, and Manning, 1974).

13. Newspaper competition also generates a statistically significant regression coefficient for partisan imbalance in news, a measure of fairness, but the overall regression equation is not significant and generalizing from the result would be hazardous.

14. As suggested by McCombs, 1987.

15. In economists' terms, we would want to know the consumers' elasticities of demand with respect to price and time, and the elasticity of supply.

16. See Harris (1978) on editors' inaccurate perceptions of reader tastes; cf. Bogart, 1981.

17. Perhaps elites exhibit ideological sophistication and clear preferences for journalistic products and take the time to monitor media content. They might have the clout in some communities to influence competitive newspapers to alter their coverage. Such processes would be difficult to confirm empirically.

18. See, e.g., Schweitzer and Goldman, 1975: 710.

19. Cf. Carey, 1982: 82–83.

20. Analogously, some analysts have called for granting television networks a monopoly on nights, not channels. On Tuesdays, for example, ABC would have three national outlets, and CBS and NBC none. In this context it might make more sense for ABC to develop three distinctive sets of shows to maximize its audience rather than to appeal to the least common denominator. The latter strategy is rational when each network must compete with the other two networks for maximum audiences on the same nights (Owen, Beebe, and Manning, 1974).

21. Broder, 1987a, describes such dynamics in coverage of the Billy-

gate case by the two Washington newspapers. Casual observation suggests the television networks, clearly in intense competition for audience share, go to extraordinary lengths to find scoops, even when they last only a minute or two before their rivals develop the same information. I am thinking of the insistence of the networks on releasing information about projected election winners instantly, even before polls close throughout the country, a practice that apparently diminished turnout on the West Coast in 1980. See Tannenbaum and Kostrich, 1983. Only after Congress applied pressure did the networks agree to withhold predictions for a state until voting is completed.

22. E.g., Bagdikian, 1987.

23. Barnett, 1978; 1980; 1988; Randolph and Behr, 1986.

6. *Faith and Mystification in Broadcast Deregulation*

1. The original doctrine is contained in 13 FCC 1246 (1949); updated in 40 FCC 598 (1964) and justified in *Fairness Doctrine and Public Interest Standards*, 48 FCC 2d 1 (1974) (hereafter FCC, 1974); sanctioned by legislation in 47 U.S.C. 315(a), 1959 Amendments to the Communications Act of 1934.

2. See FCC, 1985; 1987a; 1987b.

3. FCC, 1987a.

4. From a transcription of the proceedings of the commission's meeting on August 4, 1987, published in *Broadcasting* (August 10, 1987): 32.

5. A good synthesis of the constitutional issues is William Van Alstyne (1984). The most important constitutional puzzle in recent years has been reconciling the Court's ruling in *Miami Herald Publishing Co. v. Tornillo*, 418 U.S. 241 (1974) with *Red Lion v. F.C.C.*, 39 U.S. 367 (1969), which upheld the Fairness Doctrine. In *Tornillo*, the justices struck down a Florida statute mandating a right of reply to newspaper editorials. With newspapers seemingly scarcer than broadcast outlets, and given the priority *Red Lion* grants to the audience's First Amendment rights, scholars have found it difficult to square the difference in treatment of print and broadcast owners. One solution is to recognize that the goals of the First Amendment contain inherent contradictions, that the speaker's rights to free expression and the audience's rights of access to diverse views may at times clash. Resolution by balancing regulated and unregulated outlets might then make sense (cf. Bolinger 1976; Geller, 1985).

6. See Fowler and Brenner, 1983, *inter alia*, and FCC, 1985. Observers usually classify the Fairness Doctrine as a regulation of *content* and hence more constitutionally suspect than regulations of, say, the struc-

ture of the media industry. I believe they are mistaken. The doctrine is neither content nor structural regulation, but *process* regulation; it requires broadcasters to follow a certain process in covering public affairs. Within the process, they have almost unlimited control over content.

An example of much more direct government intrusion sanctioned by the Supreme Court is the "seven dirty words" case, in which a radio station's right to broadcast obscene or offensive words was denied: *F.C.C. v. Pacifica Foundation,* 438 U.S. 726 (1978). This ruling was based on the concept that broadcasting has a "uniquely pervasive presence" that can invade "the privacy of the home." Yet if one accepts the premise of "unique pervasiveness," it would be a basis for sustaining government regulation of broadcasting as distinct from print. Since 1978, the FCC has extended its regulation of offensive language; see "FCC launches attack on indecency," *Broadcasting* (April 20, 1987): 35–36. Notice that these rules directly intrude into content decisions, whereas Fairness rules mandated a process to ensure diversity but neither prohibited nor required any specific message.

National security prohibitions on covering intelligence activities (e.g., the Intelligence Identities Protection Act, 96 Stat. 122 (1982); *Snepp vs. U.S.,* 444 U.S. 507 (1979)) also directly curtail certain expression, even (in my view) where there is no plausible threat to national security. For example, the Intelligence Identities Protection Act prohibits Americans from publishing the names of American secret agents. But the law cannot prevent foreigners from publishing the name outside the U.S., perhaps inside the very country where the agent operates.

7. Cf. Geller, 1985.

8. The Supreme Court has strongly hinted its suspicions of the Fairness Doctrine, employing both constitutional grounds and policy analytical language that sounds like that of the Commission. Although in 1969 the Supreme Court's Red Lion decision (*Red Lion v. F.C.C.* 395 U.S. 367) did affirm the Fairness Doctrine, more recent rulings have raised doubts about the Court's attitude. For example, in *FCC v. League of Women Voters of California,* 468 U.S. 373 (1984) at 378, note 11, the Court invited "some signal from Congress or the FCC that technological developments [since *Red Lion*] have advanced so far that some revision of the system of broadcast regulation may be required." As this invitation suggests, the Court's reasoning will probably mix constitutional with policy considerations. This chapter is therefore quite pertinent to policymakers in the legal arena, not just those in Congress or the FCC.

9. E.g., Owen, 1975; Pool, 1983; Rowan, 1984; Simmons, 1978; Brenner and Rivers, 1982; Krasnow, Longley and Terry, 1982; cf. Cole and Oettinger, 1978; Geller, 1985.

10. The bible of this crusade is Fowler and Brenner, 1983. See also Kaufman, 1983.

11. The FCC produced a good summary of the doctrine that is printed in U.S. House Energy and Commerce Committee, 1987: 51–102.

12. FCC, 1974: 26374.

13. Rowan, 1984: Chap. 3.

14. *Brandywine-Main Line Radio, Inc.,* 27 FCC 2d 565 (1971), affirmed 473 F 2d 16 (D.C. Cir., 1972).

15. See FCC, 1984: 39–41.

16. FCC, 1987a: Pars. 42–51.

17. FCC, 1974: 26373.

18. FCC, 1974: 26376, cf. 26373; cf. *Red Lion Broadcasting v. FCC,* 395 U.S. at 389.

19. FCC, 1984: 28.

20. FCC, 1985: 35419. Emphasis added.

21. FCC, 1984: 23.

22. Fowler and Brenner, 1983: 647–48.

23. 395 U.S. 367 (1969).

24. FCC, 1987a: Pars. 67–68.

25. Some critics of this argument respond that scarcity demonstrably persists, based on the high price of many TV and radio stations on the open market. Independent (non-network) VHF stations in Los Angeles and New York have sold for upwards of $500 million. As a House committee reports, "These prices far exceed the value of the broadcasting facilities involved, indicating a huge premium was being paid to obtain a license to use scarce broadcast spectrum." See U.S. House Commerce and Energy Committee, 1987: 13.

26. In its decision, the FCC (1987a) backed away a bit from economic reasoning (see Footnote 88 at Par. 27 and Pars. 74–82). The commission argues that no matter what the market conditions, the doctrine exerted a chilling effect that is constitutionally impermissible.

27. McCombs and Eyal, 1980; cf. Wood, 1986.

28. "Network news confronts an era of limits, audience gets older and smaller as competition keeps growing," *Washington Post,* February 9, 1987, pp. A–1, A–4. By early 1988, the share had sunk a bit more, to 58 percent (although the method of calculating ratings also changed, which may explain some of the decrease); "A baffled Brokaw sees ratings slip," *New York Times,* March 9, 1988, p. 24.

29. For example, ABC's "Summit Analysis" program in December 1985 came in 58th out of 61 prime-time network shows that week, with an 8.4 rating and 12 percent share of the audience watching TV. The topic was the first summit meeting between Reagan and Gorbachev.

30. Further on this point, a new rating technique allows minute-by-

minute measurement of audiences. It indicates that, in the New York City metropolitan area, the rating of the CBS evening news on a typical day (March 2, 1988) was 4.4 at 7:00 p.m., which means 4.4 percent of households in the area that own televisions were watching when Dan Rather began his report. Over the next half-hour, the rating steadily rose, to 9.5, as the 7:30 beginning of the quiz show "Wheel of Fortune" approached. Not only did that show garner an audience more than twice that of Dan Rather, but it appears much of the audience for Rather tuned in so as not to miss "Wheel." See "Zapping of TV ads appears pervasive," *Wall Street Journal,* April 25, 1988, p. 29. In fact, "Jeopardy," another quiz show, attracts an average share of about 25 percent of those watching TV in the New York area during the 7 to 7:30 p.m. period, nearly as much as the CBS News and NBC News combined (29 percent). See "TV version of *USA Today* may be financial if not critical success," *Wall Street Journal,* February 4, 1988, p. 27.

31. In its decision (FCC, 1987a: Note 159 at Par. 57), the FCC explicitly says it does *not* care whether the public uses the diverse information it claims is now widely available. It says: "The Commission cannot force the dissemination of information on unwilling listeners and viewers. Our concern is properly limited to the availability of information sources, rather than whether a particular individual may choose to receive information from them." The commission can dismiss the relevance of audience behavior because it bases its decision here (unlike in its 1985 report) on the doctrine's alleged unconstitutionality. If, however, the intent is advancing the underlying goals of the Fairness Doctrine, an informed citizenry and constrained media power—goals that the 1987 decision does not repudiate—audience behavior is pertinent.

32. CNN has a sister network, CNN Headline News, that provides news summaries twenty-four hours a day. It offers no analysis or commentary, only "headlines"; the network makes an indirect contribution to diversity. Its easy availability may help some people to stay informed on major news events, and some of them may pursue detailed information in other media where once they would have remained ignorant about the new developments.

33. Media Institute, 1983.

34. About 41 million households are able to receive CNN ("Watching Cable News Network grow," *New York Times,* December 16, 1987, p. A32), 38 million can get C-SPAN-1 (U.S. House), and 14 million C-SPAN-2 (Senate), according to "C-SPAN audience," press release, C-SPAN, October 1987. As of 1987, there were about 91 million households with television sets in the United States (FCC, 1987a: Par. 69, al-

though the *Times* article just cited says 88.6 million). The FCC says 47 percent of TV households, 43 million households, subscribe to cable. On C-SPAN viewers, see Robinson and Clancey, 1985.

35. Neuman, 1986: 137, 139; Waterman, 1986: 99; see also Webster, 1986.

36. "Nightly news shows under siege—will they keep their clout?" *TV Guide*, October 11, 1986, p. 9. This decline is about the same as the average decline in network ratings for all shows; see "CBS moves do not mean end of hard times for networks," *New York Times*, September 12, 1986, p. 12.

37. "Nielsen ratings," *USA Today*, November 23, 1988, p. 3D. Ratings from November 1988.

38. As I suggest in Chapter Five, when more than one outlet exists, the power of the media may be more diffused. But diffusion of media power may not enhance the quality of the news, or the ability of citizens to hold government accountable. Nor is power reduction automatic; it is proportional to the size of the audience and prestige among elites that the competitive outlets reach. The mere number of outlets and competition among them not only fails to guarantee high-quality accountability news, it does not ensure a significant reduction of the dominant media's power. The power of the three networks is barely affected when the audiences and prestige of CNN and C-SPAN badly trail the big three.

39. FCC, 1985; 1987a; 1987b.

40. Kathy Bonk of the National Organization of Women conducted a national survey of commercial and public stations that found 40 percent offered no local news programs at all. Remarks at Wye Woods Conference of the Aspen Institute, November 19, 1986.

41. Cf. Goldenberg and Traugott, 1984.

42. The 6:00 p.m. news of WTVD (affiliated with ABC) and the 11:00 p.m. news of WRAL (a CBS affiliate) were analyzed for the weeks of October 27–31, 1986, and November 17–21, 1986. Analysis was carried out by research assistants Carrie Teegardin and Jeanne Hansell. The categories were defined as follows:

1. Human interest: features about people or upcoming events unrelated to government policy problems.
2. Disaster: stories primarily concerned with crimes, fires, or accidents, with no discussion of these events as a government policy matter.
3. Local politics and policy: stories about matters of concern to groups of local citizens that local government could act or is acting on; about actions of local officials or politicians; or about political activity by local citizens.
4. National/international politics and policy: stories about matters of concern

to groups of Americans that the U.S. government could act or is acting on, or about actions of national officials or politicians, or about foreign governments and affairs.

5. State politics and policy: stories about matters of concern to groups of state residents that state government could act or is acting on, or about actions of state officials or politicians, or about politicians running for state-level office or U.S. Senator.

6. Local economy and business: stories on local economic developments (new businesses opening and the like) that are not linked to government policy issues.

7. Mixed or ambiguous: stories that cannot be categorized in any other category.

8. Weather.

9. Sports.

43. The stations included in this study of early evening news are, except for those noted, CBS affiliates: KGGM, Albuquerque; WNCT, Asheville, NC; WAGA, Atlanta; WBRC (ABC) and WVTM (NBC), Birmingham; WBZ, Boston (NBC); WOWK, Charleston, WVA; WBBM, WLS (ABC), and WMAQ (NBC), Chicago; KTFW, Dallas; KMGH, Denver; WSPA, Greenville, SC; WFSB, Hartford; WATE, Knoxville (ABC); WHAS, Louisville; WREG, Memphis; WKRG, Mobile; WAVY, Norfolk (NBC); WCBS, WNBC, WPIX (Ind.), New York; KDKA, Pittsburgh; KIDK, Pocatello, IDA; WPTF (NBC), WRAL, WTVD (ABC), Raleigh-Durham, NC; KENS, San Antonio; KPIX, San Francisco; KOLR, Springfield, MO; KMOV, St. Louis; WIBW, Topeka, KS; WCFT, Tuscaloosa, AL; WJLA (ABC) and WUSA, Washington, DC; WXII, Winston-Salem, NC. The sample was drawn by asking student volunteers and colleagues to tape their local news shows.

Examples of the categories include the following taken from the content analysis. Coding was inclusive, with all material showing even indirect political or policy content counted. Local policy (non-crime): Santa Rosa officials dumping sewage in preparation for coming drought; Jersey City residents protesting property tax hike. Local policy (crime): family of murdered New York cop vows to fight for new laws to avenge him; Winston-Salem citizens group concerned about prison overcrowding. Local politics: San Francisco city supervisor resigns; race for clerk of Cook County Court heats up. State policy (non-crime): Missouri Attorney General cracks down on tanning salons; Hartford senior citizens rally for bill requiring post-hospital care. State policy (crime): Black activists in New York divided over Tawana Brawley case; New Jersey prisons are expanding. State politics: Connecticut Attorney General, running for U.S. Senate, refuses to attend all-male St. Patrick's Day dinner. Primary (presidential): Kemp drops out, Gart Hart expected to.

Primary (state/local/referendum): Super Tuesday vote on liquor by the drink in South Carolina recounted but measure still lost; election manuals for upcoming Illinois primaries lost. National policy: Jimmy Carter addresses Coast Guard academy on presidential race, Panama Canal, Gorbachev. International policy: Turmoil on West Bank affecting San Francisco Jewish community which is uncertain about criticizing Israel.

44. Roberts and Dickson, 1984: 396; Graber, 1984a: 80–83.

45. National news might tell a similar tale; combining the unique, unduplicated hard political news and commentary on the three commercial networks and public broadcasting in twenty-four hours would almost certainly leave one short of the amount of information contained in the same day's issues of the *New York Times, Washington Post,* and *Wall Street Journal,* to take probably the three most influential papers.

46. Bogart (1985) shows that newspapers in recent years have been increasing coverage of local news and decreasing national/international. Newspapers may thus have more importance than ever for local political information. As for the heralded "new technologies," cable TV, low-power television, and other new media offer few regular local news or public affairs shows. Cable's public access channels normally gather minuscule audiences, whether the fare is exercise classes or politics. Only newer UHF television stations are likely to have the resources to mount regular news and issue programming. But again the FCC neglects to offer evidence that they have, or that their content differs significantly from older stations'.

47. The following major national or regional newspapers were analyzed from August 5, the day the news story of the decision appeared, through August 15. Normally, one would expect editorial comment within a few days after the news story. Dates for which issues were unavailable are listed in parentheses, along with whether editorials appeared on the dates that were sampled. This information indicated that the sample probably caught almost every instance of editorializing about the Fairness Doctrine in these 39 papers: *Atlanta Journal; Baltimore Sun; Birmingham News* (Aug. 5; a pro-FCC edit appeared Aug. 10); *Boston Globe; Charlotte Observer* (Aug. 7; two pro-FCC items appeared in sampled dates); *Chicago Tribune; Christian Science Monitor; Cleveland Plain Dealer;* (Memphis) *Commercial Appeal; Dallas Morning News; Denver Post* (Aug. 9; pro- and anti-FCC pieces appeared within sampled dates); *Detroit Free Press; Los Angeles Times; Louisville Courier-Journal; Miami Herald; Milwaukee Journal; Minneapolis Star and Tribune* (Aug. 5; pro-FCC edit appeared Aug. 9); *New Orleans Times-Picayune* (Aug. 8); *New York Times; Philadelphia Inquirer; Raleigh News & Observer; Richmond Times-Dispatch; San Francisco Chronicle; Seattle Post-Intelligencer;* (Columbia, SC) *State; St. Louis Post-Dispatch;*

St. Petersburg Times; (Nashville) *Tennessean; USA Today;* (Norfolk) *Virginian Pilot; Wall Street Journal; Washington Post* (Aug. 14, 15; a pro-FCC edit appeared Aug. 6); and *Washington Times* (Aug. 5, 8, 9, 15; a pro-FCC edit appeared Aug. 12).

For North Carolina a group was available that probably mirrors the content of smaller local papers throughout the country: *Asheville Citizen* (Aug. 5; two pro-FCC items appeared on sampled dates); *Durham Morning Herald; Fayetteville Observer* (Aug. 5, 6; two pro-FCC items appeared on sampled dates); *Greensboro News & Record; Oxford Public Ledger; Winston-Salem Journal* (Aug. 5, 6; pro-FCC column appeared on sampled dates).

48. FCC, 1987b: Par. 3.

49. Cf. Hale, 1979.

50. Brenner's column strongly endorsed abolition of the doctrine but said the FCC did not have jurisdiction to do so.

51. See Cohen and Young, 1981.

52. See Sigal, 1973; Gans, 1979; Paletz and Entman, 1981; Parenti, 1985; Brown *et al.,* 1987.

53. Entman, 1981; Linsky, 1986.

54. "Network news confronts an era of limits," cited in note 28, p. A–4. See also "Fast changing channels; the future of TV news: Is it ending or beginning?" *Christian Science Monitor,* December 3, 1987, pp. 23–24.

55. Some argue that lower network budgets might actually enhance network news in two ways. First, since news programs cost so much less to produce than traditional entertainment shows, the networks may offer more programs that combine news and entertainment values, like "57th Street" on CBS; even if they garner relatively low ratings, their low production costs can make them profitable. Second, with evening news budgets tighter, campaign reporters may start doing more analysis from Washington and less following of candidates on their predictable (and media-event-laden) campaign journeys. See "Networks grow stingy with their camera crews, no longer cover every sneeze of campaign . . ." *Wall Street Journal,* January 13, 1988, p. 50. These may indeed be benefits that offset in some measure the losses that journalism suffers from heightened competition.

56. The FEDDOM, USFOR, and STLOC categories include stories whose main focus is a plan, potential policy, or action of a government official or agency. Discussions of reactions to, or attempts to influence government policy, such as rallies or bribery scandals, count. Stories about crimes, floods, earthquakes, and the like do not count unless they are predominantly about government responses to these events. If the story is purely about a foreign event with no reference to the U.S., it

counts under FOREIGN if it describes a political or policy event, idea, movement, or action in the foreign country. If the event is an earthquake, crime, or other non-government matter, it does not count. If the story is predominantly about U.S. government reaction to a foreign political or policy matter, it is categorized as USFOR. HUMAN included all apolitical material about people, including natural disasters in foreign countries where no government or policy content is apparent. Uneventful coverage of space flights (usually ten- or twenty-second announcements by anchors ("tell" stories) of progress or delay in scheduled flights) are included under human interest rather than policy. The Challenger space shuttle explosion is categorized as FEDDOM, and inflates the totals for that category in January 1986. Economic reports such as stock market results or announcements of statistics like the consumer price index are not counted if they are brief (under 20 seconds) anchor "tell" stories. NBC News was pre-empted on January 1, 1986, which is one reason for its lower total. Previews of upcoming stories and other categories of news were not counted.

57. Cf. Entman and Paletz, 1982; Paletz and Entman, 1981; Hallin, 1986; Dorman and Farhang, 1987.

58. Although 1986 was an election year, some might argue that the absence of major domestic legislative policy initiatives from the Reagan administration explains the lack of TV news in this area. That may be so, but the dearth of legislative proposals does not render government policy less significant. The administration was making enormous policy changes throughout the executive branch, from the Interior Department and EPA to the Defense Department and the independent regulatory agencies. These changes were more significant, less incremental, than any domestic policy alterations since Franklin Roosevelt. Yet, if these data are valid, the audiences of the network news had less opportunity to learn about domestic policy under Reagan than under the incrementalist Jimmy Carter. The empirical findings described in the text apparently accord with conventional wisdom in the broadcast industry. According to *Broadcasting*, "All three evening newscasts have focused less on Washington stories in the past several years . . ." (March 10, 1986, pp. 72–73). Incidentally, there is some evidence that newspapers have moved away from hard political news toward features, sports, and business coverage; but also, the number of "op ed" pages has grown significantly: Bogart, 1985: 84–85.

59. The problems in the FCC's economic analysis go deeper still. The commission's equation of the market in public affairs information with a standard product market may mislead. Even well-informed audiences cannot shop in the broadcast market for specific information the way they can in the automobile market for specific car features. If unsatis-

fied with a slanted campaign story on one station, they cannot tune to another station later that night and order up a story on the identical topic with a different tilt. They may find a station that generally takes a different view, but whether it will cover the same political story differently that night is uncertain. While some audience members may find stories on the same topic in a newspaper or magazine, most do not spend time on information searches. In any case, the commission assumes the video explosion ensures that alternative views are readily accessible on TV, not buried in other media.

60. Newspapers are already free to do this, and occasionally do. Readers may agree with the FCC that TV ought to have the same right to be unfair. Moreover, most communities have more than one TV station and only one newspaper publisher. If anything, logic would dictate applying the doctrine to newspapers, not broadcasters. That point makes sense, but tradition and court ruling (*Miami Herald Publishing Co. v. Tornillo* (418 U.S. 241 (1974)) have excluded newspapers from such regulation. Perhaps the best compromise between conflicting normative goals and constitutional principles is to regulate one medium and leave the historically unregulated medium alone (cf. Bolinger, 1976).

61. At least one network executive tacitly acknowledged ownership changes could alter the policy equation. In 1985, then-CBS chairman Thomas Wyman admitted he would not continue to favor abolition of the Fairness Doctrine were Senator Jesse Helms (R.-N.C.) to succeed in his effort to take over CBS. He said he favored elimination of the doctrine only because he accepted the integrity of current network leaders. He acknowledged different leaders might be less trustworthy. ("Technological change and business competition in the video marketplace," talk at Duke University, February 5, 1985.)

62. For example, the Roper polls reported in "Public gives TV news high rating," *Broadcasting* (May 13, 1985), which found 53 percent citing TV news as most believeable, while 24 percent cited newspapers.

63. See Clarke and Fredin, 1978; Tichenor, Donohue, and Olien, 1970; J. Robinson and Levy, 1986; but cf. Lichty, 1982; Chaffee and Roser, 1986.

64. In a public forum at Duke University on October 7, 1986, J. Richard Munro, chief executive officer of Time, Inc., said he believes the influence of newsmagazines over public opinion has already decreased compared with that of television.

65. See Bagdikian, 1974; Merron and Gaddy, 1986.

66. FCC, 1984: 32.

67. Clever manipulators have few incentives to disclose their biases (cf. Riker, 1986). Broadcasters who seek to sway public opinion would

probably attempt to render their slant subtle in order to maximize chances of converting opponents and convincing fence-sitters.

68. The power of station owners might increase, among other reasons, because they will be able to lower rates for favored groups or causes and raise rates for others. And owners can refuse to sell any advertising to enemies at all.

69. See FCC, 1985, and Rowan, 1984. ABC, CBS, and NBC all decline to take advocacy ads; but they claim that removal of the Fairness Doctrine will not change the policy. The networks feel advocacy commercials (according to *Broadcasting*, August 10, 1987, p. 62) "allows the fellow with the biggest pockets to set the agenda." Ironically, then, the networks' own reasoning contradicts the FCC's faith in a free market. If the public-spiritedness of the networks continues, elimination of the doctrine may not spur a rise in national issue ads. But the networks, pressed for revenue, may change their minds. Many local stations already ran advocacy advertising before the FCC decision, and with repeal others will probably join them.

70. See Mastro, Costlow, and Sanchez, 1980.

71. For evidence on the impact of editorial endorsements, see J. Robinson, 1974; cf. Page, Shapiro, and Dempsey, 1987. On the power of television commercials to affect referendum outcomes, even when the Fairness Doctrine was in effect, see Mastro, Costlow, and Sanchez, 1980.

72. Looking at the specific idea competition surrounding each campaign for election to Congress, the problem is already acute. Especially in House elections, news about candidates is scarce and incumbents have a great advantage in raising money, used largely for advertising. This probably contributes to the high re-election rate of House incumbents. See Goldenberg and Traugott, 1984; Clarke and Evans, 1983. If money plays a major role in production and availability of information about candidates, strengthening its role in other spheres of politics may not be desirable.

73. Some observers believe network domination of national TV news may decline or disappear. The fall in the cost of satellite time and syndicated news service reports has allowed many local stations to broadcast their own national news reports and to set up ad hoc networks. Eventually, local stations, each stitching together their own national and local news show from a variety of sources, could supplant the national networks. ABC, CBS, and NBC might no longer dominate national public affairs programming, and audiences might find more varied views on local and national issues on significantly more channels. Cf. Drummond, 1986. Although the dilemma of journalism will persist in any case, this scenario could lead to improvement in television jour-

nalism. Another view might be that replacing the wealthy network organizations and experienced network reporters with less skilled local journalists will offer little gain to the audience. Again, prognostication is difficult.

74. The commission rarely distinguishes between the impacts that abolishing the doctrine will have on the regular news shows, and the impacts on public affairs discussion shows or broadcast documentaries. I have concentrated on the news shows which garner comparatively large audiences. It is possible that abolition of the doctrine will lead networks and local stations to air more discussion and documentary programming, but there is little evidence that they will lure large enough audiences significantly to alter the conclusions in the text. And if they do not obtain good ratings, broadcasters will not continue to air them, or will put them in time slots (like early Sunday morning) where few audience members will notice.

7. *Improving Journalism by Enhancing Citizenship*

1. "Pollsters and parliaments," *Washington Post National Weekly* (July 13, 1987): 4.

2. Kernell, 1986: Chaps. 6, 7.

3. Kernell, 1986: 203. Also see Tulis, 1987, and Zarefsky, 1986.

4. Cf. Hart, 1987; Kelman, 1987: 33, 253; Linsky, 1986; Shram, 1987; Ginsberg, 1986.

5. Page, 1978.

6. Ginsburg (1986) probes some of the same issues, but with significant differences. He appears to view as quite calculated the elites' domination and use of public opinion as a self-serving political resource. This implies that elites could choose another course. I see elites more as compelled to manipulate public opinion by the operations of the media and the competition in the political market. While the hold of the elites over public opinion is considerable, they share this power with the media. On the rise of manipulation and demagoguery, see Edelman, 1988, and Tulis, 1987; cf. Lippman, 1965. See also Bennett, 1988.

7. Entman, 1981.

8. Nagel, 1975.

9. Cf. Lipset and Schneider, 1983: Chap. 10.

10. Barber, 1985.

11. Barber, 1979; Robinson and Levy, 1986.

12. Such a survey database, P.O.L.L., already exists at the Roper Center, University of Connecticut.

13. Cf. Ettema and Whitney, 1982.

14. Cf. Manoff, 1987.

15. Crouse, 1973.

16. Cf. Barber, 1985, 1987.

17. Schram, 1987.

18. The figure I suggest, $250 million, is $1 per capita. John Weisman ("Public TV in crisis: Can it Survive?," *TV Guide* (August 1, 1987, p. 6)) writes that per capita government spending on all public broadcasting (not just news) in the U.S. is 57 cents. In the UK, it is $18; Canada, $22; and Japan, $10. Part of the disparity is that these other countries have much smaller populations while confronting large fixed costs of producing programs that are the same whatever the population. But even adjusting for population differences, these other countries spend several times more than the U.S.

19. Cf. Geller, 1985.

20. Great Britain has funded an alternative channel at $150 million annually. According to one report, it "has emerged as perhaps the most exciting and varied TV channel anywhere, broadcasting much of what is at the cutting edge in the arts . . . as well as current affairs." "Channel of choice, Britain's alternative station: Low budget, high praise," *Washington Post,* November 30, 1986, p. G1. The station has an hour newscast each evening, and also welcomes "passionate partisanship within individual programs (but insists on year-round 'balance')" (p. G2).

21. Cf. Burnham, 1981a, 1981b.

22. Olson, 1965.

23. Abramson and Aldrich, 1982.

24. Of course many politicians favor the two-party system, and the U.S. erects structural obstacles to the emergence of any significant third party. But others think a dose of competition for the big two might be helpful.

25. Pickard, 1985: Chap. 5.

26. Powell, 1986.

Appendix B. *Public Opinion Impacts: Data and Statistical Analysis*

1. The study included 96 newspapers, of which four had incomplete data; readers of those four were excluded from the analysis.

2. University of Michigan Institute for Social Research, 1978.

3. The actual number of people interviewed was 1,575. The answers of some members of the sample were counted three times to obtain the weighted sample of 2,523. This was done in order to ensure adequate

representation in the sample of sparsely populated areas of the country. Thus the weighted sample is the most representative.

4. The demographics of the final reader subsample closely parallel those of the 1974 national cross-section as a whole. The mean education of the entire original sample, including non-readers (n = 2,523), is 11.5 years, the mean of the sample analyzed (n = 1,292) is 12.2; the mean income, about \$11,000 in the whole sample versus \$12,000 in the analyzed sample. On other demographic and political characteristics, the two groups are virtually identical.

5. Further enhancing confidence in the validity of the content measures is their use in such important studies as Erbring, Goldenberg, and Miller, 1980.

6. Each editorial item was coded for zero, one, or two assertions favoring or opposing liberal and conservative policy stands. The *editorial liberalism index* is a percentage formed by first counting the number of times a paper endorsed a liberal position or opposed a conservative position, then subtracting assertions favoring conservative stands or derogating liberal. The result was divided by twice the number of editorial items, since each item was coded for up to two liberal or conservative assertions. The higher the score the more liberal the editorial page. This index uses variables 21 and 28 in the *CPS Media Content Analysis Study 1974* (University of Michigan Institute for Social Research, 1978).

A second measure employed data on news (variables 27 and 34 in the CPS study). The *news diversity* measure taps a dimension of news slant that audiences are less likely to screen than editorial liberalism. Like most aspects of news slant, it is a subtle trait of reporting that few audience members would notice. The front-page news items were coded for mention of zero, one, or two problems. For each problem mention, coders noted whether two different actors overtly disagreed with each other. Each news item was coded as having zero, one, or two instances of two actors asserting different points of view. The diversity index is the number of times two actors expressed different positions divided by twice the number of stories. The higher the score, the more diversity of news.

7. Cf. Bagdikian, 1974; Radolf, 1984.

8. A competing hypothesis might be that diversity challenges initial viewpoints, so that it would promote conservatism among liberals and vice versa. That idea is not borne out by the data. Diversity is consistently associated with more liberal views.

9. Bagdikian, 1974; Merron and Gaddy, 1986. Also see Appendix C, note 2 below.

10. The surveys are described in University of Michigan Institute for

Social Research, 1979. I classified all feeling thermometers on their face for relevance to welfare state liberalism. I subjected pertinent items to the varimax technique of factor analysis. Five factors with eigenvalues over 1.0 emerged. I constructed indexes by adding together scores on all feeling thermometer responses loading above .40 on a factor. In two cases, responses loaded by over .40 on two factors. These items were included on the index where they loaded the highest. Responses to policemen and Wallace loaded negatively on their respective factors. The feeling thermometer responses to each were subtracted from the sum of the other items in forming the indexes. All dependent variable indexes had Cronbach alpha reliability scores over .80.

11. Variables 2265 2273, 2281, 2288, 2296, 2302, and 2305 in the 1974 survey.

12. Of the 1,292 readers of sampled newspapers, about 17 percent said they had not thought much about their placement on the liberal-conservative spectrum, 3.5 percent said they did not know, and 1.4 percent were not ascertained. In order to prevent attrition of respondents while still employing a control for ideology, these subjects were recoded as "moderate, middle of the road." I assumed that, lacking clear ideological self-conceptions, they would respond like moderates to messages from left or right. Regressions that exclude these 279 respondents (not shown) yielded similar results.

13. Although partisanship and ideology are not truly interval variables the results of the regressions suggest that it is quite reasonable to treat them as such. For full displays of the impacts of all independent variables, see Entman, 1985b and Entman, 1987b.

14. I omitted ideological identification from the independent variables for the policy preferences regression because that index contains the same variable (2305). If ideology is left in, the relationship between editorial liberalism and policy preferences just fails to reach significance ($p = .07$).

15. In using 1976 measures I assume that people have seen similar messages over the two years: they have not changed newspapers, and the paper has not changed its news or editorial practices. The regressions included only respondents who did not change residences between 1974 and 1976. Rating of economic performance and prospects in 1976 (variables 3137–3140) is included in this regression because it is likely to affect evaluations and voting for presidential candidates.

16. Gillespie (1977) endorses the legitimacy of employing linear regression with dichotomous dependent variables, especially when the sample is split about 50–50 as it was for the close 1976 race.

17. Another series of regressions included the 1,292 readers of sampled papers plus those who denied reading a paper (weighted $n = 733$),

the latter given codes of "0" for the two content variables. With all other independent variables the same as in Table B-1, results closely resemble those reported in the text (see Entman, 1987b, for a display of the coefficients). Giving a score of zero to those who claim not to read a paper seems to me inaccurate, so the text focuses on readers. A zero score implies nonreaders live in a world without newspapers. Yet most people are probably influenced by the paper's messages indirectly, through friends and politicians.

18. Brady and Sniderman, 1985; Conover and Feldman, 1984.

19. The standard deviations of Radical Feelings and Policy Preferences indexes exhibit more dispersion than the standard deviations of the Liberal and Poor Feelings measures.

20. As indicated by Conover and Feldman 1986: 148.

21. On the other hand, news diversity is significantly related to liberals' voting for Carter. The explanation might lie in the effect that news diversity had in cooling feelings toward Republicans and conservatives. By heightening some liberals' antagonism toward the opposite side, news diversity might have stimulated a vote against Ford, an archetypal Republican, without increasing warmth toward Carter.

22. It may seem surprising that moderates' stances toward Carter are not associated with news diversity. It turns out that news diversity fails to affect feelings or votes for him in every case but one (liberals' voting, discussed above in note 21). The finding may be traceable to Carter's blurry ideological image. For moderates, who do not think ideologically anyway, messages stimulating more liberal feelings may not have affected evaluations of this non-ideological candidate whose campaign emphasized personal themes like honesty and competence.

23. Sears and Freedman, 1967.

24. Cf. Kinder and Sears, 1985: 666–70.

25. See Entman, 1987b, for regressions within party groups; they yield nearly identical findings and support the conclusions on selectivity.

26. Cf. Conover and Feldman, 1981.

27. See Entman, 1987b.

28. "Diverse markets" are those served by two newspapers that are distinctly different in their editorial stands (scoring above the mean difference in editorial liberalism among pairs of papers in the sample). "Similar markets" are those served by two papers that resemble each other editorially (scoring below the sample mean difference in editorial liberalism) or served by a single paper. The sample was not split into groups by whether the respondent's community was served by monopoly or competitively owned papers because the research discussed in Chapter Five showed economic market structure does not significantly shape

newspaper content. Moreover, the split employed here yielded two groups that were more similar on demographic and political factors than a division into respondents served by monopoly or competitive papers.

29. There is also a logical and methodological problem since different respondents could in theory select papers based on both news diversity and editorial liberalism or on either alone, and papers could offer different packages of the two (editorially liberal but without news diversity, conservative but with diverse news, and so forth). Trying to sort all this out would be beyond the scope of this research and would add little to the basic argument.

30. Cf. Sears and Freedman 1967; Kinder and Sears 1985: 710; Chaffee and Hocheimer, 1985; Lang and Lang, 1985; Roberts and Maccoby, 1985.

Appendix C. *Newspaper Competition: Data and Statistical Analysis*

1. Illustrating the ambiguity of standards, one might argue that good local news assists readers more than national or international. It might even be more expensive for publishers. After all, most people can buy the *New York Times* or *Washington Post, Newsweek* or *Time* for non-local news, and the local publisher can simply run news service stories. Without good newspaper coverage of local affairs, audiences are likely to have very little access to information about politics and policy in the very arena where they have the greatest opportunity to participate and make a difference.

2. The imbalance indexes are formed by subtracting the percentage of coding units in which a Democratic actor was criticized from the percentage of coding units in which a Republican was criticized. Note that for this and other front-page measures, the specific messages may be an epiphenomenon of story choice. That is, an editor may have decided that two wire stories on Watergate and the election campaign merited front-page play. Given the topic, the decision to run the stories was also a decision to print critical remarks about Republicans. As we saw in Chapter Three, many of the important messages in news stories are like this: topic choice and placement dictates much of the politically influential message. On the other hand, the correlation between anti-Republican imbalance on the front page and anti-Republican imbalance on the editorial page is a significant $r = .41$.

3. I realize it could be argued that conservative policies are more responsive to the true needs of the working classes but this hypothesis

has a long tradition in political science writings on the (analogous) effects of party competition upon government liberalism; cf. Entman, 1983.

4. Entman, 1985a.

5. A comparison of the means on several key traits of competitive, quasi-monopoly, and monopoly cities reveals some large differences. For example, competitive cities in the sample are, on the average, seven times more Democratic in partisan voting habits and five times more populous than quasi-monopoly cities. Divergences between papers serving the two markets could be traceable to the size and political partisanship of the places of publication, not to competition.

6. The five other independent variables include: the 1972 *population* of the city where the paper is published (or county if city data are not available), which measures the size of the market and should have a significant bearing on the resources, and perhaps practices, of most papers regardless of competition.

Electoral conservatism is measured for the county or (where available) city of publication. The variable taps the average margin of the Republican candidate in the 1974 U.S. Senate or gubernatorial race (where there was no Senate election), and the 1972 and 1976 presidential contests. The higher the index, the more Republican the district's voting. The political culture of a paper's market area might shape and be shaped by its content.

Voting participation is the percentage of voting-age citizens in the city or county of publication who cast ballots in the 1974 U.S. Senate or gubernatorial race. All else being equal, more politically involved citizens might demand better quality newspaper coverage.

Per capita income of the city or county and percentage of the population saying they are *college educated* round out the list. More educated and wealthier readers might seek higher quality, more diversity, and the like.

Some caveats: the belief that competition affects content does not always lead to clear predictions about the direction of the effects. The regression analysis tests for direct, linear relationships. There may be little theoretical reason, for example, to expect competition to show a direct (or any) relationship to the amount of liberal editorializing. There is also scant basis for hypothesizing relationships between several of the other independent variables and content—e.g., that between per capita income and number of actors in stories. Nonetheless, the regressions include these variables as controls against attributing an effect to competition that other forces in the city actually cause.

7. Note that by any strict definition of economic competition, no newspaper exists in a competitive market. Technically, a market can be competitive only where so many suppliers are competing that none

can affect the price of the good, and where the products are identical. Newspapers operate, at best, in oligopolistic markets. But such markets are the most competitive we can hope for, and most people consider having two or more separately owned papers as competitive conditions for the newspaper industry.

8. Owen (1975) and others describe an "umbrella" model in which even monopoly newspapers face competition from nearby city journals. The daily of the central city in the metropolitan area forms the largest umbrella; underneath and competing with it, and each other, are dailies in major suburban towns; underneath these umbrellas are smaller dailies in the region, and also weeklies. The measure employed here is a good surrogate for degree of umbrella competition.

Bibliography

Abelson, R. P., D. R. Kinder, M. D. Peters, and S. T. Fiske (1982). Affective and semantic components in political person perception. *Journal of Personality and Social Psychology* 42: 619–30.

Abramson, P. R., and J. H. Aldrich (1982). The decline of electoral participation in America. *American Political Science Review* 76: 502–21.

Adams, W. C. (1984). Hart hype and media muscle: The power of status conferral in campaign '84. Paper presented at the Annual Meeting of the International Society for Political Psychology.

—— (1985). Convention coverage: Did the networks miss the big story at the conventions? *Public Opinion* (Dec./Jan.): 43–54.

Altheide, D. L. (1985). *Media power*. Beverly Hills: Sage.

Altheide, D. L., and R. P. Snow (1979). *Media logic*. Beverly Hills: Sage.

Altschull, J. H. (1984). *Agents of power: The role of the news media in human affairs*. New York: Longman.

Arterton, F. C. (1984). *Media politics: The news strategies of presidential campaigns*. Lexington, MA: D. C. Heath.

Axelrod, R. (1973). Schema theory: An information processing model of perception and cognition. *American Political Science Review* 67: 1248–66.

Bagdikian, B. (1972). The politics of American newspapers. *Columbia Journalism Review* 10 (March/April): 8–13.

—— (1973). The fruits of Agnewism. *Columbia Journalism Review* 11 (Jan./Feb.): 9–21.

—— (1974). *The effete conspiracy*. New York: Harper and Row.

—— (1987). *Media monopoly*, 2d ed. Boston: Beacon Press.

Barber, J. D. (1979). Not the *New York Times:* What network news should be. *Washington Monthly* (Sept.): 14–16.

—— (1985). The journalist's responsibility: Make reality interesting. *The Center Magazine* (May/June): 11–15.

—— (1987). Candidate Reagan and "the sucker generation." *Columbia Journalism Review* 26 (Nov./Dec.): 33–36.

Barnett, S. R. (1978). Local monopoly in the newspaper industry: Some skepticism about its economic inevitability and governmental embrace. In *Proceedings of the symposium on media concentration*. Vol. II. Washington, DC: Federal Trade Commission: 498–519.

—— (1980). Monopoly games: Where failures win big. *Columbia Journalism Review* 18 (May/June): 40–45.

—— (1988). Detroit's high-stakes "failure" game. *Columbia Journalism Review* 26 (Jan./Feb.): 40–42.

Bartels, L. (1985). Expectations and preferences in presidential nominating campaigns. *American Political Science Review* 79: 804–15.

Bayley, E. R. (1981). *Joe McCarthy and the press*. New York: Pantheon.

Becker, L. B., and D. C. Whitney (1980). Effects of media dependencies: Audience assessment of government. *Communications Research* 7: 95–120.

Behr, R. L., and S. Iyengar (1985). Television news, real world cues, and changes in the public agenda. *Public Opinion Quarterly* 49: 38–57.

Bennett, W. L. (1981). Perception and cognition: An information processing framework for politics. In S. Long, ed., *The handbook of political behavior*. Vol. 1. New York: Plenum Press.

—— (1983). *News: The politics of illusion*. New York: Longman.

—— (1988). Marginalizing the majority: The news media, public opinion, and Nicaragua policy decisions. Paper presented at the annual conference of the International Communication Association.

Bennett, W. L., and M. Edelman (1985). Toward a new political narrative. *Journal of Communication* 35 (3): 156–71.

Berelson, B., P. F. Lazarsfeld, and W. N. McPhee (1954). *Voting*. Chicago: Univ. of Chicago Press.

Berger, P., and T. Luckmann (1967). *The social construction of reality*. Garden City, NY: Anchor/Doubleday.

Bigman, S. (1948). Rivals in conformity: A study of two competing dailies. *Journalism Quarterly* 28: 127–31.

Blumler, J. G., and E. Katz (1974). *The uses of mass communications: Current perspectives on gratifications research*. Beverly Hills: Sage.

Bogart, L. (1981). *Press and public: Who reads what, when, where and why in American newspapers.* Hillsdale, NJ: Laurence Erlbaum.

——— (1984–85). The public's use and perception of newspapers. *Public Opinion Quarterly* 48: 709–19.

——— (1985). How U.S. newspaper content is changing. *Journal of Communication* 35 (2): 82–90.

Bolinger, L. (1976). Freedom of the press and public access: Toward a theory of partial regulation of the mass media. 75 *University of Michigan Law Review* 1.

Boot, W. (1987). Pre-scandal enterprise—and general indifference. *Columbia Journalism Review* 25 (March/April): 26–27.

Boynton, G. R., and C. Deissenberg (1987). Models of the economy implicit in public discourse. *Policy Sciences* 20: 129–51.

Brady, H. E., and P. M. Sniderman (1985). Attitude attribution: A group basis for political reasoning. *American Political Science Review* 79: 1061–78.

Braestrup, P. (1977). *The big story: How the American press and television reported and interpreted the crisis of Tet 1968 in Vietnam and Washington.* 2 vols. Boulder, CO: Westview Press.

Breed, W. (1955). Social control in the newsroom? A functional analysis. *Social Forces* 33: 467–77.

Brenner, D. L., and W. L. Rivers (1982). *Free but regulated.* Ames: Iowa State Univ. Press.

Broder, D. S. (1987a). *Behind the front page.* New York: Simon and Schuster.

——— (1987b). How press secrecy backfired on Reagan. *Washington Post* (March 22): C1, C4.

Brody, R. A., and C. R. Shapiro (1987). Policy failure and public support: Reykjavik, Iran and public assessments of President Reagan. Paper presented at the Annual Meeting of the American Political Science Association.

Brown, J., C. R. Bybee, S. T. Wearden, and D. M. Straughan (1987). Invisible power: Newspaper news sources and the limits of diversity. *Journalism Quarterly* 64: 45–54.

Buell, E. H. (1987). " 'Locals' and 'cosmopolitans' ": National, regional, and state newspaper coverage of the New Hampshire primary. In G. R. Orren and N. W. Polsby, eds., *Media and momentum.* Chatham, N.J.: Chatham House Publishers.

Burnham, W. D. (1981a). Shifting patterns of congressional voting participation in the United States. Paper presented at the 1981 Annual Meeting of the American Political Science Association.

——— (1981b). The 1980 earthquake. In J. Rogers and T. Ferguson, eds., *The hidden election.* New York: Pantheon.

Carey, J. (1982). Videotex: The past as prologue. *Journal of Communication* 32 (2): 80–87.

Chaffee, S. H. (1982). Mass media and interpersonal channels: Competitive, convergent or complementary? In G. Gumpert and R. Cathcart, eds., *Inter/Media: Interpersonal communication in a media world*. New York: Oxford Univ. Press.

Chaffee, S. H., and J. L. Hockheimer (1985). The beginnings of political communication research in the United States: Origins of the "limited effects" model. In M. Gurevitch and M. Levy, eds., *Mass communication review yearbook*. Vol. 5. Beverly Hills: Sage.

Chaffee, S. H., and C. Roser (1986). Involvement and the consistency of knowledge, attitudes, and behaviors. *Communication Research* 13: 373–97.

Clancey, M., and M. J. Robinson (1985). General election coverage: Part I. *Public Opinion* (Dec./Jan.): 53–57, 58.

Clarke, P., and S. H. Evans (1983). *Covering campaigns: Journalism in congressional elections*. Stanford: Stanford Univ. Press.

Clarke, P., and E. Fredin (1978). Newspapers, television and political reasoning. *Public Opinion Quarterly* 42: 143–60.

Clymer, A. (1983). Poll finds Americans don't know U.S. positions on Central America. *New York Times* (July 1): A1, A2.

Cohen, S., and J. Young (1981). *The manufacture of news*, 2d ed. Beverly Hills: Sage.

Cole, B., and M. Oettinger (1978). *Reluctant regulators: The FCC and the broadcast audience*. Reading, MA: Addison-Wesley.

Compaine, B. M. (1982). *Who owns the media?* 2d ed. White Plains, NY: Knowledge Industries Publications.

Conover, P. J., and S. Feldman (1981). The origins and meaning of liberal/conservative self-identifications. *American Journal of Political Science* 25: 617–45.

——— (1984). How people organize the political world: A schematic model. *American Journal of Political Science* 28: 95–126.

——— (1986). The role of inference in the perception of political candidates. In R. R. Lau and D. O. Sears, eds., *Political cognition*. Hillsdale, NJ: Laurence Erlbaum.

Converse, P. E. (1964). The nature of belief systems in mass publics. In D. E. Apter, ed., *Ideology and discontent*. New York: Free Press.

Converse, P. E., and G. B. Markus (1979). Plus ca change . . . The new CPS election panel study. *American Political Science Review* 73: 32–49.

Corn, D. (1987). The big ones that got away. *The Nation* (Aug. 28): 152–54.

Cornfield, M. (1988). The news story with no name: National press coverage of the Iran-contra affair/crisis/scandal, 1985–87. Paper presented at the 1988 Annual Conference of the International Communication Association.

Crouse, T. (1973). *The boys on the bus.* New York: Random House.

Dahl, R. A. (1961). *Who governs? Democracy and power in an American city.* New Haven: Yale Univ. Press.

DeFleur, M. L., and S. Ball-Rokeach (1982). *Theories of mass communication,* 4th ed. New York: Longman.

Delli Carpini, M. X., and B. A. Williams (1987). Television and terrorism. *Western Political Quarterly* 40: 45–64.

Domhoff, G. W. (1978). *The powers that be.* New York: Vintage.

Donohue, T. R., and T. L. Glasser (1978). Homogeneity in coverage of Connecticut newspapers. *Journalism Quarterly* 55: 592–96.

Dorman, W. A., and M. Farhang (1987). *The U.S. press and Iran.* Berkeley: Univ. of California Press.

Drummond, W. (1986). Is time running out for network news? *Columbia Journalism Review* 25 (May/June 1986): 50–53.

Edelman, M. J. (1988). *Constructing the political spectacle.* Chicago: Univ. of Chicago Press.

Emerson, T. (1970). *The system of freedom of expression.* New York: Vintage.

Entman, R. M. (1981). The imperial media. In A. J. Meltsner, ed., *Politics and the Oval Office.* New Brunswick, NJ: Transaction Books.

——— (1982). To vote or not to vote: Media impacts on political participation and representation in the United States. Paper presented at the conference of the International Association for Mass Communication Research.

——— (1983). The impact of ideology on legislative behavior and public policy in the states. *Journal of Politics* 45: 163–82.

——— (1985a). Newspaper competition and First Amendment ideals: Does monopoly matter? *Journal of Communication* 35 (3): 147–65.

——— (1985b). The impacts of media messages on the attitudes of the public toward welfare state liberalism. IRP Discussion Papers. Madison: Univ. of Wisconsin Institute for Research on Poverty.

——— (1987a). Affidavit in State of California v. Raymond and Peggy Buckey. Unpublished.

——— (1987b). Not agendas alone: How the media affect what people think. Paper presented at the Annual Meeting of the American Association for Public Opinion Research.

Entman, R. M., and B. Koenig (1976). Pack journalism: The "conservative" myth. *The Nation* 223 (July 17–24): 39–42.

Entman, R. M., and D. L. Paletz (1980). Media and the conservative myth. *Journal of Communication* 30 (3): 154–65.

—— (1982). The war in Southeast Asia: Tunnel vision on television. In W. C. Adams, ed., *Television coverage of international affairs.* Norwood, NJ: Ablex.

Epstein, E. J. (1973). *News from nowhere.* New York: Vintage Books.

Erbring, L., E. M. Goldenberg, and A. H. Miller (1980). Front page news and real world cues: A new look at agenda-setting. *American Journal of Political Science* 24: 16–49.

Erikson, R. S., N. R. Luttbeg, and K. L. Tedin (1980). *American public opinion: Its origins, content and impact,* 2d ed. New York: John Wiley.

Ettema, J. S., and D. C. Whitney (1982). *Individuals in mass media organizations: Creativity and constraint.* Beverly Hills: Sage.

Federal Communications Commission (1974). Fairness Doctrine and public interest standards, 39 Federal Register 26372 (also 48 FCC 2d 1) (July 18).

—— (1984). In the matter of the inquiry into Section 73.1910 of the Commission's rules and regulations concerning the general Fairness Doctrine obligations of broadcast licensees. Released May 8.

—— (1985). General Fairness Doctrine obligations of broadcast licensees, 50 Federal Register 35418 (Aug. 30).

—— (1987a). Memorandum opinion and order, in re complaint of Syracuse Peace Council against television station WTVH, Syracuse, New York. Adopted Aug. 4.

—— (1987b). In the matter of inquiry into section 73.1910 of the Commission's rules and regulations concerning alternatives to the general Fairness Doctrine obligations of broadcast licensees. Released Aug. 4.

Feldman, S. (1982). Economic self-interest and political behavior. *American Journal of Political Science* 26: 446–66.

Ferguson, T., and J. Rogers (1986). *Right turn: The decline of the Democrats and the future of American politics.* New York: Hill and Wang.

Fish, S. (1980). *Is there a text in this class?* Cambridge: Harvard Univ. Press.

Fishman, M. (1978). Crime waves as ideology. *Social Problems* 25: 531–43.

—— (1980). *Manufacturing the news.* Austin: Univ. of Texas Press.

Fiske, S. T., and D. R. Kinder (1981). Involvement, expertise and schema use: Evidence from political cognition. In N. Cantor and J. F. Kihlstrom, eds., *Personality, cognition, and social interaction.* Hillsdale, NJ: Lawrence Erlbaum.

Fiske, S. T., D. R. Kinder, and W. M. Larter (1983). The novice and the expert: Knowledge based strategies in political cognition. *Journal of Experimental Social Psychology* 19: 381–400.

Foote, J. S., and M. E. Steele (1986). Degree of conformity in lead stories in early evening network TV newscasts. *Journalism Quarterly* 63: 19–23.

Fowler, M., and D. Brenner (1983). A marketplace approach to broadcast regulation. Reprinted in E. Wartella *et al.*, eds., *Mass communication review yearbook*. Vol. 4. Beverly Hills: Sage. Originally 60 *Texas Law Review* 1 (1982).

Frank, R. S. (1973). *Message dimensions of television news*. Lexington, MA: D. C. Heath.

Funkhouser, G. R. (1973). Trends in media coverage of the issues of the 60's. *Journalism Quarterly* 50: 533–38.

Gallup, G. (1981). *The Gallup Poll 1980*. Wilmington, DE: Scholarly Resources.

Gans, H. J. (1979). *Deciding what's news: A Study of CBS Evening News, NBC Nightly News, Newsweek, and Time*. New York: Pantheon.

——— (1985). Are U.S. journalists dangerously liberal? *Columbia Journalism Review* 24 (Nov./Dec.): 29–33.

——— (n.d.). The impact of the news media on political action and communication. Unpublished manuscript.

Geller, H. (1985). The role of future regulation: Licensing, spectrum, allocation, content, access, common carrier and rates. In E. Noam, ed., *Video media competition*. New York: Columbia Univ. Press.

Gerbner, G., L. Gross, M. Morgan, and N. Signorielli (1982). Charting the mainstream: Television's contributions to political orientations. *Journal of Communication* 32 (2): 100–127.

Gillespie, M. W. (1977). Log-linear techniques and the regression analysis of dummy dependent variables. *Sociological Methods and Research* 6: 103–22.

Ginsberg, B. (1986). *The captive public: How mass opinion promotes state power*. New York: Basic Books.

Gitlin, T. (1980). *The whole world is watching: Mass media in the making and unmaking of the new left*. Berkeley: Univ. of California Press.

Glass, D., P. Squire, and R. Wolfinger (1984). Voter turnout: An international comparison. *Public Opinion* (Dec./Jan.): 49–55.

Goldenberg, E. N., and M. W. Traugott (1984). *Campaigning for Congress*. Washington, DC: CQ Press.

Gormley, W. T. (1980). An evaluation of the FCC's cross-ownership policy. *Policy Analysis* 6: 61–83.

Graber, D. A. (1984a). *Mass media and American politics,* 2d ed. Washington, DC: CQ Press.

——— (1984b). *Processing the news.* New York: Longman.

Grossman, M. B., and M. J. Kumar (1981). *Portraying the president.* Baltimore: Johns Hopkins Univ. Press.

Habermas, J. (1970). On systematically distorted communication. *Inquiry* 13: 205–18.

Haight, T., and R. A. Brody (1977). The mass media and presidential popularity. *Communication Research* 4: 41–60.

Halberstam, D. (1979). *The powers that be.* New York: Knopf.

Hale, F. D. (1979). A comparison of coverage of speech and press verdicts of Supreme Court. *Journalism Quarterly* 56: 43–47.

Hall, S. (1977). Culture, the media, and the "ideological effect." In J. Curran, M. Gurevitch, and J. Woollacot, eds., *Mass communication and society.* London: Arnold.

Hallin, D. C. (1986). *The "uncensored war": The media and Vietnam.* New York: Oxford Univ. Press.

Harris, L. (1978). Editors don't talk readers' language. *San Francisco Examiner* (Jan. 9): 2.

Hart, R. P. (1987). *The sound of leadership.* Chicago: Univ. of Chicago Press.

Hart, R. P., P. Jerome, and K. McComb (1984). Rhetorical features of newscasts about the president. *Critical Studies in Mass Communication* 1: 260–86.

Herman, E. S. (1985). Diversity of news: "Marginalizing" the opposition. *Journal of Communication* 35 (3): 135–46.

Hess, S. (1986). *The ultimate insiders: U.S. Senators in the national media.* Washington, DC: Brookings Institution.

Hicks, R., and J. Featherston (1978). Duplication of newspaper content in contrasting ownership situations. *Journalism Quarterly* 55: 549–53.

Hofstetter, C. R. (1976). *Bias in the news: Network television coverage of the 1972 election campaign.* Columbus: Ohio State Univ. Press.

Horowitz, D. L. (1987). Is the presidency failing? *The Public Interest* (88): 3–27.

Huntington, S. P. (1975). The democratic distemper. *Public Interest* 41: 9–38.

Ignatius, D. (1986). An oversight by the oversight committees? *Washington Post National Weekly* (Dec. 29): 10–11.

Iyengar, S., and D. R. Kinder (1987). *News that matters: Television and American opinion.* Chicago: Univ. of Chicago Press.

Jamieson, K. H. (1984). *Packaging the president.* New York: Oxford University Press.

Johansson, F., and D. Wiklund (1980). Competition and newspaper content: Sweden, 1912–1972. In K. E. Rosengren, ed., *Advances in content analysis*. Beverly Hills: Sage.

Katosh, J. P., and M. W. Traugott (1981). The consequences of validated and self-reported voting measures. *Public Opinion Quarterly* 45: 519–35.

Katz, E., and P. F. Lazarsfeld (1955). *Personal influence: The part played by people in the flow of mass communications*. New York: Free Press.

Kaufman, I. (1983). Should the First Amendment apply equally to the print and broadcast media? *New York Times Magazine* (June 19): 16–19.

Keeter, S., and C. Zukin (1983). *Uninformed choice: The failure of the new presidential nominating system*. New York: Praeger.

Kelley, S. (1983). *Interpreting elections*. Princeton: Princeton Univ. Press.

Kelman, S. (1987). *Making public policy*. New York: Basic Books.

Kernell, S. (1986). *Going public: New strategies of presidential leadership*. Washington, DC: CQ Press.

Kinder, D. R., and D. O. Sears (1985). Public opinion and political action. In G. Lindzey and E. Aronson, eds., *Handbook of social psychology*. Vol. 2, 3d ed. New York: Random House.

King, E., and M. Schudson (1987). The myth of the great communicator. *Columbia Journalism Review* 26 (Nov./Dec.): 37–39.

Klapp, O. (1982). Meaning lag in the information society. *Journal of Communication* 32 (2): 56–66.

Klapper, J. T. (1960). *The effects of mass communications*. Glencoe, IL: Free Press.

Kleppner, P. (1982). *Who voted? The dynamics of electoral turnout, 1870–1980*. New York: Praeger.

Krasnow, E. G., L. D. Longley, and H. A. Terry (1982). *Politics of broadcast regulation*, 3d ed. New York: St. Martin's.

Kraus, S. (1985). The studies and the world outside. In S. Kraus and R. M. Perloff, eds. *Mass media and political thought: An information processing approach*. Beverly Hills: Sage.

Kraus, S., and R. M. Perloff, eds. (1985). *Mass media and political thought: An information processing approach*. Beverly Hills: Sage.

Kritzer, H. M. (1977). The representativeness of the 1972 presidential primaries. *Polity* 10: 121–29.

Ladd, E. C. (1978). Is America going right? An editorial view. *Public Opinion* (Sept./Oct.): 33.

——— (1980). Note to readers. *Public Opinion* (April/May): 32.

Lambeth, E. (1986). *Committed journalism: An ethic for the profession*. Bloomington, Ind.: Indiana Univ. Press.

Lane, R. E. (1962). *Political ideology: Why the American common man believes what he does.* New York: Free Press.

Lang, G. E., and K. Lang (1985). Method as master, or mastery over method. In M. Gurevitch and M. Levy, eds., *Mass communication review yearbook.* Vol. 5. Beverly Hills: Sage.

Lang, K., and G. E. Lang (1983). *The battle for public opinion: The president, the press, and the polls during Watergate.* New York: Columbia Univ. Press.

Langley, M. (1988). In pre-New Hampshire flurry, images prevail, and TV coverage may be pivotal to candidates. *Wall Street Journal* (Feb. 16): 72.

Larson, J. F. (1986). Television and U.S. foreign policy: The case of the Iran hostage crisis. *Journal of Communication* 36 (4): 108–31.

Lau, R. R., and R. Erber (1985). Political sophistication: An information processing perspective. In S. Kraus and R. Perloff, eds., *Mass media and political thought: An information processing approach.* Beverly Hills: Sage.

Lemert, J. (1981). *Does mass communication change public opinion after all?* Chicago: Nelson-Hall.

Lichter, S. R. (1982). America and the third world: A survey of leading media and business leaders. In W. C. Adams, ed., *Television coverage of international affairs.* Norwood, NJ: Ablex.

Lichter, S. R., S. Rothman, and L. S. Lichter (1986). *The media elite.* Bethesda, MD: Adler and Adler.

Lichty, L. W. (1973). The war we watched on television. *AFI Report* 4 (Winter): 29–37.

——— (1982). Video vs. print. *Wilson Quarterly* 6: 48–57.

Lindblom, C. E. (1977). *Politics and markets.* New York: Basic Books.

Linsky, M. (1986). *Impact: How the press affects federal policymaking.* New York: Norton.

Linsky, M., J. Moore, W. O'Donnell, and D. Whitman (1986). *How the press affects federal policymaking: Six case studies.* New York: Norton.

Lippmann, W. (1965). *Public opinion.* New York: Macmillan.

Lipset, S. M., and W. Schneider (1983). *The confidence gap: Business, labor, and government in the public mind.* New York: Free Press.

Lodge, M., and R. Hamill (1983). Some experimental effects of ideological sophistication on the processing of political information. Report No. 19, State University of New York at Stony Brook, Department of Political Science.

Loftus, E. (1979). *Eyewitness testimony.* Cambridge: Harvard Univ. Press.

MacKuen, M. B. (1983). Political drama, economic conditions, and the dynamics of presidential popularity. *American Journal of Political Science* 27: 165–92.

———— (1984). Exposure to information, belief integration, and individual responsiveness to agenda change. *American Political Science Review* 78: 372–92.

MacKuen, M. B., and S. Coombs (1981). *More than news.* Beverly Hills: Sage.

Mann, T. E., and R. E. Wolfinger (1980). Candidates and parties in congressional elections. *American Political Science Review* 74: 617–32.

Manoff, R. K. (1987). Writing the news. In R. K. Manoff and M. Schudson, eds., *Reading the news.* New York: Pantheon.

Markus, G. B. (1982). Political attitudes during an election year: A report of the 1980 NES panel study. *American Political Science Review* 76: 538–60.

Markus, H., and R. B. Zajonc (1985). The cognitive perspective in social psychology. In G. Lindzey and E. Aronson, eds., *Handbook of social psychology.* New York: Random House.

Massing, M. (1985). The libel chill: How cold *is* it out there? *Columbia Journalism Review* 23 (May/June): 31–43.

Mastro, R. M., D. C. Costlow, and H. P. Sanchez (1980). *Taking the initiative: Corporate control of the referendum process through media spending and what to do about it.* Washington, DC: Media Access Project.

McCleod, J., and D. G. McDonald (1985). Beyond simple exposure: Media orientations and their impact on political processes. *Communication Research* 12: 3–33.

McCloskey, D. N. (1985). *The rhetoric of economics.* Madison: Univ. of Wisconsin Press.

McCombs, M. E. (1987). Comparisons of newspaper content under competitive and monopoly conditions. In R. Picard *et al.,* eds., *Press concentration and monopoly.* Norwood, NJ: Ablex.

McCombs, M. E., and C. H. Eyal (1980). Spending on mass media. *Journal of Communication* 30 (1): 153–58.

McCombs, M. E., and D. L. Shaw (1972). The agenda-setting function of mass media. *Public Opinion Quarterly* 36: 176–87.

McGuire, W. J. (1985). Attitudes and attitude change. In E. Aronson and G. Lindzey, eds., *Handbook of social psychology,* 3d ed. New York: Random House.

Media Institute (1983). *CNN vs. the networks: Is more news better news?* Washington, DC: Media Institute.

Merron, J. and G. D. Gaddy (1986). Editorial endorsements and news play: Bias in coverage of Ferraro's finances. *Journalism Quarterly* 63: 127–37.

Miller, A. H., and W. E. Miller (1977). Partisanship and performance: "Rational" choice in the 1976 presidential election. Paper presented at the Annual Meeting of the American Political Science Association.

Miller, A. H., M. P. Wattenberg, and O. Malenchuk (1986). Schematic assessments of presidential candidates. *American Political Science Review* 80: 521–40.

Miller, W. E., and J. R. Petrocik (1987). *Where's the party? An assessment of changes in party loyalty and party coalitions in the 1980s.* Washington, DC: Center for National Policy.

Miller, W. E., and J. M. Shanks (1982). Policy directions and presidential leadership: Alternative interpretations of the 1980 presidential election. *British Journal of Political Science* 12: 299–356.

Molotch, H. L., and D. Boden (1985). Talking social structure: Discourse, domination and the Watergate hearings. *American Sociological Review* 50: 273–88.

Molotch, H., and M. Lester (1974). News as purposive behavior: On the strategic use of routine events. *American Sociological Review* 39: 101–12.

Nacos, B. (1988). Press, presidents, and crises. Ph.D. diss., Columbia University.

Nagel, J. H. (1975). *The descriptive analysis of power.* New Haven: Yale Univ. Press.

Neuman, W. R. (1986). *The paradox of mass politics: Knowledge and opinion in the American electorate.* Cambridge: Harvard Univ. Press.

Neustadt, R. (1980). *Presidential power: The politics of leadership from FDR to Carter.* New York: John Wiley.

Nimmo, D., and J. E. Combs (1983). *Mediated political realities.* New York: Longman.

Noelle-Neumann, E. (1977). Turbulence in the climate of opinion: methodological applications of the spiral of silence theory. *Public Opinion Quarterly* 41: 143–58.

Olson, M. (1965). *The logic of collective action: Public goods and the theory of groups.* Cambridge: Harvard Univ. Press.

Orren, G. R., and N. W. Polsby (1987). *Media and momentum: The New Hampshire primary and nomination politics.* Chatham, NJ: Chatham House.

Ostrom, C. W., and D. M. Simon (1985). Promise and performance: A dynamic model of presidential popularity. *American Political Science Review* 79: 334–58.

Owen, B. (1975). *Economics and freedom of expression*. Cambridge, MA: Ballinger.

Owen, B., J. Beebe, and W. Manning (1974). *Television economics*. Lexington, MA: D. C. Heath.

Page, B. I. (1978). *Choices and echoes in presidential elections*. Chicago: Univ. of Chicago Press.

Page, B. I., and R. Y. Shapiro (1988). Educating and manipulating the public. In M. Margolis and G. Mauser, eds., *Manipulating public opinion*. Chicago: Dorsey.

Page, B. I., R. Y. Shapiro, and G. R. Dempsey (1987). What moves public opinion? *American Political Science Review* 81: 23–45.

Paletz, D. L., and R. M. Entman (1981). *Media power politics*. New York: Free Press.

Parenti, M. (1985). *Inventing reality: The politics of the mass media*. New York: St. Martin's.

Patterson, E. (1987). The newspaper future: Again the true mass medium? *Washington Journalism Review* 10 (Jan./Feb.): 26–28.

Patterson, S. C., and G. A. Caldeira (1983). Getting out the vote: Participation in gubernatorial elections. *American Political Science Review* 77: 675–89.

Patterson, T. E. (1980). *The mass media election*. New York: Praeger.

Phillips, K. (1987). The Reagan revolution is over—and the GOP should be grateful. *Washington Post National Weekly* (Aug. 17): 23–24.

Pickard, R. (1985). *The press and the decline of democracy: The democratic socialist response in public policy*. Westport, CT: Greenwood Press.

Pool, I. D. S. (1983). *Technologies of freedom*. Cambridge: Harvard Univ. Press.

Powell, G. B. (1986). American voter turnout in comparative perspective. *American Political Science Review* 80: 17–43.

Protess, D. L., et al. (1987). The impact of investigative reporting on public opinion and policymaking: Targeting toxic waste. *Public Opinion Quarterly* 51: 166–87.

Radolf, A. (1984). A newspaper majority for Reagan. *Editor and Publisher* (Nov. 3): 9.

Randolph, E. (1987). The story the press didn't see; the news media blew the coverage of the Iran-contra scandal. *Washington Post National Weekly* (Nov. 30): 6–7.

Randolph, E., and P. Behr (1986). Failing papers, soaring profits. *Washington Post National Weekly* (July 28): 11–13.

Ranney, A. (1983a). *Channels of power: The impact of television on American politics*. New York: Basic Books.

——— (1983b). Nonvoting is not a social disease. *Public Opinion* (Nov./Dec.): 16–19.

Rarick, G., and B. Hartman (1966). The effects of competition on one daily newspaper's content. *Journalism Quarterly* 43: 459–63.

Reese, S., and M. M. Miller (1981). Political attitude holding and structure: The effects of newspaper and television news. *Communication Research* 8: 167–88.

Riker, W. (1986). *The art of political manipulation.* New Haven: Yale Univ. Press.

Roberts, C. L., and S. H. Dickson (1984). Assessing quality in local TV news. *Journalism Quarterly* 61: 392–98.

Roberts, D. F., and N. Maccoby (1985). Effects of mass communication. In G. Lindzey and E. Aronson, eds., *The handbook of social psychology,* 3d ed. New York: Random House.

Robinson, J. P. (1974). The press as king-maker. *Journalism Quarterly* 51: 587–94.

Robinson, J. P., and M. R. Levy, eds. (1986). *The main source: Learning from television news.* Beverly Hills: Sage.

Robinson, M J., and A. Kohut (1986). *The people and the press.* Los Angeles: Times Mirror.

Robinson, M. J., and M. Clancey (1985). Who watches C-SPAN? *C-SPAN Update* (Jan. 14): S1–S4.

Robinson, M. J., and M. A. Sheehan (1983). *Over the wire and on TV: CBS and UPI in campaign '80.* New York: Russell Sage.

Rokeach, M. (1973). *The nature of human values.* New York: Free Press.

Rosenstone, S. J. (1982). Economic adversity and voter turnout. *American Journal of Political Science* 26: 25–46.

Rosse, J., and J. Dertouzos (1978). The evolution of one newspaper cities. In *Proceedings of the symposium on media concentration.* Washington, DC: Federal Trade Commission.

Rothman, S., and S. R. Lichter (1984). Personality, ideology, and world view: A comparison of media and business elites. *British Journal of Political Science* 15: 29–49.

——— (1987). Elite ideology and risk perception in nuclear energy policy. *American Political Science Review* 81: 383–404.

Rowan, F. (1984). *Broadcast fairness: Doctrine, practice, prospects.* New York: Longman.

Rusher, W. A. (1988). *The coming battle for the media: Curbing the power of the media elite.* New York: William A. Morrow.

Schiller, D. (1981). *Objectivity and the news: The public and the rise of commercial journalism.* Philadelphia: Univ. of Pennsylvania Press.

Schlozman, K. L., and S. Verba (1979). *Injury to insult.* Cambridge: Harvard Univ. Press.

Schneider, W. (1987). The Republicans in '88. *The Atlantic* (July): 58–82.

Schneider, W., and I. A. Lewis (1985). Views on the news. *Public Opinion* (Aug./Sept.): 7–11, 58–59.

Schorr, D. (1977). *Clearing the air.* Boston: Houghton Mifflin.

Schram, M. (1987). *The great American video game.* New York: William Morrow.

Schudson, M. (1978). *Discovering the news: A social history of American newspapers.* New York: Basic Books.

—— (1982). The politics of narrative form: The emergence of news conventions in print and television. *Daedalus* 111: 97–112.

—— (1983). *The news media and the democratic process.* New York: Aspen Institute for Humanistic Studies.

Schweitzer, J. C., and E. Goldman (1975). Does newspaper competition make a difference? *Journalism Quarterly* 52: 706–10.

Sears, D. O., and J. L. Freedman (1967). Selective exposure to information: A critical review. *Public Opinion Quarterly* 31: 194–213.

Sears, D. O., and R. R. Lau (1983). Inducing apparently self-interested political preferences: An experiment. *American Journal of Political Science* 27: 223–52.

Sears, D. O., C. P. Hensler, and L. K. Speer (1979). White opposition to "busing": Self-interest or symbolic politics? *American Political Science Review* 73: 369–84.

Sears, D. O., R. R. Lau, T. R. Tyler, and H. J. Allen, Jr. (1980). Self-interest vs. symbolic politics in policy attitudes and presidential voting. *American Political Science Review* 74: 670–84.

Sigal, L. V. (1973). *Reporters and officials.* Lexington, MA: D. C. Heath.

—— (1987). Sources. In R. K. Manoff and M. Schudson, eds., *Reading the news.* New York: Pantheon.

Sigelman L., and K. Knight (1985). Public opinion and presidential responsibility for the economy: Understanding personalization. *Political Behavior* 7: 167–91.

Simmons, S. J. (1978). *The Fairness Doctrine and the media.* Berkeley: Univ. of California Press.

Smith, T. J., and J. M. Hogan (1987). Public opinion and the Panama Canal treaties of 1977. *Public Opinion Quarterly* 51: 5–30.

Smith, T W. (1985). Atop a liberal plateau? A summary of trends since World War II. In T. Clark, ed., *Research in urban policy.* Vol. I. Greenwich, CT: JAI Press.

Stevenson, R. L., and M. T. Greene (1980). A reconsideration of bias in the news. *Journalism Quarterly* 57: 115–21.

Sussman, B. (1986a). Think of those 3 monkeys covering their eyes, ears, and mouths. *Washington Post National Weekly* (Aug. 11): 37.

—— (1986b). When politicians talk about the issues, people listen. *Washington Post National Weekly* (Aug. 18): 37.

—— (1987). The public hasn't been moving right, the politicians have. *Washington Post National Weekly* (Jan. 5): 37.

Tannenbaum, P. H., and L. S. Kostrich (1983). *Turned on TV/turned-off voters: Policy options for elections projections.* Beverly Hills: Sage.

Thimmesch, N. (1984). The editorial endorsement game. *Public Opinion* (Oct./Nov. 1984): 10–13.

Tichenor, P. J., G. A. Donohue, and C. N. Olien (1970). Mass media and differential growth in knowledge. *Public Opinion Quarterly* 34: 158–70.

Tuchman, G. (1972). Objectivity as strategic ritual. *American Journal of Sociology* 77: 660–79.

—— (1978). *Making news: A study in the construction of reality.* New York: Free Press.

Tulis, J. (1987). *The rhetorical presidency.* Princeton: Princeton Univ. Press.

U.S. House Energy and Commerce Committee (1987). Fairness in Broadcasting Act of 1987. U.S. House of Representatives Report 100–108 (May 27).

University of Michigan Institute for Social Research (1986). *American national election study, 1984: Pre- and post-election survey file,* 2d ed. Ann Arbor: Inter-University Consortium for Political and Social Research.

—— (1979). *The American national election series: 1972, 1974, and 1976.* Ann Arbor: Inter-University Consortium for Political and Social Research.

—— (1978). *The CPS media content analysis study, 1974.* Ann Arbor: Inter-University Consortium for Political and Social Research.

Van Alstyne, W. (1984). *Interpretations of the First Amendment.* Durham, NC: Duke Univ. Press.

Verba, S., and N. H. Nie (1972). *Participation in America: Political democracy and social equality.* New York: Harper and Row.

Waterman, D. (1986). The failure of cultural programming on cable TV: An economic interpretation. *Journal of Communication* 36 (3): 92–107.

Weatherford, M. S. (1983). Economic voting and the "symbolic politics" argument: A reinterpretation and synthesis. *American Political Science Review* 77: 158–74.

Weaver, D. H. (1984). Media agenda-setting and public opinion: Is there a link? In R. N. Bostrom, ed., *Communication Yearbook 8*. Beverly Hills: Sage.

Weaver, D. H., and L. E. Mullins (1975). Content and format characteristics of competing daily newspapers. *Journalism Quarterly* 52: 257–64.

Weaver, P. (1972). Is television news biased? *Public Interest* 26: 57–74.

Webster, J. G. (1986). Audience behavior in the new media environment. *Journal of Communication* 36 (3): 77–91.

Wilhoit, G. C., D. H. Weaver, and R. G. Gray (1985). *The American journalist*. Bloomington: Indiana Univ. Press.

Wildavsky, A. (1987). The media's American egalitarians. *Public Interest* 88: 94–104.

Wolfinger, R. E., and S. J. Rosenstone (1980). *Who votes?* New Haven: Yale Univ. Press.

Wood, W. C. (1986). Consumer spending on the mass media: The principle of relative constancy reconsidered. *Journal of Communication* 36 (2): 39–51.

Woodward, B., and C. Bernstein (1974). *All the president's men*. New York: Simon and Schuster.

Zarefsky, D. (1986). *President Johnson's war on poverty: Rhetoric and history*. University: Univ. of Alabama Press.

Index

Accountability news, 3–4, 10, 18, 21, 23, 125–26, 128–29, 135, 140, 172n, 174n; and Beirut barracks bombing, 64; and Billygate scandal, 63; and citizenship, 29, 65, 67, 139; and Donovan indictment, 63; and dependence on elites, 73; and economic competition, 119, 189n; and evaluation biases, 65; and Fairness Doctrine, 101; and Iran hostage rescue, 64; and marketplace of ideas, 68; and network news, 117, 119; and news slant, 66, 133; and watchdog standard, 46, 63, 65, 74, 101. *See also* Free press ideals

Agenda-setting research. *See* Autonomy model of audience effects

Agnew, Spiro, 31

Associated Press wire service, 131

Audience—demand for sophisticated news by, 3, 18, 93, 98, 107–8, 116, 129, 133

Audience—effects on, 41, 83, 108, 148; inattention and incomprehension hypothesis, 76, 78, 82; minimal consequences theory, 75–77; selective exposure hypothesis, 76; substantial autonomy of audience, 106, 122. *See also* Interdependence model of media effects; Public opinion

Autonomy model of audience effects, 75–76, 82, 84, 155, 180n; agenda-setting research, 75–77, 146, 181n; and democratic accountability, 88; and interdependence of audiences and media, 77, 80, 85; and schemas, 84; and selective exposure hypothesis, 78, 82, 152–155, 157, 182n, 200n. *See also* Audience—effects on; Public opinion

Ayatollah Khomeini, 69

Bagdikian, Ben, 145

Beirut Marine barracks bombing, 39, 177–178n; criticism of Reagan for, 55, 57–58; and event context, 61–62; linkage to Reagan, 55, 57, 59–60, 64, 85; *Newsweek* treatment of, 55, 57, 59, 64; press coverage of, 42; and Reagan press strategy, 61; symbolism in coverage of, 84–